On This Day

365 TALES OF HISTORY, MYSTERY, AND MORE

On This Day

365 TALES OF HISTORY, MYSTERY, AND MORE

DALE JARVIS

FLANKER PRESS LIMITED
ST. JOHN'S

Library and Archives Canada Cataloguing in Publication

Title: On this day : 365 tales of history, mystery, and more / Dale Jarvis.
Names: Jarvis, Dale Gilbert, 1971- author.
Description: Includes bibliographical references.
Identifiers: Canadiana (print) 20200258931 | Canadiana (ebook) 2020025894X | ISBN 9781771178136 (softcover) | ISBN 9781771178143 (EPUB) | ISBN 9781771178150 (Kindle) | ISBN 9781771178167 (PDF)
Subjects: LCSH: Newfoundland and Labrador—History—Miscellanea. | LCSH: Newfoundland and Labrador—History—Anecdotes. | LCSH: Newfoundland and Labrador—Miscellanea.
Classification: LCC FC2161 .J37 2020 | DDC 971.8—dc23

© 2020 by Dale Jarvis

ALL RIGHTS RESERVED. No part of the work covered by the copyright hereon may be reproduced or used in any form or by any means—graphic, electronic or mechanical—without the written permission of the publisher. Any request for photocopying, recording, taping, or information storage and retrieval systems of any part of this book shall be directed to Access Copyright, The Canadian Copyright Licensing Agency, 1 Yonge Street, Suite 800, Toronto, ON M5E 1E5. This applies to classroom use as well. For an Access Copyright licence, visit www.accesscopyright.ca or call toll-free to 1-800-893-5777.

PRINTED IN CANADA

This paper has been certified to meet the environmental and social standards of the Forest Stewardship Council® (FSC®) and comes from responsibly managed forests, and verified recycled sources.

Cover Design by Graham Blair

FLANKER PRESS LTD.
PO BOX 2522, STATION C
ST. JOHN'S, NL
CANADA

TELEPHONE: (709) 739-4477   FAX: (709) 739-4420   TOLL-FREE: 1-866-739-4420
WWW.FLANKERPRESS.COM

9 8 7 6 5 4 3 2 1

We acknowledge the [financial] support of the Government of Canada. *Nous reconnaissons l'appui [financier] du gouvernement du Canada.* We acknowledge the support of the Canada Council for the Arts, which last year invested $153 million to bring the arts to Canadians throughout the country. *Nous remercions le Conseil des arts du Canada de son soutien. L'an dernier, le Conseil a investi 153 millions de dollars pour mettre de l'art dans la vie des Canadiennes et des Canadiens de tout le pays.* We acknowledge the financial support of the Government of Newfoundland and Labrador, Department of Tourism, Culture and Recreation for our publishing activities.

Dedicated to Dr. Neil R. Jarvis
Father's Day, 2020

CONTENTS

JANUARY 1

1 Definitely Not a Caribou — London, 1638 1
2 Don't Mess With Mary — St. John's, 1833 2
3 Moose Tracks — Deer Lake, 1906 2
4 Burial of One of the Oldest Inhabitants —
   Broad Cove, Portugal Cove–St. Philip's, 1887 3
5 Boys Arrested — St. John's, 1891 4
6 Old Christmas Day — Torbay, 1891 4
7 History or Hoax — Bristol's Hope, 1920 5
8 Flooding the Outer Circle — St. John's, 1883 6
9 Fire and Brouhaha — St. John's, 1922 6
10 Rock of Gibraltar — St. John's, 1921 7
11 Goddess Chance — The Funks, 1921 7
12 Master Jack Frost — Bonavista, 1912 8
13 The Exhumation of Mrs. Nolan — Avondale, 1923 8
14 The *Runa*'s Story —
   New York to St. John's, via the Azores, 1920 9
15 Men in Uniform — From Harbour Grace to St. John's, 1884 10
16 That Stink — St. John's, 1901 11
17 Baby Stamp — St. John's, 1907 12
18 A Scandal — Francis Harbour, Labrador, 1883 12
19 A Strange Incident — St. John's, 1900 13
20 Nar Skittles — Little Bay, 1887 13
21 Footloose — Melrose, 1918 14
22 Bid Goodbye to Washday Blues — Gander, 1962 15
23 A Recluse for Five Years — St. John's, 1925 15
24 Whale Milk and Fake News — Balena, 1906 16

25 In Jail for Dancing — Conception Harbour, 1900 17
26 Jailbreak — Signal Hill, 1855 17
27 Arrival of the *Miriam* — The Azores to St. John's, 1882 18
28 Sensational Arrests — St. John's, 1916 19
29 Brained with an Iron Bar — St. John's, 1894 20
30 Ice Skating Champion and Tombstone Designer —
   St. John's, 1905 21
31 Adventure, Ho! — St. John's to Plymouth, UK, 1906 21

FEBRUARY 23

1 Danger on the Tracks — Gambo, 1906 23
2 Moose on Ice — Corner Brook, 1951 23
3 Frozen — Harbour Grace, 1868 24
4 Lost and Found, and Lost Again — Mid-Atlantic, 1920 24
5 A Pair of Grey Socks — Moascar, Egypt, 1916 25
6 A Remarkable Phenomenon —
   Off the Newfoundland Banks, 1890 27
7 Bonspiel for the Poor — St. John's, 1883 28
8 Contortionist Departs — St. John's, 1900 28
9 Touroscopic Entertainment — St. John's, 1883 30
10 Only Two Hours — Alexander Bay and Back, 1922 31
11 Blaze at Tub Factory — St. John's, 1925 31
12 Unidentified Flying Object — Goose Bay, 1956 31
13 House Haul — Twillingate, 1952 32
14 A Weighing Party — St. John's, 1899 32
15 An Apparition — St. John's, 1890 34
16 Swarms of Grubs — St. John's and Spaniard's Bay, 1888 34
17 Got a Light? — St. John's, 1902 35
18 Boats on Ice — Quidi Vidi, 1890 35
19 Railway Snow Blockade — Kitty's Brook, 1903 36

20 Wreck of the *Bessie R* — Point La Haye, 1918 36
21 In Living Colour — St. John's, 1966 37
22 Pancakes and Dancing — Brooklyn, 1941 37
23 Hearse for Hire — Twillingate, 1884 37
24 Teetotallers Rejoice — St. John's, 1872 38
25 200 Guineas Reward! — St. John's, 1846 38
26 A Farewell and a Return — Okak, Labrador, 1837 38
27 Trinity Bay Disaster — 1892 39
28 Eight Days in the Ice Jam — Gulf of St. Lawrence, 1882 39

MARCH 41

1 Champion Fog Horn — Green Island, Catalina, 1883 41
2 A Wednesday He Won't Forget — Grand Falls, 1949 42
3 Strange Lights — Eastern Newfoundland, 2009 43
4 Thrown Under the Bus — Shoe Cove, 1955 44
5 Justifiable Homicide — Harbour Grace, 1905 44
6 In Blackest Night — St. John's, 1920 44
7 Strange Holes — Central Newfoundland, 2013 45
8 Visiting Lioness — St. John's via West Africa, 1921 46
9 Pigeons on Ice — The Icefields off Newfoundland, 1894 46
10 Found Dead — Gibbet Hill, 1763 47
11 Lost 'Mid the Fog — St. John's, 1898 47
12 Promiscuous Spitting — Legislative Council, 1912 48
13 Hand Amputated — St. John's, 1925 49
14 Japanese Tea Party — St. John's, 1907 49
15 Pickled Fish Bill — St. John's, 1834 50
16 Outdoor Girl — St. John's, 1964 50
17 St. Patrick's Day Excursion — Holyrood, 1886 50
18 Sheelagh's Day — St. John's, 1829 51
19 Dog Derby — Battle Harbour to Port Hope Simpson, 1935 51

20 Young Anarchists — St. John's, 1896 52
21 Sunk in Harbour — St. John's, 1912 53
22 The Wedding of Fanny Goff — Portugal Cove, 1822 53
23 Dead in the Woods — Deer Lake, 1909 54
24 Who Are You Gonna Call? — Trinity Bay, 1926 55
25 A Strange Find — Grates Cove, 1917 55
26 Bad Gas — St. John's, 1909 56
27 Up in the Clouds — Off Signal Hill, 1894 56
28 A Long Winter Hike — Deer Lake to Norris Arm, 1912 57
29 Spontaneous Combustion — St. John's Lockup, 1920 57
30 Flippers Overboard — St. John's Harbour, 1910 58
31 Copying Pans — St. John's Harbour, 1897 58

APRIL 60

1 Exciting Chase and Capture — St. John's Southside, 1910 60
2 Flippers on the Hop — St. John's, 1898 60
3 Better Than One (So They Say) — Brigus, 1911 61
4 Caroline Brown's Raisins — Harbour Grace, 1872 62
5 Gored by a Bull — St. John's, 1889 63
6 Remains Removed — St. John's, 1905 64
7 St. Elmo's Fire — Off the Azores, 1852 64
8 Aroma of Blubber — St. John's, 1911 65
9 Window Breaker — St. John's, 1909 65
10 Preserved in Salt — Harbour Grace, 1908 66
11 Lying Down to Die — Joe Batt's Arm, 1917 66
12 Brine in a Pickle — St. John's, 1915 67
13 Southside Shark — Harbour Grace, 1890 67
14 Slate Business Under Way — Britannia, Random Island, 1900 ... 68
15 The Blind Man's Organ — St. John's, 1906 68
16 The Scamps of Coronation Street — St. John's, 1906 69

17 Runaway Bride (and Groom) — Bell Island, 1907 69
18 Two Flying Saucers — Corner Brook, 1952 70
19 Sahlstrom's Fish Biscuits — St. John's, 1897 71
20 Broom Maker's Birthday — Conne River, 1904 72
21 Michael Cullen's Hypnotic Sleep — St. John's, 1898 73
22 Born on a Train — Somewhere East of Gambo, 1918 73
23 Down She Goes — St. John's, 1897 74
24 Happy Exchange — Twillingate, 1900 74
25 Loaded Concertinas — Port aux Basques, 1906 74
26 Improving the Grounds — Government House, 1930 75
27 Ghost Trouble — St. John's, 1896 76
28 Love Conquers All — St. John's, 1898 76
29 *Felis Demulcta Mitis* — St. Bride's, 1899 76
30 A Strange Calf — Carbonear, 1899 77

MAY 78

1 Barn-Moving Drummer Boys — Harbour Grace, 1912 78
2 Should Have Called the Cadets —
   Petty Harbour to St. John's, 1908 78
3 Newfoundland War Vets' Flipper Supper —
   Cambridge, Massachusetts, 1930 79
4 First Horseless Wagon in Newfoundland — St. John's, 1903 79
5 Clothesline Thieves — St. John's, 1897 80
6 Woodpile Falls on Boy — Knight's Cove, 1908 80
7 Keeper Injured — Cape Spear, 1916 80
8 The Sleepy Stowaway — St. John's via Halifax, 1903 81
9 Meteor Observed — St. John's, 1875 81
10 Eat What You Can, Can What You Can't — St. John's, 1930 ... 82
11 Lazy Whale — Merasheen, 1897 82
12 Flying Boats and Photographed Goats — Trepassey, 1919 83

13 Riot on Water Street — St. John's, 1861 84
14 Lost Art of Letter Writing — St. John's, 1896 84
15 Transportation of the Dead —
    Statutes of Newfoundland, 1931 85
16 Holy Feast Day of St. Brendan the Navigator 85
17 Curious Find — Harbour Grace, 1893 86
18 Professor of Phrenology — St. John's, 1882 87
19 Miraculous Escape from Death — Mount Pearl, 1924 87
20 The Sowing — St. John's, 1895 88
21 Delivery Not Guaranteed — Alexander Bay, 1900 88
22 Certificate of Competency — St. John's, 1888 88
23 Hell on Earth — Somewhere in France, 1915 89
24 Trouters' Special — Gull Pond, 1930 89
25 A Wife Too Many — Little Port, Bay of Islands, 1908 90
26 Beware the Velocipede — Topsail, 1869 91
27 Killed by a Block of Ice — Gloucester, Massachusetts, 1892 92
28 Fire from the Sky — Brooms Bottom, 1908 92
29 Climbing Bird Rock — Cape St. Mary's, 1889 93
30 Watch Out for Love — St. John's, 1890 93
31 The New Coffee Tavern — St. John's, 1894 94

JUNE 95

1 Dead Man on Board — Old Perlican, 1904 95
2 Inhabited Iceberg — Torbay, 1962 95
3 Larceny of Cod Oil — St. John's, 1890 96
4 A Well-Travelled Hat — St. John's, 1890 96
5 The Concertina, Part One — St. John's, 1891 96
6 The Concertina, Part Two — St. John's, 1891 97
7 Adventure on the *Resolution* —
    To Labrador and Back Again, 1803 97

8 Crosbie's Car — Topsail, 1928 98
9 The Skull's Curse — St. John's, 1897 98
10 Message in a Bottle — Cape St. George, 1905 99
11 Starvation — Keels, 1831 99
12 Boiler Explosion — St. John's, 1897 100
13 Lord and Lady Baden-Powell — Corner Brook, 1935 100
14 Literary Kittens — Twillingate, 1952 101
15 100th Voyage of the *Harmony* — London to Labrador, 1869 102
16 Water on Tap — Windsor Lake, 1862 103
17 Bolts from the Heavens — Avondale, 1911 103
18 The Sea Recedes — St. Shott's, 1864 104
19 Burned in Effigy — St. John's, 1852 105
20 Periwinkle Baskets — Topsail, 1890 105
21 Summer Solstice Brings Winter Weather — St. John's, 1923 106
22 Queen Victoria's Diamond Jubilee — St. John's, 1897 106
23 In Want of Provisions — Waterford, Ireland, 1775 107
24 Oomancy — St. John's, 1891 107
25 From Underneath the Ground — St. John's, 1891 108
26 Battle of Foxtrap — Foxtrap, 1880 109
27 Sarsaparilla — Cupids Colony, 1628 109
28 Three Good Sheppards — Tilting, 1912 110
29 Experimental Hen Drop — Strait of Belle Isle, 1939 111
30 Forest Fires — Clode Sound to Shoal Harbour, 1892 111

JULY 113

1 A Canada Day Visitor — Cape St. Francis, 1952 113
2 Motorcycle Trip — Western Bay, 1923 114
3 A Skeleton Found — Barnes Road, St. John's, 1895 114
4 Sunk by an Iceberg — Island Cove, 1803 114

5 Seaman and the Beaver —
   Louisiana Territory (modern-day Kansas), 1804 115
6 Citizen Complaint — Rawlins Cross, St. John's, 1923 116
7 Arsonist Convicted — Jugglers Cove, 1962 117
8 New Motor Sprinkler — St. John's, 1919 117
9 Cressie Sighting — Robert's Arm, 1991 118
10 Iceberg Jesus — Battle Harbour, 1864 119
11 Sea Monster Spotted — South of Trepassey, 1899 119
12 Unlucky Lindy — Definitely Not Big Pond, 1933 120
13 A Night in the Woods — Freshwater Bay, 1908 120
14 Gnawing of Bones — St. John's, 1846 121
15 Fish-a-Trip Donation — Isle aux Morts, 1951 122
16 Died by Stroke of a Whale — Harbour Grace, 1782 122
17 Harbour Skull — St. John's, 1899 123
18 Rescued by Danes — Bay Roberts, 1908 123
19 Whaling Operations — Trinity, 1904 124
20 Flirt with Disaster — Wild Cove, 1878 124
21 Snowstorm in July — Labrador, 1886 124
22 Apparatus for Drying Fish and Other Articles —
   Washington, DC, 1890 125
23 Deleterious Matter — Windsor Lake, 1896 126
24 Peculiar Theft — St. John's, 1912 126
25 Shame! Shame! — St. John's, 1892 126
26 A Fine Chance — Somewhere in Maine, 1892 127
27 Song of Ice and Fire — St. John's to Boston, 1897 127
28 A Shower of Flies —
   Square Islands and Venison Islands, 1897 128
29 Murderer of Mary Nugent Hanged — St. John's, 1899 128
30 Shower of Honey — St. John's, 1862 129
31 A Visit from Edmond Halley — St. Mary's Bay, 1700 129

ON THIS DAY: 365 TALES OF HISTORY, MYSTERY, AND MORE

AUGUST 130

1 Lammas Day — Flower's Cove, 1938 130
2 An Alarm of Fire — St. John's, 1900 130
3 Blown Over the Parapet — St. John's, 1838 131
4 Ran Itself to Death — Torbay, 1900 131
5 A Solar Eclipse — Burgeo, 1776 132
6 Gigantic Raft — Bonne Bay, 1919 132
7 Light on His Feet — St. John's, 1919 133
8 Bootlegger Hits the Road — George's Pond, 1900 134
9 A Rolling Stone Pleases No Moss — St. John's, 1892 134
10 Wall Falls Down — Botwood, 1897 135
11 Outing at Smithville — St. John's, 1920 136
12 Youthful Sneak Thief — St. John's, 1914 137
13 Strange Signs and Tokens — Kelligrews, 1891 137
14 Attempt on the Life of Vicar-General — Shearstown, 1941 138
15 Cupid at the Picnic — Octagon Pond, 1900 139
16 Corpse Candle — St. Lawrence, 1924 140
17 A Whale of a Submarine — Bay Bulls, 1918 141
18 Complaint About the Cars — Placentia, 1899 141
19 Daring Act of Turnip Vandalism — St. John's, 1897 141
20 Terror to All Smugglers — Trinity Bay, 1881 142
21 Attacked by Devil Fish — Bay of Islands, 1912 143
22 More Vegetable Violence — St. John's, 1892 144
23 *St. John's* in St. John's — St. John's, 1899 144
24 First Chinese Laundry — St. John's, 1895 145
25 The Great Goobies Cattle Drive — Burin Peninsula, 1964 145
26 First Across the Brooklyn Bridge — New York, 1876 146
27 Billy the Newsboy — St. John's, 1807 147
28 New Era of Pleasure — St. John's, 1886 147
29 Tale of Two Hermits — Torbay and Battle Harbour 148

xv

30 A Sad and Serious Case of Insanity — Labrador Coast, 1894 ... 148
31 Young Lady Ambulance Driver — France and Belgium, 1916 .. 149

SEPTEMBER 150

1 Impaled on a Hay Fork — Torbay, 1911 150
2 Can't Say I Blame the Horse — St. John's, 1903 151
3 Work Horse Parade — St. John's, 1919 151
4 Monster in the Lake — Glenwood, 1903 153
5 A Stone Without a Tomb — St. John's, 1890 153
6 Quartz from the Moon — St. John's, 1872 153
7 Saucy Ham Thief — Topsail, 1903 154
8 A Bunch of Bad Apples — St. John's, 1890 154
9 Incorrigible — St. John's, 1925 155
10 Happy Hunting — Southern Shore, 1900 155
11 A Fracas — St. John's, 1897 156
12 Tucker's Town Torments — St. John's, 1898 157
13 UFOs Over Labrador — Goose Bay, 1951 157
14 Skeleton of a Murderer Unearthed — St. John's, 1896 158
15 Monkey Speedway — St. John's, 1917 158
16 Somnambulism — St. John's, 1879 159
17 Feline Firebug — St. John's, 1898 159
18 Lo and Behold! — Great Harbour Deep, 1902 160
19 No Big Deal — Witless Bay, 1915 160
20 Birthday of Jack Bursey — St. Lunaire, 1903 161
21 Birthday of Captain William Wilson Kettle —
   Grand Bay, 1861 162
22 The Lantern Parade — Donovans, 1896 163
23 Pea-Blowing Nuisance — St. John's, 1909 163
24 Tsunami Drawback — Bonavista, 1848 164
25 Pie-Eating Contest — St. John's, 1917 164

26 The London House Mystery — St. John's, 1896 165
27 King of Skittles — St. John's, 1898 166
28 Found in a Swoon — Mount Pearl, 1905 166
29 Not Your Average Tourist — Bound for Hebron, 1905 167
30 Kite Season — St. John's, 1897 168

OCTOBER 169

1 Best Late Excuse Ever — St. John's, 1880 169
2 Tin Men — St. John's, 1903 169
3 Grand Farewell Concerts — St. John's, 1895 171
4 Vanishing Train Jumper — Donovans, 1910 171
5 Lawless Locals — St. John's and Musgravetown, 1906 172
6 Traverspine Gorilla — Northwest River, 1906 172
7 Spying on the Sex Lives of Caribou — Sandy River, 1912 173
8 The Goat Nuisance — St. John's, 1887 173
9 Magnificent Mill Menu — Grand Falls, 1909 174
10 Logging Camp Night School — Ahwachanjeesh Road, 1942 175
11 Something Went Boom — Corner Brook, 1941 175
12 What Was It? — Portugal Cove, 1917 176
13 Luck Ran Out — Flamborough Head, 1896 177
14 Bad News — Falmouth, UK, 1696 177
15 Constable Crane Gets His Man — Bay of Islands, 1896 177
16 The Plucking — St. John's, 1895 178
17 Foote's Big Potato — Grand Bank, 1903 178
18 Killed by the Train — Gaff Topsalls, 1900 179
19 The *Africa* — St. John's, 1863 179
20 Made Right Here — Dorset, 1762 180
21 The Grandiloquent Zera — St. John's, 1879 180
22 Eel in the Plumbing — St. John's, 1906 181
23 Who Did What? — St. John's, 1902 181

XVII

24 Birthday of Private Ryan — Blackhead,
  Conception Bay, 1892 182
25 Bouncer — Bound for Portsmouth, 1901 183
26 Escaped from the Asylum — St. John's, 1903 184
27 A Tea Time Surprise — Whitbourne, 1895 184
28 Doctor Grunia Ferman — St. John's, 1995 185
29 Phantom of George Street — St. John's, 1896 186
30 Bad Doggos — St. John's, 1911 186
31 Halloween Dinner and Dance — Grand Falls, 1917 186

NOVEMBER 188

1 Resplendent — St. John's, 1886 188
2 Kelly in the Well — Southside, St. John's, 1956 189
3 Goodness, Gracious, Great Balls of Gas — Stephenville, 1997 .. 190
4 Laughter of the Dead — St. John's, 1891 190
5 Falling Rocks — Harbour Grace, 1895 191
6 An Interview with an Alchemist — Mortlake, England, 1577 191
7 Rare Birds — England, 1503 192
8 War on Shebeens — St. John's, 1894 193
9 The Amazing Miss Atlantis — St. John's, 1915 193
10 First Casket Burial — St. John's, 1878 194
11 A Whaling Yarn — Somewhere in the Arctic Seas, 1894 195
12 The Launch of the *Saint Ida* — Gambo, 1890 195
13 Unlucky — St. John's, 1899 196
14 The Chieftain of the Pudding Race — St. John's, 1890 196
15 Letter from the *Saxilby* — Irish Coast, 1933 197
16 A Mouse Twice Swallowed — Freshwater Bay, 1887 197
17 The Tipstaff's Uncle — St. John's, 1870 198
18 The *Riseover* Sets Sail — Seldom-Come-By, 1911 198
19 Phantom Ship Reappears — Near Lewisporte, 1952 199

20 St. Mary's Church — Southside, St. John's, 1859 200
21 Six Feet Under — St. John's, 1849 200
22 Death by Exposure — Goulds, 1900 200
23 Death of Richard Hakluyt — London, 1616 201
24 The Savage Pigs of King's Bridge — St. John's, 1890 202
25 Streets' Birthday — St. John's, 1855 203
26 Rare Find — Near Isle aux Morts, 1981 204
27 Stepped Into History — St. John's, 1887 204
28 Killing Dogs — St. John's, 1891 205
29 Gone with the Wind — St. John's, 1890 206
30 Captain Rupert Wilfred Bartlett — France, 1917 206

DECEMBER 207

1 Grenfell Commemorative Stamp — St. Anthony, 1941 207
2 Strongman Show — St. John's, 1909 207
3 Mules and Monkeys — Sangro River, Italy, 1945 208
4 Five Happy Couples — Garnish, 1901 209
5 Royal Designation — Cambrai, France, 1917 209
6 Marconi's Assistant Arrives — St. John's, 1901 210
7 The Waterford Kitchen — St. John's, 1914 210
8 You Will Put Out Someone's Eye — St. John's, 1907 211
9 Ice-Creepers — Washington, DC, 1873 211
10 Merry Christmas from Mr. Delgado — St. John's, 1891 212
11 Birthday of Clarence Arthur Hubley — St. John's, 1877 212
12 They Are Not Departed or Gone — St. John's, 1842 213
13 Christmas Tree and Fancy Fair — St. John's, 1880 213
14 Opening of the Bishop's Palace — St. John's, 1925 213
15 Super Speeder — Upper Humber, 1946 214
16 Strange Fish Sighted — Somewhere in the Atlantic, 1924 214

17 Dead-On — St. John's, 1862 215
18 Back to Lapland — St. John's, 1908 216
19 Saved by a Human Chain — Gulf of St. Lawrence, 1908 217
20 Christmas Windows — St. John's, 1890 218
21 Burial of John Hearn — St. John's, 1903 219
22 You Get What You Ask For — St. John's, 1863 220
23 Happy Tibb's Eve — Channel–Port aux Basques, 1971 220
24 Cantankerous Violinists — King's Cove, 1871 221
25 Birthday of Richard Brothers — Port Kirwan, 1757 221
26 Staff Night at the Newfoundland Hotel — St. John's, 1932 223
27 Device for Cutting Ships' Cables — Washington, DC, 1892 223
28 Thrilling Rescue — Between Cadiz and Baltimore, 1905 224
29 Photographic Clue — St. John's, 1920 225
30 The Garrison Hill Fire — St. John's, 1883 225
31 A Disgrace to the City — St. John's, 1897 226

ACKNOWLEDGEMENTS 227
BIBLIOGRAPHY 229

On This Day

365 TALES OF HISTORY, MYSTERY, AND MORE

JANUARY

January 1
Definitely Not a Caribou — London, 1638

On this day, King Charles I granted a coat of arms to the Newfoundland Colony. It featured two English lions (never seen in Newfoundland), two Scottish unicorns (they don't really exist), an elk (probably meant to be a caribou), and two rather fanciful depictions of what a 17th-century Englishman thought a Beothuk might look like. Not long after, a civil war broke out in England, and everyone forgot about the Newfoundland coat of arms for almost 300 years.

Coat of Arms of Newfoundland and Labrador

It was not until the 1920s that the College of Arms in London reminded Sir Edgar Bowring that Newfoundland actually had its own coat of arms. The Newfoundland government officially adopted it on January 1, 1928, only 290 years after it had been granted in the first place, which has to be some kind of bureaucratic world record.

And that, in a nutshell, sets the stage for this book: weird little pieces of half-forgotten history and folklore from all over Newfoundland and Labrador, one for every day of the year. Onward, Gentle Reader!

January 2
Don't Mess With Mary — St. John's, 1833

Governor Thomas John Cochrane opened the first Newfoundland House of Assembly in a tavern belonging to Mary Travers, near what is today the intersection of Duckworth Street and King's Road. The 14 members of the Assembly neglected to budget for rent, so the following spring, Travers ejected them from her premises. In lieu of rent, she seized the Speaker's chair and hat, the mace of the Sergeant-at-Arms, desks, and papers belonging to the House of Assembly, and tried to auction them off, setting the tone for St. John's landlords for generations to come.

January 3
Moose Tracks — Deer Lake, 1906

The Nichols boys, of Deer Lake, came across the tracks of two moose near the Upper Humber. Mr. Van Bruck, of New Brunswick, had reported seeing the tracks of two moose the early part of December at the bottom of Hermitage Bay. Locals were skeptical that moose, four of which had been introduced near Howley in 1904, would stray so far. A newspaper of the day editorialized, "This is a very unlikely story, and we do not think those animals would wander so far away from a section of the country where there is such good feed for them."

January 4
Burial of One of the Oldest Inhabitants — Broad Cove, Portugal Cove–St. Philip's, 1887

Having died at 9:00 p.m on New Year's Day at the ripe old age of 94, the late Mrs. Elizabeth Mitchell was on this day interred. Her father had been an Englishman by the name of King, and she was born at Round Harbour, near Tilt Cove, on St. Patrick's Day 1793. Reverend Walter R. Smith (Church of England) officiated over her burial and, remembering her pleasant voice and cheerful face, wrote:

> She enjoyed good health up to within a few weeks of her death. Her teeth were sound, her voice full and pleasant and her memory remarkably good. She retained distinct recollections of the Aborigines, having seen them in her childhood or about the dawn of this century. She described them to me as a tall and handsome people, both men and women. Only a short time ago she gave me a most interesting description of a visit that the Red Indians paid her father and family about the very time that Lord Nelson was fighting at Trafalgar. . . . After nearly a century of sojourning in this weary world, the feet of this Newfoundland mother have found rest in the somewhat picturesque graveyard, in the centre of which stands the church of St. Philip, at Broad Cove, in this Mission.

January 5
Boys Arrested — St. John's, 1891

A strapping policeman captured two boys and their slides and brought them to the police station. The boys were under arrest for dangerously sliding down the hills in the heart of the city and endangering the limbs of pedestrians. By the time Market House Hill was reached, a procession of small boys of every age and description were following and cheering. The published opinion was that such reckless behaviour must be punished and the boys' slides be confiscated. One anti-slider demanded that "the magistrates or the City Council should make a law defining certain limits inside of which boys should not be allowed to slide . . . and any boy who did not feel inclined to act accordingly could be appealed to with a piece of clapboard or a flour-barrel stave."

January 6
Old Christmas Day — Torbay, 1891

A Christmas tree went on display in Torbay in aid of the church. A number of items were exhibited for sale, and some of the women from St. John's who had volunteered at the St. Patrick's Bazaar the previous November travelled to Torbay to assist. Among these were "granny and her assistant," in the role of fortune teller, to enable the "blushing damsels of Torbay to take a peep into the future." Granny was possibly Miss May O'Mara, who had told fortunes at the Bazaar (for a trifling sum, we are told).

January 7
History or Hoax — Bristol's Hope, 1920

The St. John's Museum received, from Captain Nicholas Peddle, the Poet of Bristol's Hope, a historic sword that had belonged to Peddle's grandfather, Levi Peddle. Family folklore maintained that the sword had been brought to Newfoundland around 1675 by the first of the Peddle family to settle on the island, a Welsh rebel who had escaped from the Welsh Mountains. During the attack of 1696, 200 gallant Newfoundlanders barricaded themselves on Carbonear Island. A French crew got to the landing place, and one man jumped ashore at Stone Beach. A heroic Peddle ancestor drove the Frenchman back into the water with the fabled sword.

The sword had previously been on exhibition during the John Guy Celebration in 1910, where it attracted great attention. Once it entered the St. John's Museum collection in 1920, its history gets a little murky. In 1930, the Museum was closed, and the artifacts were variously dispersed and stored. As John E. Maunder writes, "an unfortunate combination of factors, including incompetent storage arrangements, a disastrous fire, and outright disposal of artifacts, decimated the collections." The Museum reopened in 1957, and The Rooms museum collection today does contain a sword that might be the Peddle weapon. One military historian, however, has dismissed it as not being a 17th-century sword at all and likely being "more of a theatrical sword." The supposed Peddle sword, as of 2020, was on loan to the Carbonear Heritage Society. You can visit and judge it for yourself.

January 8
Flooding the Outer Circle — St. John's, 1883

It was announced on this day that the "Outer Circle" of the new Curling and Skating Rink on Circular Road had been flooded, the ice had been tested, and it was deemed to be in first-rate condition. The centre ice had been open for some time, with ample accommodation for two teams of curlers to play at the same time, but this was the first day the outer ring of ice, presenting a skating area of fully 500 feet, was ready for the use of local enthusiasts. The building was lit up brilliantly for the occasion, with Professor Bennett's band furnishing music for the multitude that gathered. A gallery running completely around the interior of the structure allowed visitors to watch the busy brooms of the curlers as well as the graceful movements of the skaters.

January 9
Fire and Brouhaha — St. John's, 1922

A great row broke out this morning, causing a large number of people to gather to watch the pugilists. Two labourers named Teens and Sheean got into fisticuffs, and when Sergeant Furlong and several constables appeared on the scene, Teens kicked out and struck Furlong. Teens was nevertheless quickly brought to jail. It is said that the row started over the origin of the fire at the Longshoremen's Protective Union (LSPU) Hall.

The Hall had been built by the Sons of Temperance after the Great Fire of 1892 and had been used as a Congregationalist church and as a Presbyterian Sunday school before being purchased by the Union. Earlier that morning, at three o'clock, Mr. E. Skiffington, the night watchman, had noticed the glare of the flames in the sky on Victoria Street. He ran to the box at the foot of Prescott Street and sent in the alarm.

The blaze was a most spectacular one, and firemen worked for two hours before their efforts began to prove effective. By this time the roof was a mass of flames, and the roof and floors gradually began to fall in, sending flankers and flames hundreds of feet in the air. At a quarter past four, the entire top front of the hall, including the flagpole, crashed down across Victoria Street. The cause of the blaze, which started near the boiler room, was never confirmed.

January 10
Rock of Gibraltar — St. John's, 1921

Blinding snowdrifts prevailed, with drifts of 10 and 12 feet deep not uncommon. On Pennywell Road, the snow piled up in one thoroughfare and shaped itself to a resemblance of the Rock of Gibraltar. Dwyer's Hill on Carpasian Road was completely blocked, with the snowbank presenting a wall on one side difficult for pedestrians to climb. Two men on Long Pond Road came near losing their horses. In one instance, the animal was shovelled out and left to find its own way home, while the harness and catamaran were left behind.

January 11
Goddess Chance — The Funks, 1921

The Newfoundland sealing fleet was already preparing for the spring trip to the ice. It was announced that, this year, airplanes would be used to scour the ice surface off the Funks, with any news of the discovery of seals to be flashed to the hunters by wireless. Formerly, the chance of obtaining a cargo rested entirely on the captain's intuition as to where the herds were located. It was noted that "last year the hunt was a failure owing to the fact the masters could not locate the herds, but the advent of the airplane should eliminate the success of the industry depending on the fickle Goddess Chance."

January 12
Master Jack Frost — Bonavista, 1912

James Ryan Limited included the following in the company diary:

> Cold weather with a western wind blowing a good stiff breeze but not by any means so hard as yesterday's wind. The train at noon was jamming between Trinity East and Port Rexton and at 6:30 p.m. it is said she has not yet reached the latter place. Nothing new to record but hard cold weather is upon us and we are in the grip of Master Jack Frost.

January 13
The Exhumation of Mrs. Nolan — Avondale, 1923

Early on this morning, Detective Constable Bennett journeyed to Avondale by train, taking with him an empty coffin. He returned to St. John's that evening at 9:15 p.m., the coffin much heavier. It was part of a particularly sad case, an investigation into the death of a woman identified in the press only by her husband's last name.

A few days previously, Mrs. Nolan had perished in the nine-foot-by-five-foot shed, where she was living after having been turned out of her house early January by her husband, Peter Nolan. The shed had previously been used as a shelter for cattle, its seams stuffed with straw. It was not watertight, and ice and snow had formed on the floor. For a week or more, Mrs. Nolan and her children slept on the hay that was stored there. Neighbours provided her with a bed, a couple of blankets, a small stove, and some food and firewood. A few days before Bennett's arrival, she had given birth to a child, and though a midwife neighbour was present, the mother and her baby could not be saved. They were buried together in the local churchyard.

News of the husband's alleged brutality had spread, and so the detective was dispatched to exhume the corpse of Mrs. Nolan and bring it to St. John's for a post-mortem. The remains were brought to the morgue by Murphy the undertaker, and Doctors Anderson and Greeve conducted the examination. The results of this did not disclose sufficient evidence to make a charge of manslaughter against Peter Nolan. A warrant for his arrest was issued, however, charging cruelty under the Delinquent Neglected and Dependent Childrens Act. He was held for a few days at the penitentiary, then released on a $3,000 bail. In February, he was acquitted on all charges and went home a free man.

The remains of his wife were returned to Avondale by train and reburied with their child.

January 14
The *Runa*'s Story — New York to St. John's, via the Azores, 1920

The Gulf of St. Lawrence Shipping Company's steamer *Runa* arrived in port this morning, covered with ice and frozen snow and telling a dramatic story.

Laden down with Christmas goods, the *Runa* had left New York on the seventh of December, 1919, for St. John's under the command of Captain Gunnerson, a native of Norway, with a crew of mostly black sailors. Four days out, she struck a storm, which developed into a raging blizzard lasting five days. During the blizzard, a Norwegian member of the crew was washed overboard and drowned. Blown off course and running short of coal, the captain decided to head to the Azores, the nearest port. The weather was still very stormy, and the passage to the Azores proved to be more difficult than anticipated. Their remaining coal was used up quickly. Desperate to reach land, the crew began to cut up all the woodwork on the ship to use as firewood. The crew dismantled what they could and burned every scrap of wood available, including the deckhouse and two derricks (hoisting apparatus employing a tackle rigged at the end of a beam). Only the lifeboats were saved from the furnace. Even with this, only half speed could be made. When they reached the Azores—which is not normally a coaling station—the *Runa* had to wait several days to collect coal from passing ships. She eventually left the port of Fayal and again met heavy storms. Eight days later, she arrived in St. John's in a sorry state. Her deck cargo was completely washed away, the mail she carried was wet, and some of her cargo was damaged, including a shipment of grapefruit and filbert nuts. The crew, at least, was reported as being well and fit.

January 15
Men in Uniform — From Harbour Grace to St. John's, 1884

On this day, the cavalry branch of the police force rode back into St. John's, having spent the New Year in Harbour Grace. Though they rode through a heavy snowstorm on their return trip, they arrived "without a feather out of their plumes." It was said that the cavalrymen had been the special objects of admiration by the fair sex of Harbour Grace, what with their noble bearing, gay trappings, jingling spurs, and bright sabretaches (leather pouches worn hanging from a cavalry officer's belt). Their commander claimed to have never received so many New Year cards and congratulations and invitations to call again. He considered the belles of Harbour Grace a little shyer than those of St. John's but surpassing the latter in terms of good looks and symmetrical proportions.

Royal Newfoundland Constabulary on horseback at the Parade Grounds, circa 1910s

January 16
That Stink — St. John's, 1901

A cesspool located behind the post office was the cause of local concern. "All kinds of nuisance is thrown there, and the stench arising from the grating, when the weather gets mild, is abominable."

January 17
Baby Stamp — St. John's, 1907

A funeral of a young girl was held on this day, made all the more tragic by the confusing proceedings of the previous few days. Two days before, it had been reported that Aggie Stamp, a little girl about a year and a half, had died at the hospital of scarlet fever. The girl's father had been called home from work in order to prepare for the funeral. The following day, it was revealed that the reported death of baby Stamp had been a terrible mistake and that the child was still living, in spite of the fact that Mr. J. T. Martin already had her coffin made. On the 17th, Aggie Stamp died at the hospital (for certain this time). Her funeral took place that afternoon, the grave for her burial having been dug two days previously.

January 18
A Scandal — Francis Harbour, Labrador, 1883

As the steamer *Hibernian* arrived in St. John's, constables were waiting to arrest one Frank Bransfield and take him directly to Judge Prowse, who charged him with obtaining $1,400 under false pretences and abandoning his wife and four children. Bransfield was a resident of Carbonear, from where he ran a trading business in the summers along the Labrador coast.

At the time of his arrest, Bransfield was accompanied by a young woman, of about 17 years of age, whom the newspapers described as "a rather good-looking girl." The young woman had been employed by him for two years to keep his store, trade, and cook for him at a place called Francis Harbour, a short distance from Battle Harbour on the Labrador coast. Bransfield was described as being "very kind to her," while the girl herself was described as being "enciente"—an expression in Victorian English meaning that Bransfield's kindness to the girl had resulted in an unplanned pregnancy.

Hoping to avoid a scandal, Bransfield had given them both assumed names and sailed out of Francis Harbour. He attempted to take the girl to Halifax, "intending to place her in a comfortable position till after her trouble." Authorities there found out about the situation and promptly sent him back to the attention of Judge Prowse.

January 19
A Strange Incident — St. John's, 1900

A resident of King's Bridge Road received a surprise by post. Opening a letter that she received through the mail from Salem, Massachusetts, a live butterfly flew out. The writer of the letter neglected to mention anything about the butterfly, so it was presumed that it must have gotten into the envelope by itself. The butterfly had been in the letter for nearly two weeks, and the envelope had been stamped five times.

January 20
Nar Skittles — Little Bay, 1887

A sad day for the Friends of Temperance in Little Bay, as they watched the local skittle alley burn to the ground. The skittle alley had been opened by watchmaker, jeweller, and cricketing enthusiast John Lamb. Lamb had opened the business in 1883 as a combination skittle alley, billiard room, shooting gallery, rental space, and jewellery store. Skittles was originally an old lawn game of European origin, from which the modern sport of nine-pin bowling is descended.

The building had been 100 feet in length and 20 feet in breadth, and at the time of its opening, it had been noted that

"A good deal of taste has been displayed by the builder, and the erection is quite an ornament to the place. It will thus be observed that the young people of Little Bay are not so very deficient as regards to amusements after all." Local teetotallers had heartily approved of the business, as it had provided an alcohol-free place of entertainment for the workers at Little Bay Mines.

What was perhaps not as well understood by the enthusiastic Friends of Temperance was that Mr. Lamb had been bankrolled (and the building had been owned) by Mr. John Lindberg, Esquire, brewer, saloon owner, and crafty entrepreneur. Owner of the Bavarian Brew Depot on Duckworth Street in St. John's, which also featured a skittle alley, Lindberg had seen an opportunity and had funded the construction of the Little Bay enterprise, happy to separate leisure-deprived miners from their hard-earned cash wages. Wisely, Lindberg had insured the building with the Phoenix Assurance Company, so he likely made a profit on the entire affair.

January 21
Footloose — Melrose, 1918

A dance was organized by the local teacher in the financial aid of one Miss Moore, a blind girl. Doors opened at 7:00 p.m., and the hall was soon packed with men, women, and children, some walking upwards of four miles to attend. The dancing continued until 2:00 a.m., at which point it was discovered that some of the young men had danced the very soles from their shoes. The dance was followed by the performance of songs by several attendees, to great applause and much stamping of feet.

January 22
Bid Goodbye to Washday Blues — Gander, 1962

With much fanfare, the Blue Ribbon coin-operated laundry opened on Pine Tree Road. It was the first self-service laundry store of its kind in the area. The laundry was designed to meet "the demands of modern-day living" and featured the following ultra-modern conveniences: 14 top-loading automatic Blue Ribbon washers with the 4-Way Washing Action of wash, spin, rinse, agitate, and spin rinse, made by the Marquette Corporation of Minneapolis; six Safe-T-Steam Coin Operated Laundry Dryers with the all-new Ultra-Violet Ray Clothes Purifier; the "famous" Natco Tankless Water Heater; plus a coin change maker, a plastic laundry bag dispenser, a bleach dispenser, two recommended brands of laundry soap, and a bright, cheery waiting area with comfortable chairs "for the convenience and pleasure of customers."

The first coin-operated self-service laundry had opened on the west coast of the United States in 1951. By the time the Blue Ribbon Laundry opened in Gander, there were over 15,000 such laundries in operation across North America.

January 23
A Recluse for Five Years — St. John's, 1925

A resident of the Dardanelles was examined at the lockup and then ordered to be sent to the Lunatic Asylum by a local doctor. The man, thought to be about 25 years of age, had not been outside his home for five years. The man appeared to be in perfect physical health, though during that period he had entirely ignored all rules of hygiene: "With his hair long enough to plait and his face hidden behind a forest of whiskers, he presented a frightful appearance, resembling more a cave dweller of prehistoric days than a resident of a civilized community."

January 24
Whale Milk and Fake News — Balena, 1906

On this day, the *Western Star* newspaper in Corner Brook took to task their fellow journalists at the *North Sydney Herald* for presenting an outlandish story as a true piece of news. The *Herald* had printed a story that had started out as a joke: that a company in Balena had started to milk the lacteal glands of female whales, can the product, and market it as a new brand of condensed milk.

"Just fancy a whale coming onshore every day to have her milk squeezed out by machinery or human hands," exclaimed the *Western Star*. "We thought our North Sydney contemporary was more fair-minded than to endeavour to mislead its readers with such nonsense."

The story had started to make the rounds the previous year, some newspapers obviously presenting it as a joke, with others like the *Herald* apparently not realizing it was fiction. The *Harbor Grace Standard*, for example, had in August printed an article entitled "Professor Muller's Tame Whales," which credited the story as a "hot weather story" having been originally printed in the *Bangor Daily News*:

> Professor Muller has succeeded in domesticating a herd of fifty sulphur bottom cow whales and has perfected an apparatus for milking the mammoth cetaceans. The yield of milk from the full-grown whale is from five to seven hogsheads a day. The milk is fresh and sweet, and peculiarly rich in nutritive and medicinal qualities. It is much thicker and richer than the best Jersey milk, and possesses a peculiarly pleasant and distinctive flavour which those who have tested it pronounce it superior to any known product of the lacteal variety.

In spite of the debunking attempt made by the *Western Star*, the whale of a tale did not stop there. The *St. John's Daily Star* elaborated upon the urban legend in 1918, adding that Professor Muller had trained the whales to swim around to orchestral music, as well as compete in races, tug-of-war, and water polo. The character of Professor Muller was likely intended as a parody of Doctor Rismuller, a German-American chemist, who had introduced to Newfoundland in 1902 a system of converting whale carcasses into fertilizer. And in case you are tempted to add a drop to your tea, whale milk has a fat content between 35% and 50%, with a consistency more akin to toothpaste than your tin of Carnation.

January 25
In Jail for Dancing — Conception Harbour, 1900

On this day, a number of young men found themselves locked up in prison, tried, and found guilty of the crime of dancing. The previous spring, Benjamin Toole, John Gushue, and Mike Wade, along with two fellows named Griffin and Power, had been sentenced at the Brigus court to one month's imprisonment for dancing on the St. John's Bridge near Conception Harbour. As it had been the busy fishing season, the punishment was postponed. The women who took part in the dance, shockingly including a local official's wife, were allowed to go free.

January 26
Jailbreak — Signal Hill, 1855

On a Friday night, between nine and ten o'clock, an imprisoned cow thief pulled off a quick-thinking escape from the Signal Hill jail. When the jailer and his assistant went upstairs to lock the cells for the night, the prisoner was already lurking behind the door. As the two officials unbolted the door and entered, he darted out, slammed the door shut, and locked them inside. There was still a bolted trap door on the stairs to the lower level, but the prisoner rang the bell, the usual signal to the jailer's family below. They unlocked the trap door, and the prisoner threw the trap door open and walked out of the prison as free as a lark.

January 27
Arrival of the *Miriam* — The Azores to St. John's, 1882

The waterfront at Delgada, in the Azores, between 1909 and 1919

The clipper brigantine *Miriam*, under the command of Captain Manning, arrived from the Azores early this morning after a very boisterous passage of 20 days. During the first two or three days of the voyage, she experienced rough seas and high, variable winds. Then, on their 11th day out, a terrific hurricane fell upon them. Huge waves crashed over the vessel, causing her to tremble violently and threatening to wash everything movable from the deck. On the next day the bulwarks, stanchions, and skylights were all swept away, and the weather continued to be frightfully severe for the remainder of their passage. On the Wednesday night before her arrival in St. John's, a new danger threatened the *Miriam*—the frost became so intense that before morning the sides of the vessel were covered with ice, in some places 18 inches thick. The rudder could not be moved for several hours, though as the day progressed, her hardy crew regained control of the vessel. They steered her to St. John's without further complications, to the delight of Alan Goodridge & Sons, the firm that owned her.

January 28
Sensational Arrests — St. John's, 1916

Following up on a series of clues, the ever-vigilant Detective Byrne on this day visited the home of Walter LeGrow and, in doing so, put a stop to a rash of thefts. As a result of his search, two clerks (LeGrow and a Mr. Reid) and two teamsters (Frank Bugden and Samuel Clarke) were arrested. All four were employees of the Honourable George Knowling's Dry Goods Department on Spencer Street.

Detective Byrne confiscated the following list of goods with Knowling's stamp on them: 1 pair of boots valued at $4.50, 1 boy's overcoat $6.10; 1 pair blankets $4.50; 1 lady's coat $21.00; 1 felt hat $2.20; 2 books 70¢; 1 carpet square $30; 2 hearth rugs $14, 2 tablecloths $17; 2 doormats $1; 1 lady's fur-lined coat $25; 2 quilts $6; 1 trunk $6; 2 books $2; 1 dressing gown $15; 1 overcoat $6.10—at a total value of $161.10.

Knowling's teamsters were charged with receiving goods given to them by LeGrow. Bugden was charged with receiving one suit of clothes, one tweed suit, a cap, a pair of boots, an overcoat, and a quantity of flannelette. Teamster Samuel Clarke, 23 years old, was charged with having received one suit of underclothing.

(*Jump ahead to April 1 if you want more adventures with Detective Byrne.*)

January 29
Brained with an Iron Bar — St. John's, 1894

A brutal murder was committed this evening, the victim of the crime a man well-known in the city as William "Billy" McCarthy. "MURDERED!!" screamed the newspaper headline the next morning, with an article that described him in this way:

> ```
> He was an aged, miserly individual, near-
> ly 80 years old, and not over appreciated
> in the community, as he was remarkable for
> hardness of heart, and exacted his pound of
> flesh in his dealing with everyone he had to
> do with. Yet with all his faults one can
> scarcely help a feeling of regret at his
> violent and unprepared death, for he lived
> hard, and the few years yet remaining to
> him might have sufficed to better prepare
> him for the great hereafter. He was his own
> worst enemy and bitterly has he paid for it.
> He carried on business as a junk dealer and
> lived in a house in Springdale Street, one
> of a number of tenements belonging to him.
> He was a hard landlord, always in trouble
> with his tenants, and constantly at law with
> them, and it may be found that wrongs of
> this character had something to do with his
> killing.
> ```

McCarthy was found in a pool of blood in his own house and had been "brained" with a hollow iron bar, likely a section of gas pipe. His murder was never solved.

January 30
Ice Skating Champion and Tombstone Designer — St. John's, 1905

The remarkable Frederick G. Chislett won a six-hour-long skating race at the Parade Rink on this day, achieving a distance of 71 miles. In 1897, at the age of 17, Chislett had become the long-distance skating champion of St. John's by defeating F. Donnelly and W. Smithwicke, covering eight kilometres (five miles) in 19:48. He defended his title many times, often against competitors brought in from outside Newfoundland.

By 1912, Chislett had decided to retire from skating and made a professional shift, beginning his career in the monument business. He worked for a while as the manager of Muir's Marble Works and then set up his own business on McMurdo's Lane. He pioneered the use of design books and photos, which allowed prospective customers to peruse marker shapes, motifs, and epitaphs, and place orders for cemetery markers and monuments by mail. This allowed Chislett to expand the business beyond the local St. John's market, and Chislett stones can be found in many cemeteries across the province.

January 31
Adventure, Ho!   St. John's to Plymouth, UK, 1906

Two young lads, Walter Andrews of McFarlane's Lane, and John Richardson of York Street, did not return home for supper. It was later discovered they had stowed away on the *Gra-*

tia. The day before, the ship had been tied up at the wharf of A. Goodridge & Sons, loading fish for Europe and having just discharged its cargo of salt from Cadiz. It set sail on the 31st with 4,000 quintals of fish, bound for Plymouth, and arrived after a fine run of 17 days, the stowaways none the worse for their voyage.

FEBRUARY

February 1
Danger on the Tracks — Gambo, 1906

A section foreman working on the railway line just east of the community of Gambo heard a thunderous crash. He hurried out along the track and found a large landslide had just taken place. Hundreds of tons of rock, clay, and earth had been dislodged from the hill, in places burying the tracks to a depth of 12 feet. Knowing this would spell disaster for any train approaching, he turned and hastened back the way he came. In the nick of time, the telegraph operator was able to wire ahead and hold up the outgoing freight train, thus averting an accident.

February 2
Moose on Ice — Corner Brook, 1951

General Foreman Tom Power caused a stir when he announced to paper mill workers that the motor vessel *Trepassey* had made a very unusual catch in the frigid waters of Humber Arm. The crew had come upon a large, two-year-old cow moose in the open channel, where she had fallen through the ice. The crew looped ropes under the fore- and hindquarters of the moose, lifted her into the ship's hold, and steamed for the mill dock. There, several of the dockworkers assisted in tying the bedraggled-looking cow's hooves securely. She was lifted from the *Trepassey* and transferred to a game warden's truck for a jaunt toward the new Trans-Canada Highway. The rescued cow was released in the forest along Pinchgut Road, with a photographer and friends following her for a mile to make sure she was fully mobile.

February 3
Frozen — Harbour Grace, 1868

Thirty men set out to cut firewood for fuel when a terrible and sudden snowstorm descended upon them. The tempest raged all day, and the woodsmen were forced to remain out in its fury all night. Not all survived. The following morning, when the community went out to search for the men, eight of the 30 were found frozen and cold in death's embrace. In the neighbourhood of Riverhead, two men named Quilty and Smith were found, exhausted. They were carried into a nearby home and died shortly after. In the days that followed, other communities reported losses: Joseph Drover, Joseph Hussey, Jane Messer, and Grace Lundrigan were all found dead in Upper Island Cove, with a John Combs reported missing, and a man working for the Rorkes of Carbonear was also found frozen. The total number of those lost remains unknown.

February 4
Lost and Found, and Lost Again — Mid-Atlantic, 1920

Happy news was received by a Halifax radio operator. The steamer *Persian Prince* reported the rescue of the crew of the Newfoundland three-masted schooner *Monchy*, abandoned in mid-Atlantic. The *Monchy* was a new vessel of about 100 tons. She was constructed at Harbour Grace and then towed by the SS *Ingraham* to Catalina, where she was loaded with 4,000 quintals of fish from the Union Trading Company.

With a full hold, she set off on her maiden run across the Atlantic. Only four days out, she ran into trouble and was abandoned on January 28. The six-man crew was picked up by the passing *Persian Prince*, 26 days out of Liverpool, and transported safely to New York. Two months later, the Danish schooner *Hamlet* was en route to Lisbon. Near the Azores, she sighted an abandoned ship. The vessel was covered with shells, with water washing over the deck amidships. The main deck was underwater, the afterdeck and forecastle head were only barely visible, and the masts and the rigging gone. The cabin doors were broken away, and the cabin was full of water. The *Hamlet* sailed around the derelict three times and identified it as the abandoned *Monchy*. After making sure there was no sign of life on board, the *Hamlet* left it adrift and continued on its journey. The *Monchy* was never seen again.

February 5
A Pair of Grey Socks — Moascar, Egypt, 1916

Mrs. M. Bastow of St. John's received the following letter of thanks from Private Carroll, an Australian soldier, thanking her for the pair of socks she had knitted.

> Dear Margaret Bastow,
>
> I am writing to let you know that in a pair of socks I got on the Peninsula or better known as the Dardanelles I found inside a piece of paper and on reading it I learn that you are the good hearted friend and I feel it my duty to write and thank you for the gift which the boys appreciate. It makes a fellow proud to think that someone takes an interest in the welfare of the men at the front. I suppose you have read all about

our evacuation of the Dardanelles which was a great bit of work. I see by your note that you have a son at the front in the second contingent. I am sorry to say that it would take a lot of enquiry to find him . . . but I will try and find him.

I myself am an Australian and belong to the 15th Battalion which comes from Queensland, Australia. I was on the Peninsula for three months and I was not sorry when we left. It was very cold when we were there and in the end of November we had about six inches of snow and it lasted on the ground for a week. You can imagine what the Australians would think of snow considering about only one out of every hundred had seen it before. We have it very hot where we are now and I hope we are away before the summer sets in properly. Well, I think I have told you all the news for the present so I will conclude by saying ta-ta till the next time and don't forget to write and let me know if you receive this.

I remain your soldier friend,

Jim Carroll
Address 2564 Private J Carroll,
C Co. 15th Battalion, 4th infantry brigade,
Australian Expeditionary Force on active service.

James Carroll had enlisted for the war at age 22, along with his only brother, Joseph. The letter was written at the Moascar Isolation Camp outside of Ismailia, Egypt. Isolation camps screened soldiers arriving in Egypt, checking for illnesses such as measles. Carroll was wounded at Pozières, France, on August 8, 1916, again at Zonnebeke, Belgium, on September 26, 1917, and was awarded the Military Medal October 1, 1917. He received shrapnel wounds in his jaw and leg, but he survived the war to return home, marry, and have children and grandchildren. His brother, Joseph, was not so fortunate and lies buried in a war grave in England.

February 6
A Remarkable Phenomenon — Off the Newfoundland Banks, 1890

Captain Trennery of the steamer *Queensmore* arrived in Baltimore and was given a warm reception by a large circle of friends. As they chatted, he shared a story of an event that had badly frightened all hands aboard the *Queensmore* during their recent Atlantic crossing. It had been blowing a gale when something eerie transpired:

> "Off the Newfoundland Banks a phenomenon was witnessed, it being nothing more or less than a rain of blood apparently, and covered the decks, bridge, masts, stacks, boats and every exposed part. When it came down it was of a dark rich colour, like human blood, but soon dried up and assumed the colour of bird dust."

Trennery's tale was corroborated by Captain Inch of the *Rossmore*, who witnessed the same remarkable sight.

February 7
Bonspiel for the Poor — St. John's, 1883

Civic-minded curling enthusiasts gathered to join in "the Noble Game" for a good cause at the new Parade Grounds Curling and Ice Rink. The rink, on the site now occupied by The Rooms and the Royal Newfoundland Constabulary (RNC) Headquarters, had opened the previous December. Play commenced at 10:00 a.m., and then again at 2:00 p.m., with Professor Bennett's Band performing that evening from 8:00 p.m. to 10:00 p.m. The entire rink was marked off for curling, and the proceeds raised were devoted "to the Poor."

February 8
Contortionist Departs — St. John's, 1900

Local admirers of the female form were saddened to see the leaving of one Miss Castano for New York. Castano, a serpentine dancer for the Metropolitan Dramatic Troupe, had been greatly hyped by the local press, and her arrival in St. John's had been hotly anticipated. Serpentine dance was a form of dance popular throughout the United States and Europe in the 1890s, becoming a staple of stage shows and early film. The dance was a form of burlesque performance, often employing a costume of gauze fabric combined with lighting that allowed the audience to glimpse the shapely form inside.

A curious St. John's audience had gathered, and her first performance at the Total Abstinence Theatre was attended by one of the largest audiences to ever fill the hall. The Metropolitan Dramatic Troupe performed a vaudeville concert consisting of songs, dances, sketches, and the like. But it was Miss Castano's "contortion specialty" and graceful movements that were most admired. As the premiere danseuse, her gyrations provoked vociferous demands for encores.

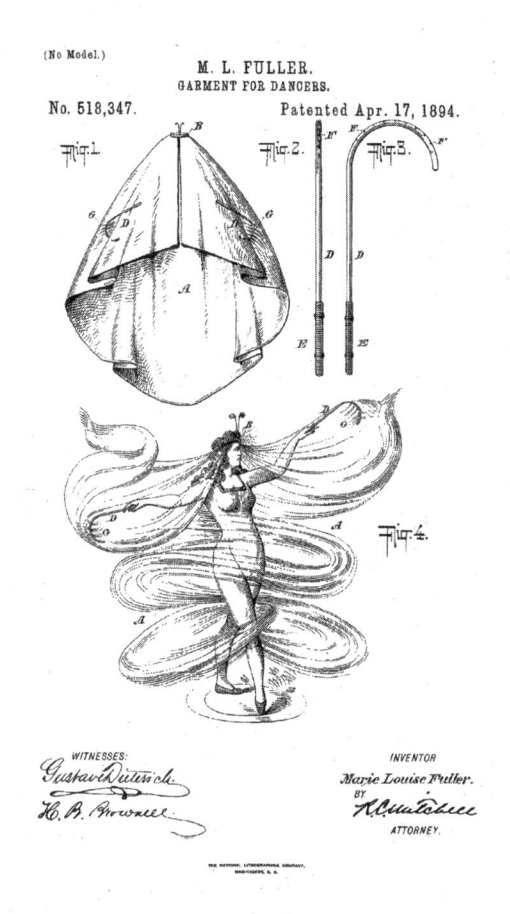

Garment for serpentine dancing, invented by Marie Louise Fuller of New York, 1894

"She is, without doubt, the best contortionist that has ever been seen in St. John's," exclaimed one journalist, while another enthused, "The feats executed by her are indeed marvellous, and her pleasing appearance tends to make her still more attractive to an audience." One writer, either missing the point entirely or immune to the dancer's charms, noted that "Miss Castano's singing was only poor." Castano performed to several packed houses during her month in St. John's before departing by express train, chastely chaperoned by her mother.

February 9
Touroscopic Entertainment — St. John's, 1883

A Touroscopic Entertainment was held at the Athenaeum Hall on Duckworth Street, featuring an all-new dissolving process. The Touroscope was an instrument designed to project plain and coloured transparencies and slides, like a Magic Lantern. On one hand, the event was deemed highly successful, financially speaking, as the organizing committee made approximately £19. On the other hand, it had been promised that strict order would be enforced, yet those who attended deluged the floor of that beautiful building with tobacco juice. It was hoped that common principles of order and decency would not be violated during future performances.

Illustration of the new Touroscope, 1880

February 10
Only Two Hours — Alexander Bay and Back, 1922

Mr. Blackstad, manager of the Terra Nova Sulphite Company, was anxious to get to Alexander Bay quickly and asked Major Cotton to take him there in his aeroplane. The flight took two hours, travelling approximately 125 miles in a straight line, and setting a record time for travel between the two points. On the return flight, the distance from Harbour Grace to St. John's was covered in 10 minutes. During the flight, newspapers were dropped over Bell Island and Carbonear. Aeroplane enthusiasts believed the flight demonstrated the potential benefit of an aerial mail service.

February 11
Blaze at Tub Factory — St. John's, 1925

At 3:00 p.m. yesterday the Central and East End Fire Companies were called to Harvey's Tub Factory, situated on Water Street East, where a slight blaze was in progress. Firemen worked for nearly an hour before the blaze was finally extinguished. A disarrangement of electric wires was believed to be the cause. The Tub Factory operated for decades, producing flour barrels, puncheons, and other barrels for the fishery and local businesses. The company sponsored several boats in the St. John's Regatta.

February 12
Unidentified Flying Object — Goose Bay, 1956

On a routine mission 38 miles southwest of Goose Bay, at around 11:25 p.m., two American servicemen aboard a Northrop F-89D Scorpion all-weather interceptor had a close encounter over central Labrador. A United States Air Force pilot named Bowen and a radar observer named Crawford saw a green and red object rapidly circle their jet. They were able to track the object on radar before it vanished completely. The entire encounter lasted approximately one minute.

February 13
House Haul — Twillingate, 1952

Starting the previous morning at the Arm and finishing at noon on the South Side, Mr. William Lambert and his willing assistants engaged in "Twillingate's Favourite Winter Occupation"—the house haul. The company dragged a house that had been recently purchased from Harry Cooper from its original location to its new site. A few weeks later, Mr. Stan Curtis, with the hearty co-operation of friends, hauled a different house from Davis Cove to Back Harbour.

House hauling in Twillingate was often done to the refrain of "Johnny Poker, Ohhhhh!"—a hauling shanty most often associated with the launching of wooden boats.

February 14
A Weighing Party — St. John's, 1899

A "gay time" was held at St. Andrew's Presbyterian Hall, attracting a company of about 200 persons. The crowd was chiefly attracted by the novelty of a new type of social activity known as a "weighing party," described as "an entertainment unique, unprecedented, the ripe product of the 19th century in its last year." The event was organized by the Ladies of the St. Andrew's Church Aid Committee, who had sent around an invite with the following verse:

> 'Tis something novel and decidedly new,
> This weighing party we invite you to.
> We send you each a little sack,
> Please either bring or send it back.
> With one cent for every four lbs., this we ask;
> You surely won't find it a very hard task.
> Kind friends will give you something to eat,
> And others will furnish a musical treat;
> So come to this party, feel perfectly free,
> And the heavier you are, the more welcome you'll be.

The evening started at 8 o'clock with a variety concert hosted by the Honourable James Baird and included songs, instrumental selections, and recitations. Refreshments (tea, coffee, cake, and sandwiches) were served around ten o'clock, after which the main attraction took place—the weighing—which is exactly what it sounds like.

The Ladies' Committee had procured a weighing machine, and for five cents, participants could ascertain their weight. The lightest single lady present was identified as Miss May Duder, weighing in at 92 pounds. She was awarded a penny-bun as a prize. In contrast to Miss Duder, the heaviest single gentleman was Doctor McKenzie at 288 pounds, who was given three all-day suckers. Heaviest married lady, Mrs. Baxter, at 202 pounds, received an undefined prize. The lightest single gent, E. Henderson, at 137 pounds, got a candy walking stick; the lightest married couple, Mr. and Mrs. Hepburn, at 218 pounds, took home a cake. The grand finale was the heaviest married couple, a Mr. and Mrs. Sclater, topping the scales at 310 pounds. Their appropriate, starch-friendly prize? A potato masher.

February 15
An Apparition — St. John's, 1890

Courthouse officials report seeing a ghost on the premises. Of the event, historian Paul O'Neill wrote:

> There were many who felt it was that of Catherine Snow who had been hanged from a window of the old Court House next door for the murder of her husband. Others wondered if the spirit which was troubling the officials did not originate from the consumption of bottled spirits.

February 16
Swarms of Grubs — St. John's and Spaniard's Bay, 1888

A myriad of grubs appeared on the surface of the snow covering a piece of agricultural land between Torbay Road and Portugal Cove Road, and in Spaniard's Bay. They were over an inch long and resembled a large butterfly caterpillar. Unfazed by the cold, they crawled across the snow full of vitality. According to one account, "there were countless millions of those grubs on the snow and were as thick as the grass in the fields." It was unknown if they had come up from the earth or had fallen from the sky.

This was neither the first nor the last time this happened. Fourteen years previously, the same thing had happened in the same locality. Then, in January 1941, a shower of grubs fell from the sky on a St. John's field during a snow shower and were identified by the Department of Agriculture as the cutworm *Noctua clandestina*, not known in Newfoundland, but which could be found over the northern US and throughout Canada. Another shower of grubs fell in

St. John's at Robinson's Hill in February 1946, wriggling actively on the snow.

February 17
Got a Light? — St. John's, 1902

The Imperial Tobacco Company, established by James H. Monroe, opened. When in full swing, it could process over 300,000 pounds of tobacco leaf imported from Kentucky and Virginia and churn out over 800,000 cigarettes per year. The original building was destroyed by fire and rebuilt in 1910.

Imperial Tobacco Company building, prior to its conversion to residential units

February 18
Boats on Ice — Quidi Vidi, 1890

An ice boat race was held on the frozen Quidi Vidi Lake. A boat operated by a man named Stewart took the prize.

Winter on Quidi Vidi Lake

February 19
Railway Snow Blockade — Kitty's Brook, 1903

The express train from Port aux Basques to St. John's became blocked by snow halfway between Howley and Gaff Topsails. For 17 days, most of them in blizzard conditions, the train was trapped by snow 15 feet deep. The relief train sent to rescue the passengers derailed, and the relief party was frostbitten. The train eventually reached town on March 10.

February 20
Wreck of the *Bessie R* — Point La Haye, 1918

When the *Bessie R* was wrecked at Point La Haye, quick-thinking fisherman Richard Manville brought a rope to the beach and, after three or four attempts, got the rope aboard the vessel. He was able to pull all seven crewmen to safety. The people of Point La Haye and St. Mary's took the men home, stripped them of their wet clothes, brought them dry clothing, and did everything they could for their comfort.

February 21
In Living Colour — St. John's, 1966

CJON Television signed a contract with the RCA Company for the installation of coloured television equipment. Saturday mornings would never be the same again.

February 22
Pancakes and Dancing — Brooklyn, 1941

In keeping with the Newfoundland traditions of their homeland, the Original Newfoundlanders club held a celebration of Pancake Night (and Washington's Birthday) at their club rooms, Tivoli Hall, 51st St. and 4th Ave, Brooklyn, NY. True to custom, prizes and favours were included inside every pancake. As if prize-filled pancakes were not enough of a draw, the event also included a dance with music provided by the Gades Orchestra and Maurice Powers. Tickets to the event set hungry dancers back 50¢ each.

February 23
Hearse for Hire — Twillingate, 1884

W. J. Scott, committee secretary, advised the public that the United Society's hearse was available at any time upon application to Reuben Blackmore or John Lunen, for a fee of three shillings, in advance. Horses and harnesses not included.

February 24
Teetotallers Rejoice — St. John's, 1872

The Newfoundland Temperance League was organized on this date. They were real downers at parties for decades to follow.

February 25
200 Guineas Reward! — St. John's, 1846

On this Wednesday evening, some "Evil-Disposed Person or Persons" did maliciously break and otherwise destroy the windows of the Scottish Church. The church managers offered a reward of 100 guineas to anyone who could give information that would lead to an arrest or conviction of such persons. The publishers of the *Patriot and Terra-Nova Herald* printed the notice for free in aid of discovering the delinquents, while His Excellency the Governor added his own 100 guineas and a promise of a pardon to any confederates in the deed who would turn evidence against their own. A guinea was equal to one pound and one shilling (21 shillings), and 200 guineas in 2019 currency would be roughly equivalent to £1,000. Even with that amount on the table, it is unclear if the window-breakers were ever caught.

February 26
A Farewell and a Return — Okak, Labrador, 1837

The married Moravian Brother John Koerner was called into eternal rest in his 56th year after a faithful service of 23 years in the Labrador mission. Koerner, a teacher and violoncello player, passed away after suffering for several months from a

complication of disorders. His widow and two children returned by ship to London and thence to Germany.
Twelve years later, much to the pleasure and surprise of those in Labrador, a cheerful widow Sister Koerner disembarked from a returning mission ship to assist with Moravian affairs. She stayed for two more years before travelling to Hamburg, chaperoning four of the missionary children going to Germany to attend school. She continued to travel and do missionary work, dying in the West Indies at the age of 80.

February 27
Trinity Bay Disaster — 1892

A blizzard struck suddenly, with around 215 men and boys from Trinity Bight sealing on the ice in the bay. Of those trapped on the ice, over 20 perished, most of them from English Harbour and Ship Cove (Port Rexton).

February 28
Eight Days in the Ice Jam —
Gulf of St. Lawrence, 1882

The fast mail steamer *Newfoundland*, the "greyhound of the Atlantic" under the command of Captain Charles Mylius, left on this day for a short passage from Halifax to St. John's. The *Newfoundland* left Halifax on a Tuesday. The weather was fine, and everything seemed to indicate the probability of a good run. The next morning, she struck ice in the Gulf, which she passed through, but then encountered thick fog and heavier ice than usual. It was loose enough for the steamer to make some progress for a time before becoming completely jammed. During the next few days, several efforts were made to move forward, but without avail. While jammed, 36 icebergs could be seen from the deck of the steamer. Eventually, a heavy swell hove in through the ice pack and broke it up. The normally quick voyage ended up taking eight days.

MARCH

March 1
Champion Fog Horn — Green Island, Catalina, 1883

The Champion Automatic Fog Horn, patented in Canada in 1876

On this day in 1883, a "Champion Fog Horn" began its work on Green Island, near Catalina, Trinity Bay. It was a steam-powered horn, producing its sound through the use of compressed air, and an additional water tank had to be constructed on the island to provide the needed fresh water for the steam engine. The device was housed in a wooden one-storey building on a point of the island northeast of the lighthouse. A notice to mariners advised that the horn would be sounded during "thick weather" and snowstorms, for periods of five seconds, with intervals of silence of 35 seconds. It was estimated that the range of the foghorn would be from half a mile to 10 miles, depending on the weather at the time.

The foghorn, however, had different ideas and refused to properly sound at that interval. In 1885, it was modified to sound for 10 seconds, followed by 37 seconds of silence. Possibly just as contrary was the lightkeeper himself, widower Peter Woods, who kept the station running for 25 years. In 1893, an inspector noted, "The keeper's dwelling internally is in a very dirty condition. The keeper, now an old man, as he gets older is less and less attentive to cleanliness."

March 2
A Wednesday He Won't Forget — Grand Falls, 1949

Wednesday was not a good day for local taxi driver Mr. Elliott. That morning, he was involved in a collision with a station wagon. The vehicle was taken to a garage for repairs, and heated words developed between Elliott and the male driver of the other car. It seemed as if the two were close to coming to blows, but before things could develop, the statuesque wife of the other driver pulled her husband aside.

"I think I'm more qualified than you are to handle this situation," she said.

Forthwith, she led off with a right-handed upsweep to the other taxi driver's noggin. She followed this up with a body attack and a few sharp punches delivered at close range. The cabbie had the wind knocked out of him before he knew what was happening.

The combatants were dragged before Magistrate Abbott that afternoon. When questioned, the woman declared she had fought for her husband out of love. Unimpressed by the romantic gesture, the judge gave her a fine of $10 and ordered her to keep the peace in the future.

March 3
Strange Lights — Eastern Newfoundland, 2009

The main gossip of the day was a strange aerial flash of light. A man working at St. Clare's Hospital saw a bright white flash that lit up the skyline above St John's, while a Pouch Cove woman saw a blue flash. Two bright flashes of white and purple were reported by a woman in Bonavista, while an eyewitness in Paradise saw the sky turn orange, an effect that lasted for at least a couple of seconds before it faded out. Another person claimed the sky changed from white to blue to pinkish-purple and that the light seemed to last for ages. A woman from Carmanville saw something light up the sky as she was driving through Lethbridge, while a woman driving near Clarenville saw a flash that she described as "like a bomb without the boom."

Local radio stations reported that officials were baffled. Internet discussion ranged from the serious to the outlandish, putting the blame variously on the Russian Mafia, meteors or asteroids, space debris, missile launches, aliens, and too many baked beans. The probable cause was cloud-to-cloud lightning.

March 4
Thrown Under the Bus — Shoe Cove, 1955

A licensed brewer's agent from Shoe Cove ended up in court before Magistrate O'Neill, charged with two counts of selling India Pale Ale from his shop outside of legal operating hours. The gentleman pleaded guilty to the second charge but insisted that he was not guilty of the first. When asked why he had not pleaded guilty to the first charge, the man argued that the sale had not been made by him but rather by his wife. He was fined $25, and a new summons was issued for his spouse.

March 5
Justifiable Homicide — Harbour Grace, 1905

Do you feel your spouse never notices you? Take pity on Mrs. Catherine Kane, wife of James Kane, of Harbour Grace. She left her house on a Thursday morning to go to the root cellar nearby to get potatoes for dinner. In some way, she barred herself in. Raw potatoes were her only food the next three days, and she was trapped in the cellar until the following Sunday. Her husband did not seem to be concerned at all about her absence. When she came home, he looked up and said: "Did you get the potatoes, Kate? If you did not turn up I was going to look for you tomorrow."

March 6
In Blackest Night — St. John's, 1920

Businessman Mr. George Hierlihy, the owner of the Oyster Bay Parlour, opened an ice cream parlour on Theatre Hill known as The Green Lantern. The spacious parlour could seat at least 85 customers, and the ice cream plant in the rear of the business featured a new electrical freezer that could turn out 250 gallons a day. The parlour also boasted a splendid line of chocolates and fruit. Green electric lanterns adorned the store outside and were situated at various points throughout the interior. One writer promised that the lights "will shed a green, soothing, eerie light on the cafe and an air of novelty will at night pervade," while another suggested the lights "no doubt will give the establishment that uncommon touch which always appeals to modern citizens."

On August 9, 1922, the building was completely gutted by fire, cause unknown, and The Green Lantern's lights went out for good.

March 7
Strange Holes — Central Newfoundland, 2013

Locals reported hearing a loud noise, and a cabin owner found a large, partially iced-over hole in Dawe's Pond, located off a woods road just off the Trans-Canada Highway 15 minutes west of Badger. Jim Gillard of the Twillingate Observatory investigated the mysterious crater and suggested a meteor or piece of space junk had fallen through the ice. Amateur astronomer Gary Dymond studied photographs of the Dawe's Lake site and spoke to nearby residents. Rather than blaming the crater on something crashing into it, he suggested that the hole could have been created by a buildup of methane gas that exploded, rupturing the ice from below. A few days later, a cabin owner on Powderhorn Lake, about six kilometres away, noticed a strange hole in the centre of the icy pond. That circular crater measured about 30 metres across, with ripples in the ice along the edge of the hole.

March 8
Visiting Lioness — St. John's via West Africa, 1921

A crowd of people gathered to visit the Norwegian steamer *Venus 2*, which was busily discharging coal at the harbourfront. The reason for the excitement was a nine-month-old female lion cub that had been brought by the steamer from West Africa. The cub had been taken on as the ship's mascot, but the plan had not been fully thought out. The animal was attached to the smokestack with a chain and was reported as being anything but friendly. Members of the crew had decided the animal's bad temper could be improved with a good whipping, and one crewman sported a scar on his hand as the result. The captain intended to sell the lioness at the first opportunity.

March 9
Pigeons on Ice — The Icefields off Newfoundland, 1894

A novel idea was suggested in the local press: that carrier pigeons might be used during the seal fishery, which could be released to announce where seals had been found on the ice. Inspired by this, Job Brothers & Company imported a number of trained pigeons for the seal hunt of 1896. Off steamed Captain Sam Blandford with his trial pigeons in search of seals, and eventually two birds were let loose. One was sent off on March 20, and the other on April 2. Neither pigeon was ever seen again, thus ending the experiment and the far-too-brief history of seal hunt pigeons in Newfoundland and Labrador.

Engraving of "carrier pigeons" (most likely homing pigeons), with messages attached.

March 10
Found Dead — Gibbet Hill, 1763

According to the Church of England registers, one Thomas Mead, of Coffin's Well, Devon, was found dead by the gibbet above Maggotty Cove. There was a Thomas Mead, son of John Mead, christened at Coffinswell, Devon, on October 23, 1730. It is uncertain if this is the same person.

March 11
Lost 'Mid the Fog   St. John's, 1898

A young lady stopped at the house of two friends on King's Bridge Road and asked them to accompany her home, a distance of about a 10-minute walk. The three women proceeded on their way, but in the fog, they took a wrong turn and went off in the direction of Torbay. After groping along in the fog, they discovered a house by the roadside and found that they were three miles from town. They retraced their steps when the fog lifted and got home at 10 o'clock the following morning.

March 12
Promiscuous Spitting — Legislative Council, 1912

The Honourable John Harvey introduced "An Act to Prevent Promiscuous Spitting" to the floor of the Legislative Council. The act was designed to curb the pernicious habit of spitting in meeting places and public thoroughfares believed to aid the spread of tubercular disease. Harvey spoke, saying:

> "As far as I know, the first great blow to be struck in this direction was by His Grace Archbishop Howley several years ago. The Archbishop had noticed that among his own congregation, even within his own beautiful Cathedral, the offensive habit of spitting on the floor was far too common an offence against the sacred character of the building and against social well-being, and His Grace did not hesitate to give a very strong address to his people on the subject, pointing out its repulsiveness as a habit and its danger from a health viewpoint. The address had a most beneficial effect, which was not confined to that time and place."

Harvey's anti-spitting law was defeated in the House of Assembly, which believed that education rather than compulsion was a more appropriate measure.

March 13
Hand Amputated — St. John's, 1925

Mr. James Sullivan was using the hard bread mixer at Harvey & Company's bakery. Just as he was about to shut off the machine, his hand, in some unaccountable way, became caught in the cogwheels. His cries of pain alerted his co-workers, who quickly stopped the gears, but not before Mr. Sullivan's hand had been badly mangled. Doctor Knight was called, who bandaged the wound and drove the injured man to the General Hospital. There, Doctor Keegan and his staff attempted to save the injured member, but to no avail. The decision of the physicians was to amputate the hand above the wrist in order to save the rest of the arm. Sullivan was a trusted employee, and the firm was said to have felt the incident very keenly, though probably not as keenly as Mr. Sullivan.

March 14
Japanese Tea Party — St. John's, 1907

The spacious lecture room of Cochrane Street Methodist Church was taxed to its utmost capacity for its annual entertainment. For this year, it took the form of a Japanese Tea Party, with over 70 performers in kimonos and brightly coloured gowns. There were choruses, solos, and recitations, followed by refreshments. Tickets cost 10¢ each, and as the event had sold out completely, it was repeated the following Saturday afternoon.

March 15
Pickled Fish Bill — St. John's, 1834

W. Beckford (elected for Trinity) introduced "An Act to Regulate the Packing and Inspection of Pickled Fish, for Exportation from this Colony." It set rules for the production and sale of salted, pickled, and preserved fish and the various aspects of the salt fish trade. It also defined rules for such things as barrel-making, noting that "New Casks . . . shall be made of sound and well-seasoned wood, free from sap-knots, and bug or worm holes."

March 16
Outdoor Girl — St. John's, 1964

Miss Virginia Elaine Martin of St. John's was named "Outdoor Girl of Canada" in a contest organized by the Ontario Federation of Anglers and Hunters. A year previously she had been one of five finalists in the Kinsmen Club's search for the Newfoundland entry to the Miss Canada competition. Pageant life seems to have struck a chord with Miss Martin—in 1965, the 20-year-old store clerk became the new Miss Toronto, the first Newfoundland native to win the title.

March 17
St. Patrick's Day Excursion — Holyrood, 1886

Sixty jolly passengers, many sporting bulky protuberances in their coat pockets, boarded the train for a special excursion to Holyrood. Huge banks of snow were encountered in many places, but the Eagle Wing snowplow on the front of the train performed its duty admirably. Enlivening the party were some of the best singers in town, who shared songs of the Emerald

Isle along the route. The return trip encountered even larger mountains of snow, so the train reversed a distance, then tore through all obstacles with increased speed. Meanwhile, in St. John's, travel on suburban roads had ground to a standstill due to the day-early arrival of "Sheila's Brush."

March 18
Sheelagh's Day — St. John's, 1829

The members of the Benevolent Irish Society in St. John's were out on the town until six o'clock on Sheelagh's morning, at which hour a few of the campaigners might have been seen employed in "drowning the shamrock." Sheelagh's Day, the day following St. Patrick's Day, has a long history in Newfoundland and Labrador, including the tradition, among some, of getting piously and patriotically drunk.

March 19
Dog Derby — Battle Harbour to
Port Hope Simpson, 1935

Newfoundland and Labrador's first "dog derby" was held over 45 miles of extremely rough trail, starting from Battle Harbour, up Alexis Bay, through the woods to St. Lewis Inlet, and finishing at Port Hope Simpson. A total of 14 teams and 110 dogs started the race. The winner was Robert Russell with a time of five hours and 25 minutes. Charles Russell came in second, only three minutes behind, and Samuel Russell was third, arriving 34 minutes later. The Russells were from Williams Harbour, where the family had settled over 100 years previously. All three winning Russells were employed by the Labrador Development Company pit prop–cutting operation, which had sponsored the race.

Sybil Hillier with Don and Edgar, Great Northern Peninsula

March 20
Young Anarchists — St. John's, 1896

At about four o'clock, William Hackett was met on Princess Street by three boys between the ages of 10 to 14 years. They asked Mr. Hackett for a match, saying they wanted to set off a "fire cracker." Hackett asked to see the firecracker, and one of the boys produced from under his coat a large dynamite cartridge measuring about two feet with a long fuse attached.

Mr. Hackett took the infernal machine from the boys and brought it to the West End Fire Station, where it was determined that the cartridge was one of the largest used for heavy blasting purposes. Their "fire cracker" contained sufficient dynamite to "blow the three boys and half the block to Jericho."

The firemen decided to get rid of the device by sinking the dynamite at the mouth of the Waterford River.

March 21
Sunk in Harbour — St. John's, 1912

A forty-ton schooner, which had been anchored off the Horwood Lumber Company's wharf all winter, sank this morning. The continual chafing of the harbour ice had cut through the hull, causing her to fill with water and sink. Her topmasts were visible above the surface, and it was worried she might prove to be a dangerous obstacle for cargo steamers coming up the harbour.

March 22
The Wedding of Fanny Goff — Portugal Cove, 1822

According to a popular local legend, Tryphena (Fanny) Goff was said to have been the most beautiful woman in the Newfoundland of the early 19th century. One enamoured young clerk wrote,

> Let others praise the city maids—
> At outport beauties scoff:
> For voice, for grace, for charming face,
> There's none like Fanny Goff.

Miss Goff was pursued by many, but she gave her heart to John Barton (or Barter) of Brigus. A date was set for their union, but typhoid fever took Fanny, tragically, on the same day she was to be wed. Her groom, unaware, had ridden his horse from Brigus to Portugal Cove, where he learned the sad news. He returned home and died soon after, possibly of a broken heart. Fanny was laid at rest under an apple tree in her father's garden. In the early 1960s, her headstone was moved to St. Peter's Anglican Church for safety and preservation.

March 23
Dead in the Woods — Deer Lake, 1909

A young man named Frank Penny received the scare of his life in a disused camp of the Humber River Pulp and Lumber Company. Penney discovered the body of a man lying on a camp berth with its knees bent up and arms folded across the breast. The body was dressed in two suits of underwear, three coats, and a heavy pair of trousers, and the stench was almost unbearable, as decomposition had set in.

The manager of the mill notified Judge March by wire, who, accompanied by Inspector Bartlett, Constable Quintan, and Doctor Fisher, left for the scene on the next train. On their arrival, Doctor Fisher pronounced the cause of death as exhaustion and exposure. The remains of the man, about 45 years of age, had evidently lain in the bunk for several days.

The mill manager sent five men to assist the doctor and police in moving the body, but not one of them would handle the remains "on account of superstitious fears." The police and Doctor Fisher were obliged to carry the body to the ice, where a sleigh was waiting. The driver of the sleigh refused to drive the corpse, so the police took charge, and the body was taken to a house and prepared for burial.

There, the mystery deepened. In the man's pockets were found numerous astronomical drawings and plans for airships, as well as imaginative descriptions of planets and "crazy philosophical dissertations on the relations between humanity and the heavenly bodies." Another paper bore a crude likeness of himself drawn with indelible pencil and the name "Jas. R. Millere" written beneath the portrait. There was also a post office receipt, issued at Summerside, PEI, indicating the deceased had sent a registered letter to the Duke of Orleans in Paris. In his pockets were found a few crusts of bread and a package of dates.

The body was buried in the Catholic cemetery at Birchy

Cove. The papers found on the body of the unfortunate wanderer were retained by the police. The mystery of the man's identity and history remains unsolved.

March 24
Who Are You Gonna Call? — Trinity Bay, 1926

Phantom ships by sea, and ghosts by land, were the order of the day (or night) in Trinity Bay. "If these reports are correct, this is very alarming," stated the *Daily Globe*. A Trinity correspondent noted that mysterious lights in the Bay were on the increase, and the threat of supernatural interference needed to be taken seriously: "The fishery has been very poor in Trinity Bay for the past few years, may not the beginning of the poor fisheries correspond with [when] phantoms first appeared? This would indicate that they are destroying our fish, in which case steps should be taken for their immediate suppression."

March 25
A Strange Find — Grates Cove, 1917

Mr. Joshua Stanford and crew picked up a drifting 12-foot-long boat, painted green with a black bottom. In the boat were found three seals, three men's coats (much worn), two oars, powder and shot, one axe, one pocket knife, and one partially filled breadbox. The theory was that the boat became jammed in the ice whilst sealing, and the occupants decided to walk to the shore, bringing their guns and some food in their pockets. The coats were examined, but they contained no identification. It was hoped that the seal hunters would turn up, though there was no word of their ever reaching land.

March 26
Bad Gas — St. John's, 1909

It was reported on this day that Mrs. Foran and Miss Barter were gradually recovering from the effects of gas. Miss Barter, the worst affected, was still confined to her bed. The previous evening, a successful pork and cabbage supper had been held at the Alexander Street Hall, and it was said that the organizers had done their utmost to ensure that all participants had "a good blow-out."

It is unknown if the two stories were related.

March 27
Up in the Clouds — Off Signal Hill, 1894

Frank Scott, a signalman working at the Block House on Signal Hill, witnessed a curious phenomenon. He saw, about 18 or 20 miles distant, what he took to be a very large steamship travelling quickly through the ice. The vessel had a long black hull, two masts, well apart, with yards on the foremast. In spite of her great speed, Scott saw no smoke coming out of her funnel. In a letter to the newspaper, he wrote:

> I have frequently heard of such things having been seen by mariners and others, but it has never been my lot to see it so plainly before. During my twelve years' service at this station, I have often seen the reflection of icebergs and ships high up on the horizon, and sometimes in an inverted manner, and at one time saw Baccalieu Island, perfect in all its outlines, "up in the clouds," which every visitor to the Block House knows is completely hid from our view by the intervening high land.

Scott watched the speeding steamer for upwards of 45 minutes before it vanished suddenly. He surveyed the ice for several more hours, but no steamship was spotted.

March 28
A Long Winter Hike — Deer Lake to Norris Arm, 1912

Mr. Mitchell, the Inspector of Postal Telegraphs, arrived in St. John's by the morning train. The inspector had been away for some time and had walked the entire distance from Deer Lake, over the Gaff Topsails, to Norris Arm, a distance of about 100 miles. Mitchell was caught in three severe snowstorms and reported he had never seen so much snow. In some places the drifts were 25 feet high, and along the Topsails, in several locations, the telegraph poles were completely covered.

March 29
Spontaneous Combustion — St. John's Lockup, 1920

A prisoner who was brought in to the lockup told the police that he had gotten drunk on what he called "canned heat"— most likely Sterno, a fuel made from denatured and jellied alcohol. The prisoner had dissolved the solid Sterno in a jug of hot water before drinking it. Subsequently, he began to swell, and thinking a smoke would do him good, he took out the stump of a pipe. When he lit up, the air seemed to catch fire, and in the man's own words, "he had to close his mouth to keep his stomach from going alight." The story was corroborated by the police, and the gentleman's face was all red, which was taken as proof.

The practice of drinking Sterno became popular during Prohibition years. The Sterno would be squeezed through cheesecloth or a sock and the resulting liquid mixed with fruit juice to make "squeeze." The methanol it contains can cause permanent blindness, so don't try this one at home.

March 30
Flippers Overboard — St. John's Harbour, 1910

The crew of the *Viking* had lifted up two barrels of seal flippers in a sling and were in the process of swinging them out over the gunwales of the ship to load into a boat below when the sling broke. Both barrels dropped with a crash into the boat, narrowly missing the two men within, and splitting the side open and turning her over. The men were thrown into the water but held onto the wreckage of their boat until they were fished out. The flippers, worth $10, went to the bottom of the harbour.

March 31
Copying Pans — St. John's Harbour, 1897

Two boys were seen on a pan of ice, which they propelled by means of two birch brooms. Their pan was caught in the current and swept out to sea. Two men from the Southside set off in a dory and rescued the two boys a quarter-mile outside of Chain Rock. Meanwhile, four boys were spotted working themselves along with short sticks on a small, thin pan of ice near Job's premises. That evening, two young lads named Walsh and Summers also had a narrow escape from drowning. They were copying on the ice near Harvey's wharf, and one lost his foothold while jumping from one pan of ice to the other. He grabbed the other boy's arm, but both fell in. A boat with two men went to their rescue.

"They seemed to be courting death," it was reported. "Strange that there is such fascination where an element of danger exists."

APRIL

April 1
Exciting Chase and Capture —
St. John's Southside, 1910

For a few days previously, Detective Byrne had been on the lookout for a man wanted for stealing cash and goods from various stores on New Gower Street. At 9.30 a.m., he eyed his quarry near Bowrings's premises on the Southside. The thief, spying the officer, took off running east down Southside Road toward Job's premises. Byrne gave chase, but when he got close to Job's, the thief ran up the hill and doubled back on his tracks, running back west with the intrepid Byrne close at his heels. All morning, hunter and hunted kept up the back-and-forth. The pursuit lasted over three hours, the officer eventually cornering the man at Fort Amherst lighthouse. The man was completely exhausted but was still desperate enough to attempt a leap off the cliffs before Byrne nabbed him. It was 1:00 p.m. by the time the miscreant was brought to the city jail.

April 2
Flippers on the Hop — St. John's, 1898

As the crew of the steamship *Algerine* was unloading in port, one of the crew took a barrel of seal flippers onto the dock. A small boy came along, reached into the barrel, and made off with one of the flippers. The owner immediately gave chase and, after running a considerable distance, managed to catch the boy and snatch back his flipper. However, upon returning to his barrel, he found that half of them were gone. He looked up the hillside to see a number of young boys, presumably companions of the young scamp, running off with his flippers as fast as they could.

A group of men on a St. John's dock processing seals

April 3
Better Than One (So They Say) — Brigus, 1911

Mr. G. A. Roberts, a resident of Brigus, made his way to St. John's with a curiosity to be put on exhibition, to wit, a lamb (dead) with one body and two heads. The animal had been stillborn the previous Thursday. A sibling born at the same time, of the same mother, was perfectly normal, healthy, and alive.

April 4
Caroline Brown's Raisins — Harbour Grace, 1872

Under the command of Captain John Kennealy, with a sealing crew of 24 men, the schooner *A. T. Stone* of Harbour Grace came across an abandoned vessel drifting in the ice 60 or 70 miles to the southward of Cape Chapeau Rouge. The crew succeeded in boarding her and found her to be a schooner bearing the name *Caroline Brown*. Upon further examination, they found that her hatches were open and that she had been stripped of sails, rigging, and provisions. Her masts and anchors were gone, and she had several feet of water in her hold from a continuous leak. The crew of the *A. T. Stone* patched the leak as best they could, jury-rigged a mast with materials from their own ship, and fastened a tow line to the *Caroline Brown*. Nine sailors were put on board the *Caroline Brown*, and at the risk of their own lives, they towed her back to St. John's, where the crew of the *A. T. Stone* claimed salvage rights.

It was discovered that the primary cargo of the ship was raisins—boxes upon boxes of raisins from Spain's Costa del Sol. These delicacies were auctioned off upon the return of the *A. T. Stone*, much to the delight of local cooks and bakers. Historiographer H. F. Shortis remembered:

> I was a boy at the time, and you can readily imagine the excitement in the old town when the news went round. There was no scarcity of raisins in Conception Bay for the next two years, and figgy duff was the order of the day, from the highest to the lowest. I can well remember Alexander Clift, the auctioneer, selling those raisins in large or small lots, and they went as cheap as two cents per pound. As everyone knows, the Malaga raisins are the finest quality to be had anywhere, and the Nine Crown raisins were as large as figs.

April 5
Gored by a Bull — St. John's, 1889

Two men, Myrick and Halliday, were seriously injured by an attack of a savage Holstein bull, which broke loose on Military Road after being brought down from Connor's Farm on Signal Hill Road. Myrick escaped with minor wounds. Halliday, however, received a terrible wound in his forehead, had his nose pierced by the bull's horns, and had one of his eyes "started from its socket." A policeman ran for a rifle and, returning, fired three or four shots at the bull. The bullets lodged in its flesh and did not pierce any vital part. Eventually, the creature was driven down to Mr. Denis Dooley's premises at King's Bridge, where it was auctioned off for the benefit of the Agricultural Society.

Three-year-old Holstein-Friesian bull, 1887

April 6
Remains Removed — St. John's, 1905

Undertaker Carnell on this day exhumed the mortal remains of the late Mrs. Lamb from the General Protestant Cemetery. The previous Christmas Day, in the afternoon, Mrs. Lamb, the wife of Doctor Lamb, had passed away at the General Hospital after a protracted illness. Her remains had been embalmed, placed inside a hermetically sealed casket, and then only temporarily buried. It had been decided that Mrs. Lamb, a native of Philadelphia, should have her hometown as her final resting spot. Once her casket was excavated, it was sent on the steamship *Bruce* for reinterment at the home of the deceased.

April 7
St. Elmo's Fire — Off the Azores, 1852

Two days before Good Friday, journalist and man of letters Henri Emile Chevalier was witness to an eerie sight. He was en route to Newfoundland on board the *Western World*, a transatlantic passenger ship carrying 700 passengers. It was a stormy night, and as passengers and crew watched, strange, bluish flames wrapped themselves around the top of the ship's mast. Chevalier wrote:

> "'Tis the devil dancing up there, beware!" said an Irish sailor, crossing himself, to anyone who cared to listen. It was nothing more than St. Elmo's fire, a natural, electric phenomenon known by ancient navigators as Castor and Pollux. However, its appearance had a harrowing effect on most passengers aboard the *Western World*. While I was not at all perturbed, I had neither the age nor authority to reassure them.

April 8
Aroma of Blubber — St. John's, 1911

A Letter to the Editor:

> Dear Sir,
> In the interest of health, and for the benefit of residents and pedestrians, I would ask the Public Health Officer to visit Leslie Street. To the westward of it on a meadow has been deposited a quantity of blubber, the aroma of which floats over that section of the city. Perhaps it is the business of the Sanitary Inspector to attend to this important matter, at any rate, whoever's business it is I would ask him to take a car and arrive on the scene quickly and confer a favour on the suffering residents by having it removed **immediately**. This is not a matter to be treated indifferently, as goodness knows we have enough sickness in our midst already without courting a wholesale epidemic.
> Yours sincerely.
> LESLIE STREET.

April 9
Window Breaker — St. John's, 1909

For about a week, the residents of Ansel Place had stones thrown at their doors and their windows broken. The mischief was generally done at night, and locals believed a man was the culprit. Finally, the perpetrator was caught in the act—a young girl, about 11 years old, who lived in the vicinity. She was forgiven but was warned not to do it again.

April 10
Preserved in Salt — Harbour Grace, 1908

The sealing ship *Algerine* arrived in port with a dead man on board. The unfortunate man had been working before the bow of the ship on March 29. When he jumped on the ice, an ice pan was suddenly thrust upward in the floe ahead of the ship. The man was pinned between the sheets of ice, which moved with such force they cut off the poor fellow's two legs. He died shortly after, and the body was placed in a coffin and preserved in salt for the return journey.

Breaking out through the ice: the sealing fleet leaving St. John's

April 11
Lying Down to Die — Joe Batt's Arm, 1917

In June, a man picked up a sealing gaff near Moreton's Harbour, which had belonged to Joseph Jacobs. A message scratched into the wood read, "April 11, lying down to die."

Previously, on April 7, three brothers, Joseph, Stephen, and Walter Jacobs, and their friend, Francis Pomeroy, had gone to the ice in search of seals. All were from Joe Batt's Arm. A thick fog rolled in. The wind changed direction, blowing the ice away from the shore and trapping the four on the ice pans. Poor weather and ice conditions continued for more than a week, making rescue impossible. Time passed, and the families of the men gave them up for lost. The gaff found that June was given to Thomas and Mary Jacobs, the parents of the Jacobs brothers.

April 12
Brine in a Pickle — St. John's, 1915

Patrick Brine, aged 28, an employee of the City Council, was excavating for new sewer pipes at the eastern end of Duckworth Street. As he was digging with his pickaxe, the earth caved in, and Brine was left standing to his chin in clay. He attempted to free himself but was too tightly pinned to move. He shouted to three fellow workmen, who rushed to his assistance. It took three hours to remove the clay and release Brine from his predicament. Exhausted, he was taken to the General Hospital, where his injuries were found to be slight. He left the hospital at noon and resumed work immediately.

April 13
Southside Shark — Harbour Grace, 1890

A young Southside man watched a large shark following a piece of paper floating in the harbour. The creature followed the floating paper so far inshore that it nearly grounded. The enterprising young man fetched a grapnel and proceeded to hook and haul the monster ashore. At that point, it was the largest shark that had been seen in Harbour Grace for some time, measuring 25 feet in length with a tail nearly four feet across. When cut, the shark meat filled six flour barrels.

April 14
Slate Business Under Way — Britannia, Random Island, 1900

Mr. D. Currie of Britannia Cove, Trinity Bay, was in St. John's and staying at the Waverley Hotel. Mr. Currie was in town to drum up business for the family slate quarry, announcing that work had commenced with A. W. Harvey acting as agent. He proclaimed the Smith Sound slate to be the best in the world, superseding even the celebrated Welsh slate. The Currie family had been on Random Island since 1852 when Welsh quarry workers Pierce and David Currie arrived to operate a slate quarry at Britannia. The community was originally called Porridge Cove, but a visit from the warship HMS *Britannia* inspired a new name.

April 15
The Blind Man's Organ — St. John's, 1906

Mr. Michael Power, a blind man, was out with his new organ on Wafer Street for the first time. The music was so good that it attracted hundreds. The hand piano-organ had been presented to Mr. Power in the British Hall a few nights previously by Mr. A. H. Martin. The *Telegram* newspaper had advocated for the purchase of the organ to assist the destitute Mr. Power. W. Clouston, J. Vey, Ayre & Sons, Bowring's, and

Reid's had all been generous in their contributions, and on his first day out with his new instrument, Mr. Power serenaded each of their establishments in thanks.

April 16
The Scamps of Coronation Street — St. John's, 1906

Residents of Coronation Street complained that their street was in a frightful condition, with mud several inches deep. The only respite from mud came when the street was frozen solid. Furthermore, neighbourhood women and girls were afraid to leave their homes at night, even to cross the streets, without an escort, as "scamps have on more than one occasion insulted them." Locals felt that the lack of a street light in the area made matters worse. Council was encouraged to see to the matter at once.

April 17
Runaway Bride (and Groom) — Bell Island, 1907

Following the wedding of Miss Annie Fitzgerald to Mr. Michael Bower at the Roman Catholic Church, the bride and groom got into the first sleigh to return home at the head of a procession of 10 sleighs. When passing through the meadow near the church, the horse became frightened and started off at a mad gallop. In full flight, the sleigh struck against a post, the harness broke, the sleigh turned over, and the bride and groom were thrown out. They escaped without any broken bones and were taken home on one of the other vehicles, where the wedding celebration continued. The horse ran on to the end of the island, where it fell, exhausted.

April 18
Two Flying Saucers — Corner Brook, 1952

Clarence Hamilton, of Empire Street, was awakened by a howling dog at 4:00 a.m. He leaned out of his window in time to see what he could only guess to be "a Flying Saucer." He watched as a yellowish sphere the size and shape of a football, with a short tail of light, circled Corner Brook twice, very rapidly, then shot off in a northeasterly direction. Hamilton stated it was travelling faster than any plane he had ever seen. Ernest Harmon Air Force Base, Stephenville, stated that none of its planes were in the air over Corner Brook at that time. A second sighting was made that evening at 10:00 p.m. by an ex–air force pilot. He reported the encounter as follows:

> There was a plume of smoke stretching across the sky from the paper mill, and glancing up I detected a bright spot near the edge of the smoke about the size of a manhole cover. It was so much brighter than the rest of the smoke trail that I thought at first it was caused by a powerful spotlight, but could not detect any beam from ground to air. I watched it for about a minute and a half and it remained motionless but the outline remained well defined and bright. Suddenly the spot climbed in a slow spiral at the rate about 3,000 feet a minute. . . . The manoeuvres it executed were definitely controlled, but at speeds that no human could withstand. I do not claim it was a saucer, but it was definitely a disc of light—controlled—and travelling at fantastic speed.

April 19
Sahlstrom's Fish Biscuits — St. John's, 1897

The energetic Professor C. A. Sahlstrom convened a meeting of probable shareholders in a bold new scheme—a factory to produce fish biscuits. Biscuits. Made of fish. Let the professor explain, in his own words:

> A biscuit, you say. Well, a pound of these biscuits—which contain fish and vegetables, with flavouring matter—the preparation of these is a secret at present, because a company is about to be floated to put them on the English market shortly—when soaked will give 2 pounds of food, which, when fried, will furnish a palatable meal. A pound of these biscuits costs the consumer about sixpence. One or two biscuits will give a solid meal—at the cost, say, of a penny. The portability of these biscuits—they will, of course, keep as long as you like—has already attracted the attention of military and naval authorities; and as regards the merits of fish food as nourishment, you can ask any man of science you care to mention.

The professor had blown into town not long before. He was (so he claimed) by birth a Swede, but by inclination a Briton, and educated in the splendid school of natural science of the University at Berlin. Before he was out of his teens, he had received a gold medal for his discoveries in the science of pisciculture at the 1862 Great Exhibition and had visited almost every court in Europe as the private secretary of the Grand Duke of Tuscany.

Sahlstrom unhesitatingly predicted that Sahlstrom's Fish Biscuits would soon take a most important place among the "Fish Products of the World." He produced a letter from a Captain Collins, the chief of the American Fisheries Bureau, who declared them to be the best-prepared fish food he had ever tasted. It would only, the professor imagined, require $100,000 in capital to get the venture off the ground before he headed for Europe to open up markets for the disposal of his biscuits.

"We should be foolish indeed to allow the opportunity to pass us by," opined the *Evening Telegram*. The business community of St. John's agreed, meeting to form the Sahlstrom Fish Biscuit Co. Ltd., with various merchant tycoons of the best families lining up to support the fishy business, with E. R. Bowring, Esquire, at the helm as chairman of the new venture. All the investors agreed there were immense possibilities ahead.

By September, the professor's mail had gone curiously unclaimed at the General Post Office, and by the following year, no one seemed to know of the whereabouts of the professor nor the cash. The Sahlstrom Fish Biscuit Co. Ltd. sank as quickly as it had risen.

In 1902, the professor was in British Columbia, pitching a scheme to sell local peat as fuel. Under the magic wand of science, the professor promised to transmute the brown peat of the bog into gold, in the form of fuel, wood spirit, acetic acid, ammonia, tar, fibre for papermaking, even a brown colour for dye.

There was no mention of fish biscuits.

April 20
Broom Maker's Birthday — Conne River, 1904

Nigola "Nickly" Jeddore was born on this day, the third child of five born to Steven Jeddore and Mary McDonald. Jeddore became a well-known maker of birch brooms and eel spears and was also remembered as a carver of axe handles and other sundry items. He was a noted hunter, camp cook, canoeist, and snowshoer. Into his eighties, he would walk the road from Miawpukek (Conne River) to St. Alban's at least once a week to shop, visit friends, or to attend bingo. Jeddore was buried on his own birthday in 1991, after dying from a heart attack in hospital following a tragic house fire. It was said that when he died, a vast wealth of unrecorded Mi'kmaq history of the district of Taqamkuk (Newfoundland) was lost with him.

April 21
Michael Cullen's Hypnotic Sleep — St. John's, 1898

Michael Cullen was woken from a hypnotic sleep by Professor Lawrence at the Total Abstinence Hall. A full 22 hours previously, the young man had been hypnotized and placed on a cot in the window of the hall by the professor, a gentleman of medium height, about 40 years of age, with bright, hazel eyes, and well-cut features. Hundreds of people had crowded outside the window to eyeball the young man as he slept, attendants turning his body every two hours. Not a sound was heard in the audience that night when the professor bent over him, counted to three, and clapped his hands. At this, Cullen woke and calmly walked across the stage "amid such a storm of applause as was never known in the city before."

April 22
Born on a Train — Somewhere East of Gambo, 1918

An unusual incident occurred on board the incoming express. During the run across the island, passenger Doctor Chisholm was called to attend to an emergency patient. Under his ministrations, the wife of a section man (a railroad worker who maintains and patrols the track) gave birth to a son. It was a happier outcome than the doctor's previous case: he happened to be on the train as he had been called to Gambo to inspect a young fellow whose finger had been badly lacerated by a saw. The finger was amputated.

April 23
Down She Goes — St. John's, 1897

A terribly windy night in town, so windy that a house being erected on Mundy Pond Road was blown down completely. It roared so ferociously on Cook Street and Merrymeeting Road that windows and doors were blown in by the gale, and residents were worried about remaining in their houses. Meanwhile, an old lady on her way home from prayers fell into the open sewer at the corner of Deady's Lane and New Gower Street. Today's pedestrians need not fear, as Deady's Lane is long gone—it was located on the north side of New Gower Street running to Casey Street, in the area east of Brazil Square.

April 24
Happy Exchange — Twillingate, 1900

The *Virginia Lake* arrived at 9:00 p.m., and the enterprising Purser Webber and Chief Steward Cunningham soon initiated an interesting trade. The duo had brought along a barrel of turnip seed and distributed them to the locals, taking payment in mussels. Both sides of the exchange were delighted, as mussels were plentiful and seed scarce.

April 25
Loaded Concertinas — Port aux Basques, 1906

Three Norwegians arrived in port, each carrying an innocent-looking concertina. Collector Pike became suspicious when the first would not let the inspector handle the instrument. When Pike took up the concertina, he was surprised at its great weight. He had the end taken off and found it filled with watches and jewellery. The other two accordions were found to be similarly loaded. Another passenger, rather bulky around the waist, was found to have his clothing stuffed with watch chains and other items. The goods, valued close to $1,000, were confiscated, and the parties arrested.

April 26
Improving the Grounds — Government House, 1930

Some alterations were under way on Government House grounds. The fence along Military Road was moved back a couple of feet, and the main entranceway was altered.
The "orderly's garden" at the corner of Military Road and Bannerman Road was being set out with ornamental trees.

Royal Visit of Queen Elizabeth and King George V to Government House in St. John's, 1939

April 27
Ghost Trouble — St. John's, 1896

The young ladies of a retail showroom in the city were "afflicted with ghost trouble." They declared that they heard steps adjacent to their department, "in a place where mortal man does not exist, and they are alarmed accordingly."

April 28
Love Conquers All — St. John's, 1898

A labourer returned from work, drunk and disorderly, to his house on Cabot Street. His wife, having had enough, locked him in the house and fetched the police to arrest him. The next morning, perhaps after a peaceful night's sleep, she broke down completely when she appeared in the witness box. As she was unwilling to give evidence against her erring husband, Judge Conroy allowed her to leave the witness box and dismissed the case, expressing his hope that the pair would settle the matter amicably between them. They left court together "as happy as two turtle doves."

April 29
Felis Demulcta Mitis — St. Bride's, 1899

Mr. W. J. Allan, the watchmaker, reported he had in his possession a curio that had been lately dug up in St. Bride's, Placentia Bay. It was a silver plate of an oval shape, with a shield bearing three fishes, surmounted by a cat holding a flag. Allan surmised the plate was "probably a relic of the French occupation" and asked the public for their help in identifying the crest. It is uncertain if Allan ever uncovered the lore behind the plate. The design, however, sounds remarkably like the coat of arms of the Keane Baronetcy, Cappoquin House, Belmont, in the County of Waterford, to wit: "Gules three Salmon naiant in pale Argent; Crest: A Cat-a-Mountain sejant proper supporting in his dexter paw a Flagstaff thereon a Union Jack proper." The family motto was *Felis Demulcta Mitis* (the stroked cat is gentle). How an Irish silver plate ended up buried in St. Bride's is uncertain, but there are certainly Newfoundland connections to Cappoquin. The village is believed to be home to one branch of the Tobin family, and the 1846 Newfoundland will of John Cronin, which left half his estate to his sister, Elinor Cronin alias Condon, noted her as living in Afahan, near Cappoquin, County Waterford.

April 30
A Strange Calf — Carbonear, 1899

The stuffed calf of Mr. William Taylor, Burnt Head Road, was put on display and seen by hundreds of Sunday gawkers. The calf had been born with two heads, "perfect in every particular; one turned to the right and the other to the left, and joined at the junction of the ears, from whence they form as one to the neck." Each head was said to have two eyes, two ears, with mouth and teeth all alike, the only difference being in that one head was a male and the other female. The owner consented to skin the animal and stuff it at the request of several friends.

MAY

May 1
Barn-Moving Drummer Boys — Harbour Grace, 1912

Mr. George Whelan decided to move his barn from its old site on Military Road to the site of his new house on Bennett's Lane. He had the barn prepared, and rollers ready, when a bright idea struck him. Whelan called on Colonel Kennedy of the Catholic Cadet Corps and asked if the lads would give him a hand. At seven o'clock they left their Armoury and marched, proceeded by the beating of their drums, to the barn. The cadets grabbed hold of the ropes, and after an order of "quick march," the boys, drums, and barn made their way along Military Road, down Garland Street, up Harvey Street, and down Bennett's Lane. The barn was in its new location before dark, much to the satisfaction of its owner.

May 2
Should Have Called the Cadets — Petty Harbour to St. John's, 1908

Things did not go quite so smoothly with the house haul of Mrs. Halley, milliner. Her house needed to be moved from Petty Harbour to a new location in St. John's in order to build a new house on the old site. The men she contracted had hauled the house as far as Waterford Bridge Station but slightly miscalculated their timing as they started to drag the house across the railway tracks. It was noon hour, and the Carbonear train was making its run for the St. John's station.

By the time the train was within sight, it was too late to stop the locomotive or move the house. The train smashed into the end of the house, spinning the building 90 degrees. The side of the locomotive cabin was almost demolished, and the engineer slightly injured. The end of the building had to be cut away before the train could continue its journey.

May 3
Newfoundland War Vets' Flipper Supper — Cambridge, Massachusetts, 1930

Eighty people sat down at the Odd Fellows' Hall to enjoy their annual flipper supper, cooked and served in Newfoundland style. From the way the food disappeared, "it was evident that the guests had not lost their taste for the succulent Flipper." After the meal, there was a short concert with music and recitations, followed by a dance. The prize for the evening (a lampshade) was taken home by Miss Margaret Miles.

May 4
First Horseless Wagon in Newfoundland — St. John's, 1903

The first automobile in Newfoundland arrived by the SS *Rosalind* from New York:

> The new horseless wagon is of the single-seat order and is capable of being driven at great speed. Mr. Reid will manipulate the machine himself just as soon as the weather and roads will permit and will certainly attract much attention as he speeds along over the city and suburban roads.

May 5
Clothesline Thieves — St. John's, 1897

An old woman from Freshwater Road placed her week's washing out on a clothesline and let them remain out all night. In the morning, the majority of her washing was gone. It was not the first time clothesline thieves had been at work in the neighbourhood.

May 6
Woodpile Falls on Boy — Knight's Cove, 1908

The five-year-old son of James F. Ricketts was playing about the door of his home when a pile of about 400 "turn" of wood fell on him. The first sticks to fall fell crosswise, and it is this happenstance that saved the child from being crushed to death. When the wood was removed, the father expected to find a dead body, but the boy was taken out from under the woodpile with life still in him. A hurried call brought Doctor Levisconte from King's Cove. After tending the boy for a few hours, the doctor brought him around.

A "turn" is a Newfoundland expression used variously to mean either so much wood as a man can carry at one time or one stick of wood made from a fair-sized tree with its limbs lopped off.

May 7
Keeper Injured — Cape Spear, 1916

Harold Cantwell, the 21-year-old son of lightkeeper James Cantwell, was badly injured when his coat caught in the belt of the machinery used to operate the steam fog whistle at

Cape Spear. He received a severe fracture of the skull, but after a short stay in the hospital, he was sent home.

May 8
The Sleepy Stowaway — St. John's via Halifax, 1903

Thomas Healy, of Halifax, was arrested for being a stowaway when he disembarked on this morning from the *Virginia Lake*. He was charged with obtaining a passage by fraud and brought before Judge Conroy. Healy protested his innocence, claiming he had gone aboard the ship in Halifax to see some friends and had fallen asleep. While he was in the depths of his slumber, the *Virginia Lake* steamed away. A dubious Judge Conroy advised the police to make further inquiries.

May 9
Meteor Observed — St. John's, 1875

At a quarter past nine, at an altitude of about 40 degrees above the eastern horizon, a brilliant and beautiful meteor was spotted proceeding in a northerly direction. It was the second dramatic meteor reported over St. John's that week. One local skywatcher gave an excellent description of the phenomenon to the *St. John's Advertiser*:

> At first sight the nucleus appeared of a yellowish colour bearing a long trail of luminous matter, which, however, faded away at the same time as the nucleus which suddenly changed in all respects as regards appearance to what is termed pyrotechnically a "squib," emitting a bright green lustre of variegated hue, shooting in variable lengths and directions, sometimes to the north, at other times directly downwards or towards the earth,

when, just before it disappeared, it again resolved into the nucleus form, but without any trail as it had on its first appearance, and then suddenly divided into two parts of almost equal size, one slightly diverging to the NW the other smaller part to the NE; but only proceeded for a very short distance, when they seemed to be extinguished.

May 10
Eat What You Can, Can What You Can't —
St. John's, 1930

It was reported that several parties were contemplating a new industry for the upcoming berry season. Instead of shipping them in a frozen state, it was suggested that blueberries be canned in gallon containers instead: "It is pointed out that in tins the berries would keep indefinitely, there would be no loss of juices and storage expenses would be less."

May 11
Lazy Whale — Merasheen, 1897

While the *Pride of the West* was becalmed in Placentia Bay in the same line of latitude as the island of Merasheen, a large whale came to the side of the craft and remained there for three hours. Mr. Patrick Gaulton, master of the vessel, judged it to be nearly 100 feet long. Every now and again it rolled up against the *Pride of the West*, so close that the crew could easily place their hands upon its back.

The men tried to scare the whale off, but it would not leave the side of the ship, even when sticks and bilge water were thrown at it. The skipper was tempted to fire a shot into the whale, but cooler heads prevailed, fearing a destructive blow from the whale's tail. Eventually, the whale swam off a short distance, and as the wind picked up, the ship sailed on. The whale seemed unconcerned and lingered behind "in a lazy mood."

May 12
Flying Boats and Photographed Goats — Trepassey, 1919

Three Navy Curtis Seaplanes arrived at Trepassey, where they joined a dozen naval vessels and approximately 8,500 American crewmen. They had flown in from Halifax, a seven-hour flight, in order to make an attempt at a transatlantic flight to the Azores. One of the "flying boats," the NC-4, took off from Trepassey and completed the first transatlantic flight between North America and Europe, albeit not non-stop. The first true non-stop flight was made by pilots John Alcock and Arthur Whitten Brown two weeks later.

Navy-Curtiss Flying Boat NC-1 in Trepassey, Newfoundland, Canada, on a leg of its transatlantic journey in May 1919

The residents of Trepassey were curious about the American machines and sailors; the Americans, apparently, were curious about the Trepassey goats. One reporter noted, "as in nearly all outports the goats 'wear' big, heavy wooden collars to prevent them from going through fences, it was most amusing to see a gang of gobs [American sailors] surrounding a pack of goats and driving them into a herd so that the men with cameras could snap them."

May 13
Riot on Water Street — St. John's, 1861

A serious riot erupted, after a contentious election, as a mob broke into the premises of Nowlan and Kitchen. The soldiers were ordered out, and officials did all they could to calm the violence. The magistrate read the Riot Act, but to no avail: stones were thrown at the soldiers, and the mob tried to drag Colonel Grant from his horse. It is alleged a shot was fired at the soldiers, and the commander gave the order to fire on the crowd. Three people were killed and 20 wounded.

May 14
Lost Art of Letter Writing — St. John's, 1896

Thirteen-year-old Bella Parrell was arrested for sending notes "of a most revolting and obscene character" to a woman named Mrs. Beck, who had received three of the letters in one day. Bella had been in service to Mrs. Beck, and when she left, she had taken one of her employer's hats, and references in the letters to this hat led the police to make the arrest. Bella denied the charges.

Sadly, no record of the letters' contents remain.

May 15
Transportation of the Dead — Statutes of Newfoundland, 1931

An updated Act Respecting Health and Public Welfare was passed on this date, which included detailed rules for moving bodies of those who had died of infectious diseases. For example, the bodies of persons who died of diptheria, scarlet fever, anthrax, or leprosy could not be transported unless they were thoroughly disinfected by arterial and cavity injections of an approved disinfectant fluid, all orifices blocked with absorbent cotton, and washed externally with a disinfectant by a licensed embalmer. This was just the start of the procedure. The body then had to be completely wrapped in a sheet saturated with an approved disinfectant, encased in an airtight zinc, tin, copper, or lead coffin, or an iron casket, hermetically sealed, all of which was to be enclosed in a stout outside wooden box. The Act also covered transit permits for the diseased dead, the licensing of embalmers, and the correct procedures for the destruction of infected property. The Act makes excellent reading for anyone wanting to know how to lessen the chances of a zombie outbreak.

May 16
Holy Feast Day of St. Brendan the Navigator

One of Newfoundland's possible first European tourists, St. Brendan the Navigator made a legendary seven-year voyage across the Atlantic Ocean in a curragh, a wood-framed boat covered in sewn ox hides, travelling to a new land and returning home to tell his tale. Whilst exploring the North Atlantic, the good Saint and his men stopped on a small island to celebrate Easter Mass. The next morning, the brethren put a cauldron on a fire to cook. As the pot began to boil, the island began to move. The monks rushed back to the curragh, and the "island" lifted up its great tail and swam off into the distance. St. Brendan is the patron saint of boatmen, divers, mariners, portaging canoes, and, appropriately, whales.

St. Brendan's legendary voyage, showing Mass being said on the back of a whale. Image circa 1621.

May 17
Curious Find — Harbour Grace, 1893

While digging in a garden on Noad Street, which he had been cultivating for 18 years, a gentleman unearthed a plain gold ring. Inside was stamped: "Mary Andrews 1730." It was found exactly where a portion of an old house once stood. It was deduced that the ring had been the property of the maiden aunt of the late Mrs. Captain Nathaniel Davis, who had lived in the former building.

May 18
Professor of Phrenology — St. John's, 1882

Noted American phrenologist and lecturer Orson Squire Fowler appeared at the Star of the Sea Hall, much to the appreciation of the large audience that had gathered. Phrenology is a pseudo-science that involves observing or feeling the bumps on the skull to predict mental traits or psychological attributes of the individual. Professor Fowler started his lecture by arguing that it was not the heart that caused the circulation of blood, but air taken into the lungs that caused blood to flow. Next, he lectured on phrenology proper, asking a man from the audience to come to the front to have his skull read. Mr. Michael Dea volunteered for the test, and eyewitnesses said the professor was "generally accurate in his description of Mr. Dea's leading traits of character." The professor had checked in to the Avalon Hotel, and over the next few days, he did a lively business directing his attention to the bumps of local politicians.

May 19
Miraculous Escape from Death — Mount Pearl, 1924

Mr. Scott, the officer in charge at the Mount Pearl Wireless Station, and his wife had driven into St. John's to purchase their week's supply of groceries. Driving back to the station, around 3:00 p.m., Scott slowed the car down as he drew close to Paddy Coughlan's Crossing, as the crossing had a reputation of being dangerous. As he started to cross, the oncoming train, travelling at a rate of between 30 and 35 miles per hour, collided with the car. Scott swerved his car to the left, and the train ripped along the side of the machine, smashing both wheels and axles, and driving some of the ironwork a foot deep into the ground. The train stopped about 50 yards farther on, and the crew hurried back to the car, expecting to find the occupants terribly injured. To everyone's surprise, Mr. and Mrs. Scott had received only a few bruises.

May 20
The Sowing — St. John's, 1895

Mr. Edward Hanrahan planted some turnip. It wouldn't be ready for plucking till October 16.

May 21
Delivery Not Guaranteed — Alexander Bay, 1900

A traveller found a bag that had been thrown behind the door of a railway shanty in Alexander Bay. At first he thought it was a bag of moss, used as insulation for stuffing chinks in the walls of cellars or camp bunkhouses. It was, instead, the postal bag containing all the mail for Glovertown, which had been missing for a week.

May 22
Certificate of Competency — St. John's, 1888

Abram Kean, of Flowers Island, passed his examination and was awarded a Master's Certificate of Competency. Within a month, he had his first ship, the SS *Curlew*, on the Labrador Mail Service. He would go on to become famous for his success in sealing, and infamous for his part in sending 78 men to their deaths in the 1914 Newfoundland Sealing Disaster, at which time he was captain of the *Stephano*.

May 23
Hell on Earth — Somewhere in France, 1915

Campbell "Cam" Philips, while serving with the Canadian contingent in France, wrote to his father in St. John's:

> I came out of the trenches last night unscathed but believe me it was hell on earth while we were there. My first day in we had to bury some dead. It was an awful sight as many were blown to pieces. My nerves were almost completely shattered before we got out. We lost every officer in our company, four killed and the others wounded. We were supposed to have a double company of 200 going in but we really had 150, and out of this, we had 9 casualties. When on our way to the trenches we halted a mile in the rear to receive our rations and wait for dusk. A small shell (about 18 pounder) hit in amongst us and killed outright a man not 10 feet from me and wounded four others.

May 24
Trouters' Special — Gull Pond, 1930

For many, Victoria Day by tradition means the first trouting expedition of the year. One Victoria Day weekend in the 1920s, a man was drowned in Gull Pond, near Windsor Lake, just outside of St. John's. He had waded out from shore, in search of elusive trout, and had sunk down into a deep hole in the pond and drowned. Within a year, rumours began to float around that the pond was haunted by the man's ghost. In 1930, a St. John's man was fishing at the far end of the body of water. Finding himself without matches to light his cigarettes, he noticed another man fishing not far away, thigh deep in the water. The matchless man called out, asking for a light. The second man acted as if he had not heard the question, and when the first looked back a moment later, the stranger had vanished. It was not until much later that a friend told him of the ghostly fisherman who had been seen in that section of the pond.

May 25
A Wife Too Many — Little Port, Bay of Islands, 1908

Constable Quinlan travelled to Little Port and arrested Frank Wilson on a charge of bigamy. Wilson, true name Kenneth LeDrew, was a native of Alexander Bay, Bonavista Bay, where his first wife (formerly Miss Wells) resided with one child. Things had not gone well with Mrs. LeDrew No. 1, and he had left for the United States. There, under a false name, he married another young woman and brought her to reside in Petrie Crossing. Mrs. LeDrew No. 2 also bore him one child, and it was said she was "in a sorry plight."

Petrie Crossing, passenger train shot, May 1959

May 26
Beware the Velocipede — Topsail, 1869

Curious citizens witnessed the first velocipede ever ridden in public in Newfoundland. Mr. R. H. Earle ventured on his bicycle to Topsail and beyond before returning to St. John's. There were apparently some doubts about the safety of this new kind of conveyance. A few days later, the *Patriot and Terra-Nova Herald* printed the following cautionary tale, a parody of a popular folk ballad:

- The Velocipede -

Lord Lovell, he stood by the garden-gate,
With his shining velocipede.
And whispered farewell to his Lady Bell,
Who wished for his Lordship good-speed, speed, speed,
Who wished for his Lordship good-speed.

"When will you be back, Lord Lovell?" she said.
But he gave her question no heed —
Placed his feet in the stirrups and galloped away
On his famous velocipede, pede, pede,
On his famous velocipede.

Then Lady Bell cried in frantic alarm,
"What a monster my Lord is indeed.
To ride thus away from his loving young wife,
On that horrid velocipede, pede, pede,
On that horrid velocipede."

Lord Lovell returned, broken-hearted and sore,
Broken-armed and, alas! broken-kneed;
For he struck on a post, nearly gave up the ghost,
And smashed his velocipede, pede, pede,

> And smashed his velocipede.
> Remember the fate Lord Lovell hath met,
> Let this be your warning and creed;
> Stay at home with your wife for the rest of your life,
> And beware of the velocipede, pede, pede,
> And beware of the velocipede.

May 27
Killed by a Block of Ice — Gloucester, Massachusetts, 1892

Eli Rowe, 21 years old, expired at Gloucester from the effects of an injury received while taking ice on board a fishing vessel. Eli was a native of the South Side, Trinity, the son of the widow Anne Rowe. He had left the previous year for work in the herring fishery in Placentia Bay, but as the catch was not successful, he had signed on as crew with an American vessel. While loading ice in a schooner, he slipped and fell. The block of ice slid against him, striking him in the abdomen. He continued to work till that evening but did not feel well the next day. He took to his bed and could not eat. A week before he died, he ran a high fever, and a doctor said he had contracted pneumonia on top of his injury. He started coughing constantly and spitting blood. He grew worse very rapidly and died peacefully on this date at 4:00 p.m. The Rev. William F. Cook, of the Methodist Episcopal Church, performed the funeral service and wrote to Mrs. Rowe, explaining the mournful particulars.

May 28
Fire from the Sky — Brooms Bottom, 1908

Before the shades of night had closed in, Bay of Islands witnessed a strange phenomenon. What appeared to be a large shooting star appeared out of the western sky and descended in the direction of Brooms Bottom, leaving a long fiery trail behind it. A forest fire that broke out around the same time between Brooms Bottom and Lark Harbour was blamed on the meteorite.

May 29
Climbing Bird Rock — Cape St. Mary's, 1889

The steamer *Caspian* arrived from Halifax after being detained a few hours by fog. Among her passengers was J. C. Cahoon, an American ornithologist. Cahoon made headlines a few months later when he made a successful hour-long barefoot climb of Bird Island (or Bird Rock) at Cape St. Mary's, a rock-climbing feat that had killed the men who made the two previous attempts. The rock formation rose 300 feet from the ocean and was nearly perpendicular for 200 of those feet. Millions of birds swarmed around him as he climbed, and he defended himself with a club. "With death staring him in the face, he was quite cool and collected, talking with the men below," wrote one eyewitness, adding, "He is a man of splendid nerve power."

In April 1891, Cahoon was killed by falling 80 feet while attempting a similar climb to recover a crow's nest from Shag Rock near Placentia. His name, however, lives on in the scientific name for one of the subspecies of Brown Wren, *Troglodytes aedon cahooni*, native to northern Mexico.

May 30
Watch Out for Love — St. John's, 1890

What must have been a very interesting case to witness unfolded before Judge Conroy at the police court. In summary, a woman had brought her was-to-have-been daughter-in-law before the court in order to recover a watch. The girl had been introduced to the woman's son the summer previously, and they became "very intimate." The son was going away and therefore stole the watch from his mother and gave it as a present to his lady love, saying "keep it in remembrance of me until the day of your death." Memory, apparently, was not the girl's strongest suit, and while her love was away, she took up with another fellow, forgot the first, and married the second. Meanwhile, the mother, upon finding her watch missing, had written to her son asking of its whereabouts. The son wrote two letters in return: one to his mother telling her where the watch was to be found; and one to his sweetheart, telling her that if she had another beau, to return the watch. The girl, however, refused to return the watch, unless she was paid the sum of seven shillings, the amount she had spent on gifts to her former lover.

Judge Conroy ruled that the watch was to be returned and that the girl was to be paid seven shillings.

May 31
The New Coffee Tavern — St. John's, 1894

A distinguished company gathered on Adelaide Street to attend the opening of a new type of institution in Newfoundland, a Coffee Tavern. The tavern was equipped with a modern kitchen, which meant edibles of all kinds could be served with the greatest ease, including tea, cocoa, cold meats, luncheons, chops or steaks, pastry, temperance drinks of all kinds, and, of course, coffee.

"Every hour spent by young men in a tavern of that kind was an hour gained in keeping them from the influence of drink and bad company," enthused Lady O'Brien, the wife of the Governor, as she officiated over the opening.

JUNE

June 1
Dead Man on Board — Old Perlican, 1904

The banking schooner *Snowbird* arrived in port bearing 250 quintals of fish, and one dead body, preserved in salt. The body was that of Mr. Joseph Snook, of Old Perlican, who had been sick for only two days before dropping dead. The cause of death was given as dropsy (edema). The body was placed in a coffin and sent by train to Old Perlican the same day.

June 2
Inhabited Iceberg — Torbay, 1962

An iceberg inhabited by some strange denizen of the north drifted into Torbay. Jack Dodd, a local fisherman, approached the berg in his boat and saw the creature resting at the water's edge. Dodd claimed the creature looked like it weighed approximately a ton and was dark grey or black, with a face like a cow and eyes as large as a man's clenched fist. It also had a mane like a horse and seven or eight white whiskers sprouting from its chin. As Dodd approached, the beast seemed to rise up, so he veered off, and as he did, the creature started to climb the berg. From Dodd's description, it may have been a sealion or walrus, but the authorities of the day made no attempt to determine what it was. Within a few days, a strong breeze propelled the small iceberg far from shore, and the beast was not spotted again.

June 3
Larceny of Cod Oil — St. John's, 1890

Henry Taylor, an employee of A. Goodridge & Sons, was arrested for larceny of cod oil. Taylor had made away with several casks of cod-liver oil belonging to his employer and then was brazen enough to sell the same casks back to the same company. The master cooper became suspicious when he recognized the cask as his handiwork, and the police were called in. Taylor was sentenced to 12 months imprisonment. It was felt that Taylor must have had an accomplice, as the oil was evidently lowered over the wharf into a boat at night. If there was an accomplice, Taylor refused to reveal who it was, and they were never brought to justice.

June 4
A Well-Travelled Hat — St. John's, 1890

An 89-year-old passenger arrived on the SS *Caspian* and caused quite a stir on the harbourfront, largely due to his sartorial sensibilities. Most noticeable in his attire was his hat, which he claimed was 25 years old. He wore serge pants and shirt, with an English oiled jacket. A native of Waterford, Ireland, he had taken up farming in America and had returned home to visit friends. His crossing marked his eighth passage across the Atlantic.

June 5
The Concertina, Part One — St. John's, 1891

The following notice appeared in the *Evening Herald*:

> The individual who promenades Water Street every night grinding out discordant airs from that modern instrument known as the concertina, had better take himself to some wider field where his musical talents will be more appreciated.

June 6
The Concertina, Part Two — St. John's, 1891

The following (smug) notice appeared in the *Evening Herald*:

> The little item in yesterday's Herald had its effect on the concertina fiend. He made no appearance last night.

June 7
Adventure on the *Resolution* — To Labrador and Back Again, 1803

The *Resolution* left London and proceeded with the Hudson's Bay convoy to the Orkneys, and from there onward to the Moravian mission at Okak, Labrador. The "Brethren's Society for the Furtherance of the Gospel among the Heathen" had purchased her in 1802 for service as a mission ship. She had been built in Spain but had been captured by the English and sold as a prize to the Society. As the *Resolution* set sail for Labrador, it would become clear that her adventuring days were far from over.

Her voyage to Okak took three weeks more than anticipated because of the heavy ice along the Labrador coast. The ship visited a number of Moravian communities, and then on October 10 bid farewell to Hopedale for a return trip to Orkney. When the ship was only three days' sail away from

Orkney, strong easterly gales drove the ship back and kept it three weeks longer at sea. Then, on November 18, the *Resolution* was chased down by a French frigate, which brought up alongside. The seas were so high, however, that it was impossible for the French to get a boat over to the *Resolution*. This continued during the night and the following day, and when the second night fell just as dark and boisterous, the captain set as much sail as the ship would carry and made their escape. When dawn broke, there was no sign of the French frigate. Two days later, the two ships met again, and the *Resolution* was chased and brought to a second time. Again, the wind was so violent that the frigate could not put out a boat, and the following night, the captain escaped again and saw no more of the enemy. The *Resolution* reached Stromness on December 2, almost two months after it had left Labrador.

June 8
Crosbie's Car — Topsail, 1928

Sir John Crosbie and his son were returning from a trouting excursion around 9:00 p.m. As they were driving back from Topsail, their Stutz motor car caught fire and was destroyed completely. The cause of the accident was not known, but the blaze created a traffic jam on the road, with about 25 cars held up for more than an hour.

June 9
The Skull's Curse — St. John's, 1897

A young lad discovered a round object near the top of the wall on Long's Hill, where the government of the day had been making some alterations to the cemetery. The object was covered with an accumulation of clay, and the boy and his friends used it as a football, and then set it up and threw stones at it. This continued until the earth was knocked away and revealed the "grinning emblem of mortality." The skull was reported to authorities, and Constable Murphy investigated. Parts of the bone had been knocked away by the stones, and Murphy gathered together what he could, placed it in a small box, and had it respectfully reburied. Later, it was reported that the boy who had unearthed the human skull had taken ill and was suffering from diphtheria.

June 10
Message in a Bottle — Cape St. George, 1905

It was reported from Port Saunders that the Saint Pierre banking schooner *Madeline*, under the command of Captain Leflem, picked up the following note in a bottle, about 13 and a half miles west of Cape St. George:

> 6th May, 1905. The finder of this can have the best wishes for good-luck and prosperity from the undersigned: Jack Sutherland, 287 Dufferin Ave., Winnipeg, Can.; Jas. T. Freer, Captain; W. McGregor, Richard Anderson, Wm. Melville Macpherson, Edinburgh; G. Smart. "All Scotchmen trying to better their luck in Canada; good luck till we meet again. God be with us till we meet again. *SS Corinthian*, left Glasgow, 22 April, 1905."

June 11
Starvation — Keels, 1831

A group of men from Keels, who had journeyed to King's Cove and failed to get supplies there, then made a 15-mile trek to Bonavista over the ice in search of food for their families. Once they reached Bonavista, they reported that conditions in Keels were so dire that a woman and three children had died there from hunger.

June 12
Boiler Explosion — St. John's, 1897

The train to Harbour Grace was minutes out of the station when the boiler of the locomotive exploded, killing the engineer, Fred Glasgow, and injuring several others. The accident took place just east of Allandale Road along what is today Empire Avenue, just opposite the Newfoundland Brewery on Circular Road. The explosion was as loud as a cannon, and the force of it completely flipped the engine, twisted the rails, and blew the wooden sleepers apart like matchsticks. Glasgow was blown 50 feet up the steep hill and landed in a terribly gruesome condition in J. Dwyer's potato field:

> He was torn in several places and his clothes ripped as with a knife, while he was literally par-boiled from scalding water and steam. His skull was severed, and although alive when help reached him, he did not live beyond a few minutes; a portion of his skull was picked up about 10 yards from where his body lay.

June 13
Lord and Lady Baden-Powell — Corner Brook, 1935

A Scout and Guide rally in Corner Brook received two distinguished visitors, Lord and Lady Baden-Powell. The couple were on a British Empire tour and spent two weeks in various parts of Newfoundland, including two days at Corner

Brook. Following his retirement from the British Army, Lord Baden-Powell had founded the Boy Scouts in 1908, to "promote good citizenship in the rising generation," and to further peace through the advancement of international understanding.

Lady Baden-Powell

June 14
Literary Kittens — Twillingate, 1952

The printing press at the *Twillingate Sun* decided it needed a rest and shut down completely in the middle of printing an issue. Only after 24 hours of tinkering did the staff get her rolling again, and then frantically worked to get back on schedule. By a strange coincidence, they discovered that a cat had given birth to four kittens in the basement at the exact same time. Once the next issue went to press, it included this notice:

> Whether there is any connection between the two we don't know for sure, but as this is the first time the press has given real trouble in its long history and the first time kittens have been born in the office, it seems more than coincidence. We hope it doesn't happen again. Anyone interested in owning a young kitten which can lay claim to such distinguished parentage, is asked to get in touch with the Editor at the very earliest opportunity.

June 15
100th Voyage of the *Harmony* — London to Labrador, 1869

A meeting was held on board the Moravian mission ship *Harmony* at the West India docks before the vessel's departure for Labrador. The on-board, pre-departure meeting was a usual custom for the Moravians, but this event attracted a large number of friends of the mission, as it marked the *Harmony*'s 100th trip to Labrador. A new flag had been procured for the voyage, featuring the figure of an angel and an angelic message on a scroll, but the weather was so unfavourable that it could only be unfurled for a short time. If 100 voyages across the North Atlantic seems like a lot, it is important to note that the Moravian missions had five different ships all named *Harmony* between 1787 and 1926, so it is likely the 100 voyages were divided among several ships of the same name.

The Moravian mission ship *Harmony* somewhere near Nain on the coast of Labrador

June 16
Water on Tap — Windsor Lake, 1862

Water for the first time was conveyed through the pipes to St. John's from Windsor Lake. The General Water Company advised all parties interested in having an indoor source of water to make the necessary arrangements in their respective dwellings. The branch pipes were furnished and laid by the company, but all internal pipes and fittings had to be provided by the house-keepers at their own expense.

June 17
Bolts from the Heavens — Avondale, 1911

The most severe thunder and lightning storm in living memory swept through Avondale. Peals of thunder shook the dwellings, and lightning flashes "like tongues of fire" lit up the firmament. At 11:00 p.m., as one of the most severe bursts of thunder and lightning shot over the place, flames were seen issuing from the spire of the church on the hill. Almost instantaneously, fire burst from all parts of the sacred edifice, amidst peals of thunder and lightning flashes that illuminated the darkness. Father Sheehan rushed into the burning church and made several attempts to save the vestments and sacred articles, with partial success. Pieces of the tower were driven several yards from the site of the building as if blown there by dynamite.

Meanwhile, lightning entered the house of Edward Cook and broke through the chimney. Four people in the house were rendered unconscious. Mrs. Cook was sitting in the kitchen reading a book and had her feet on the fender of the stove. The lightning drove the boots clean off her feet and then shot through the kitchen floor, tearing a wide hole in the floorboards. Mrs. Cook swooned from the pain and fright, and her feet were badly burned. Two miles away, in Harbour Main, the house of Peter Walsh was broken to pieces by the storm.

June 18
The Sea Recedes — St. Shott's, 1864

At 7:00 pm, the ocean at St. Shott's receded 250 yards beyond where the wreck of the HMS *Drake* lay submerged in about five fathoms of water. For 10 or 12 minutes, the wreck of the *Drake*, which had been wrecked with the loss of 13 men in 1822, was entirely visible, including its cannons. The water eventually returned in a great rush, pushing in enough stones and gravel to fill the gut.

June 19
Burned in Effigy — St. John's, 1852

Opponents of Governor LeMarchant recreated his figure in effigy and dragged it through the streets:

> On the breast of the effigy glistened a star, and two ornamented his coattails, epaulettes, military boots, silver laced trousers, a cocked hat and plumes completed his habiliments. The crowd passed up Military Road and down Garrison Hill, through Water Street and up Cochrane Street, where they halted before the Government House. The effigy was then fastened to the palings of the fence on the Mall. A match was put to the fuses between the stars on his coat-tails, and with a loud explosion, he was blown into the air, while the crowd cheered.

June 20
Periwinkle Baskets — Topsail, 1890

A large number of withrod baskets, made for the purpose of periwinkle fishing, were exhibited from the deck of a schooner at Job's wharf. The baskets had been made by the women of Topsail, and Job Brothers intended to fit their banking schooners out with them. "Should they come into general use," it was suggested, "the industry will be a large one, and will afford the women folks of Topsail and other places a means of employment." In the 1890s, periwinkles (also known as "wrinkles" or "snagles") were often used as bait, notably by the Saint Pierre fishermen, while Fortune Bay fishermen of the same period used periwinkles when there was a shortage of other baitfish such as herring.

June 21
Summer Solstice Brings Winter Weather —
St. John's, 1923

Summer arrived in Newfoundland with the ferocity of an October gale. The green foliage of the trees in and around the city was hurled in heaps into the gutters as though autumn had come. Fences blew down along the country roads, while traps, boats, and stages were wrecked along the east and northeast coasts.

June 22
Queen Victoria's Diamond Jubilee — St. John's, 1897

Queen Victoria (who reigned 1837–1901) celebrated 60 years on the throne. St. John's celebrated with music, military displays, fireworks, and decorated buildings. Of particular grandiosity was the Colonial Building, which made fine use of modern technology:

> The front was a mass of beautiful designs done in the vari-coloured incandescent electric lights, 12 ordinary arc lights descended on either side from the flagpole and on the facade appeared a crown beautified with myriad coloured lights, with two Union Jacks, crossed over a shield bearing the letters V.R., the whole surrounded with a bordering of beautiful electrical lamps. The grounds were beautified by hundreds of Chinese lanterns hanging from the trees and numbers of people inspected the brilliant room of the interior. The pillars were draped with bunting and entwined around with festoons of evergreen. About 800 candles were burnt in the windows and the building presented a perfect appearance.

June 23
In Want of Provisions — Waterford, Ireland, 1775

The *Hercules*, under Captain Thompson, and the *Byron*, under Captain Reeves, arrived in Waterford from St. John's. They had arrived to purchase 40 tons of bread and a number of other necessities, with an eye to returning to St. John's as quickly as possible. The day before, the *Valentine*, under Captain Nowlan, had also arrived from St. John's looking for bread. This was due in part to the American War of Independence, which had caused a disruption in shipping from the Colonies to Newfoundland. As a result, the people of Newfoundland were in extreme want of provisions, so ships had been sent to Ireland in search of food.

June 24
Oomancy — St. John's, 1891

June 24 marks both an old midsummer celebration across many cultures and the Feast Day of St. John the Baptist. It is a day with a complex folklore and a myriad of traditions. In many Catholic parts of the province, this was a day for bonfires. For the young ladies of the city, this was the day they were ready with eggs and tumblers to divine their future husbands. The usual method was to drop the egg white in a tumbler of hot water and then pick out the shapes revealed in the swirls of the egg white in order to foretell the profession of their future partners, not that dissimilar from other kinds of divination like tea-leaf reading. An anonymous writer in the *Colonist* offered up some tongue-in-cheek tips for young ladies who wished to interpret their eggy signs:

> If the outlines of a ship can be traced in the tumbler, the future head will be something between the cap-

tain of a man-of-war and the skipper of a banker. If a tall structure with spires shooting up from it should be traced in the tumbler, the shadowy head will be in the Church, or keeper of a light-house. If many short spires are seen, the future lord of the blushing fair one will own an ancestral estate in England, or a farm on the Topsail road. If numbers of small bars are noticed in the tumbler, they denote bridges, which the future husband will have something to do with the construction of, or Chairman of an outport Road Board. . . . The broken egg takes many other forms, but the above are fair samples.

June 25
From Underneath the Ground — St. John's, 1891

While undertaking some excavation work along Water Street, Mr. W. Donnelly and his work crew struck a very curious find. In one spot the men unearthed the following items: a number of cups and saucers; a brass tap; two clay pipes; a pendulum of a clock; a pair of scissors; a poker; a pair of tongs; a 14-pound weight; a pork barrel; and a brass coin. It was presumed that all these things had been in a house that had tumbled down during the Great Fire of 1846. Found with the other objects was a bed key, which is a small metal combination tool used to disassemble the wooden frame of a bed and to tighten the ropes that supported the mattresses. The tightening of bed ropes was often a weekly task, though rope beds fell out of fashion after the invention of the coil spring mattress in 1865.

June 26
Battle of Foxtrap — Foxtrap, 1880

A group of surveyors set out to conduct a location survey for a proposed railway from St. John's to Halls Bay, a very contentious political issue. As the surveyors approached the community of Foxtrap (now part of Conception Bay South), a crowd of over 500 irate residents, most of them women, armed with splitting knives, pitchforks, and rocks, refused to let the surveyors pass through.

June 27
Sarsaparilla — Cupids Colony, 1628

Regarding the John Guy Company, Doctor Meadus wrote to Lady Conway:

> Have conferred with Mr. Paine about the Newfoundland business; he will part with his Presidentship if John Slaney, the Governor of the whole land, consents. Hopes of mines of iron and silver in Newfoundland; present profit by fishing, furs and sarsaparilla.

Fishing, of course, and furs, yes, but sarsaparilla? The Mi'kmaq used the root of wild sarsaparilla crushed into a powder and steeped in water as a medicine for colds. In the 17th century, wild sarsaparilla (or American sarsaparilla) was imported into Europe, where it was used as a treatment for various complaints, including sexually transmitted diseases. Sarsaparilla was later believed to serve as a blood purifier and was a popular additive to health tonics. Think about that next time you are drinking your root beer.

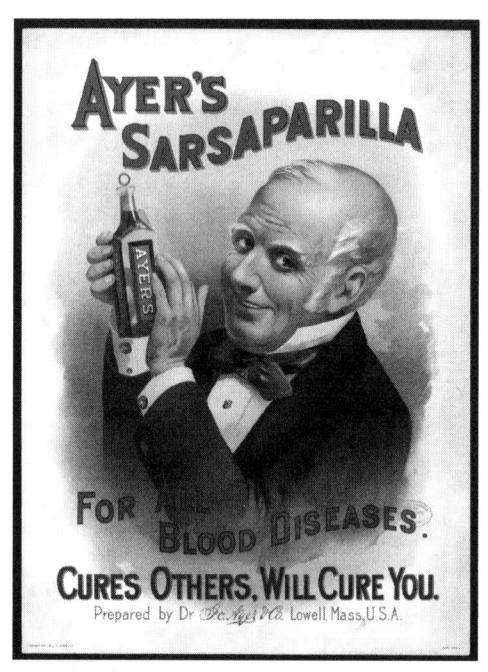

Advertisements like this one for Ayer's Sarsaparilla were common in the Newfoundland newspapers of the 1890s.

June 28
Three Good Sheppards — Tilting, 1912

Nicholas Keefe and Thomas Keefe were fishing off Fogo Island when their boat struck a small iceberg and started to take on water. The Keefes were rescued by three members of the Sheppard family: Nathaniel, aged 60; Mark, aged 30; and Henry, aged eight. When a piece of plank punched a hole in the side of the Sheppards' boat during the rescue, a quick-thinking young Henry Sheppard stuffed his coat into the hole, giving them enough time to make it back to Tilting. The parish priest heard their story and sent it to the Carnegie Hero Fund Commission in the United States. In November 1915, the Sheppards received by post two medals of bravery and $1,000, a remarkable sum of money for the day.

June 29
Experimental Hen Drop — Strait of Belle Isle, 1939

Henry H. Anderson, Jr. was a crew member on board the *George B. Cluett* steaming between Boston, Massachusetts, and Mugford Tickle, Labrador. Anderson wrote the following on this date about the ship's mate, whom he described as a burly fellow:

> He delighted in plucking a freshly laid egg from one of our crated hens, biting off the end and sucking it down in one swallow. Of scientific bent he frequently experimented with the hens, determined to find out whether they could swim, by dropping one overboard in the Strait of Belle Isle. Poor visibility meant that the fog swallowed up the hen before the sea.

June 30
Forest Fires — Clode Sound to Shoal Harbour, 1892

Fires raged between Trinity and Bonavista Bay, consuming 25 miles of woods. In the midst of the fire, two men walked to safety. The first man left Point of Beach, Clode Sound, Bonavista Bay, on the last day of June, where the fire was raging between the northwest and southwest brooks. All the stores belonging to the Railway Company at Point of Beach had already been destroyed. He walked two miles on the railway track toward Thorburn Lake and came to a large fire burning across the track. He crossed Thorburn Lake and walked four and a half miles to Seven-Mile Camp, the fire raging on both sides.

Along the track, he met up with Mr. George Gushue, the mailman for the Halls Bay Railway. The two of them left the camp at 7:00 a.m. and walked five miles between the fire on either side of the track until it cut them off again. At 5:00 p.m., they decided to ford down a large river, through a raging fire of pine, birch, and spruce, the flames 40 and 50 feet high. The men had to wet their clothes to keep them from burning. The smoke was so thick they had to stoop down to the surface of the river to get relief. Eventually, they were able to get back on the track, but after half a mile, they were forced back into the river by the flames. It wasn't till they reached Shoal Harbour, outside Clarenville, that they were safe, as the fire had already swept through, burning the church and eight houses. The Lower Soal Harbor church had burnt as well, along with two or three more houses. The only casualties were two or three horses, and a fine pig belonging to Mr. Gushue.

It was, claimed the first man, "one of the most unpleasant and laborious days I ever spent, and I shall long remember the last day of June, 1892."

JULY

July 1
A Canada Day Visitor — Cape St. Francis, 1952

At 9:30 a.m., nine Convair B36 "Peacemaker" bombers based out of Carswell Air Force Base, Fort Worth, Texas, were engaged in a high-altitude simulation, circling around Cape St. Francis. The group was being tracked by three radar instructors and 12 Army Signal Corps radar students out of Fort Monmouth, New Jersey. Somewhere between Newfoundland and the continental US, the radar operators picked up two slow-moving unidentified targets. The objects were moving much slower than the aircraft, then stopped and hovered at an altitude of 50,000 feet for about five minutes. Then, they took off in a "terrific burst of speed" and disappeared to the southwest. The mysterious flying objects were never officially identified.

Convair B-36 Peacemaker in flight

July 2
Motorcycle Trip — Western Bay, 1923

Mr. C. R. Tuff, his brother, and Mr. James Snelgrove made a run by motorcycle from St. John's to Western Bay. Upon their return, they noted that the roads were in very good condition. The exception was the almost-impassible Spout Cove Hill, which they deemed "not fit for a wheelbarrow."

July 3
A Skeleton Found — Barnes Road, St. John's, 1895

In opening a sewer near the Thompson property, a Council workman named Thormey made a curious find: the skeleton of a body. Most of the bones were recovered, plus a green coat with brass buttons thought to be part of a military uniform. The body was found about three feet underground.

July 4
Sunk by an Iceberg — Island Cove, 1803

Two small boats, a jolly boat and a cutter, arrived at Island Cove, Conception Bay, with their passengers in a terrible condition. On June 22, the *Lady Hobart* had sailed out of Halifax, bound for England, carrying a few passengers. On the 26th, they captured a French schooner with a load of salt fish and took the crew on board. Then, on the 28th, some 350 miles off the coast of Newfoundland, the *Lady Hobart* struck an iceberg and quickly started to take on water. The crew, passengers, and captured Frenchmen took to the ship's two small boats, frantically adding what provisions they could grab. No sooner was everyone in the boats than the *Lady Ho-*

bart gave a great lurch to port and sank beneath the waves. Over the next few days, the castaways suffered through terrible storms, cold, and severe rationing of their provisions. The captain of the French schooner went mad and jumped overboard. One of the French sailors became "so outrageous" that it was necessary to tie him to the bottom of the boat. When they made land on July 4, the entire population of Island Cove came to the shore to help them up over the rocks, where they were brought into their homes. The only food the Island Cove people had to share was salt fish and potatoes, and there was no medical care available, so the next day the captain of the *Lady Hobart* hired a schooner and sailed the three boats and the survivors to St. John's. The 28 survivors were so terribly frostbitten that they needed surgical attention, and many of them had lost their toes. They stayed in St. John's for some time before they had the strength to return to Halifax.

July 5
Seaman and the Beaver — Louisiana Territory (modern-day Kansas), 1804

Seaman, a Newfoundland dog, became famous for being a member of the Lewis and Clark overland expedition from the Mississippi River to the Pacific coast and back. Seaman served as a guard and hunting dog, and on this date, William Clark recorded in his journal that: "We came to for Dinner at a Beaver house. Capt. Lewis's Dog Seaman went in & drove them out." Squirrels were Seaman's favourite prey, but he also caught geese, was adept at ferreting beavers out of their lodges, and could take down larger animals such as deer and pronghorn antelope. Seaman had been purchased for $20 in Pittsburgh, Pennsylvania, by Captain Meriwether Lewis in August 1803, prior to their expedition. Seaman was the only animal to complete the entire trip. His hunting prowess was probably part of what saved him—Lewis and Clark's Corps of Discovery ate over 200 dogs during the course of their explorations.

Newfoundland dog, lithograph created between 1830 and 1835

July 6
Citizen Complaint — Rawlins Cross, St. John's, 1923

A cranky St. John's resident wrote a letter to the editor to register the following complaint:

> Dear Sir.—A great deal of annoyance is caused by the streetcars at Rawlin's Cross. When taking the curve to Military Road they screech, bawl and howl. Many of the resi-

dents of this part of the city are in bed by eleven o'clock, people may be ill, and the terrific noise caused by the cars causes untold misery. There is one car especially, which must have square wheels as the pounding on the track can be heard from Garrison Hill to Government House. A little grease on the track at Rawlin's Cross would remedy the first trouble, and a round wheel on the cars would remedy the second.

July 7
Arsonist Convicted — Jugglers Cove, 1962

A 20-year-old man from Bay Roberts was convicted of deliberately setting a grass fire at Jugglers Cove on June 10. The fire burnt over an acre before it was put out by area firefighters. The firebug was given two weeks in jail.

July 8
New Motor Sprinkler — St. John's, 1919

The Municipal Council's recently imported motor sprinkler went out for a trial run across Duckworth and other streets. It was a 1,000-gallon Mack truck, built by the International Motor Company, and could be used for oiling as well as watering. It featured a "force flusher," which was used every morning at 5:00 a.m. for flushing down Water Street. The "Mack-Car" set municipal taxpayers back $3,000 but was said to do the work of six ordinary sprinkling cars.

A 1,000-gallon Mack sprinkler in action, 1917

July 9
Cressie Sighting — Robert's Arm, 1991

A slim, black shape rose up from a patch of churning water before sinking out of sight beneath the depths of Crescent Lake. It was the latest in a long series of sightings of the Crescent Lake Monster, dubbed "Cressie" by locals. Sightings of the lake monster date back to the start of the 20th century. One of the first residents of the community, a lady remembered today as Grandmother Anthony, was startled from her berry-picking by a giant lake serpent. Eyewitness Fred Parsons described Cressie as "similar to a giant eel, but more than a dozen feet long." Others have described the creature as looking long and shiny and having a fish-like head.

July 10
Iceberg Jesus — Battle Harbour, 1864

The fabulously named Anglican missionary Reverend Ulric Zuinglius Rule, writing about his life's work, reported on a miraculous ice formation he had seen on this day:

> The views over the sea from Battle Harbour were very beautiful, and wonderful was the appearance of icebergs passing, some near some far out at sea, in all kinds of fanciful forms. One fine sunshiny morning . . . looking from the cliff at six o'clock, I saw at a short distance an iceberg which presented the stately figure of a man in a long white robe, as it were standing on the water, just on the line where two fields of colour met, a field of gold and a field of silver. The water was neither smooth nor rough, but rippling. It was indeed a most beautiful sight; and if one had but been a good painter, or sculptor, no better model could have been imagined of a figure of Christ walking on the sea.

July 11
Sea Monster Spotted — South of Trepassey, 1899

Two days out from Boston, the steamship *New England* made the acquaintance of an uncanny-looking creature. "Mind, I don't say it was a sea serpent," said Captain McAulcy, hedging his bets, "but the strangest animal I have seen in forty years at sea." The captain described the smooth grey mystery animal as being about 40 feet long. Its neck, with a keel-like ridge, projected about six feet out of water. As the ship approached, it raised its head from the water for a few seconds to gaze unconcernedly at the passengers. When it stopped, it seemed to snort and sent up a jet of spray. The first officer said it "was a rum-looking fish." Others thought it looked "something like a hippopotamus" or postulated it might have been an emaciated whale. Father Deming, of New York, corroborated the story but said its shape was like a lizard with an elongated neck and a very large tail, which it kept below the surface of the water. Whatever the beastie was, it was entirely uninterested in the *New England* and swam away as steadily as a steamer till it was lost from sight.

July 12
Unlucky Lindy — Definitely Not Big Pond, 1933

Amateur aviator Mr. Ches Mills of Forest Road had an unexpected encounter with Charles Lindberg. Everyone in St. John's had gone to Bay Bulls Big Pond to await Lindberg's arrival, but Ches was at Quidi Vidi on that day. Who should land on the pond to ask for directions but Lindberg himself.

"He landed in a Ryan Mono," remembered Ches. "I went out in the boat, shook his hand, and spoke to him. I told him to go west, and I could have flown with him but I was afraid of losing the damned boat. It was stupid, the boat couldn't have got out of the lake."

Lindberg took off and eventually landed in the right place to the delight of the gathered spectators.

July 13
A Night in the Woods — Freshwater Bay, 1908

Michael Kerivan, eight years old, had gone into St. John's with some men. He was on an errand for his sister, with whom he was staying in Freshwater Bay. His errand done, he went to the Long Bridge at the head of the harbour to meet the men, but they were not to be seen. He concluded they had left, so he set off to overtake them, taking a shortcut behind St. Mary's Church on the South Side. That evening, when there was no sign of him, the family got worried and called the police. Two officers searched all night without success. At 11:00 a.m., in walked young Michael in torn clothes, his legs, hands, and face cut and bleeding. He had gotten lost the previous evening, yet kept on through the bush through the night, until he came out by the settlement of Freshwater Bay the next morning, exhausted.

July 14
Gnawing of Bones — St. John's, 1846

During the Great Fire of June 9, 1846, the churchyard fences of St. John's Church (the site of the present Anglican Cathedral) were pulled down to arrest the progress of the flames. It had an expected consequence, that being "scenes repulsive to decency and humanity." The rector, church wardens, and vestry of St. John's requested the House of Assembly to consider a grant to restore the fence, for the following reasons:

> . . . the troops of starving dogs infesting the tombs have become dangerous as well to the living as to the dead, and have commenced desecrating the tombs, and may be seen gnawing the bones of those who have been buried in the said Churchyard. Pigs and Goats infest it in great number, and the grave-stones and monuments of the deceased are daily violated.

A new fence was approved.

July 15
Fish-a-Trip Donation — Isle aux Morts, 1951

Right Rev. Philip Abraham, Bishop of Newfoundland, consecrated the fourth church to be built by Church of England members at Isle aux Morts. The previous church was blown down in 1946, and Rev. George Martin had come up with a plan to fund the replacement. He suggested to the fishermen of his congregation that each time they went out to fish, they bring back one for the church. The manager of the local fish filleting and freezing plant had his staff look after the records and keep an account of the pounds of fish contributed. By the end of the first year, $2,000 was raised on the "fish-a-trip" method. A total of 62 members of the church agreed to carry on with the program, and the women of the parish got busy with their own fundraising efforts. Their combined work raised $18,000 in five years. That, added to an immense amount of contributed labour, allowed Bishop Abraham to consecrate the new church without a cent of debt.

July 16
Died by Stroke of a Whale — Harbour Grace, 1782

Missing at sea after four days, the corpse of Jonathan Webber was finally found on this day, then transported back to Harbour Grace and interred in St. Paul's Churchyard. Jonathan, aged 18 years and nine months, was, according to his tombstone, "drown'd by the stroke of a whale." It is likely that young Webber was engaged in the family whale fishery. By 1750, the Webber family of Boston had set up business in Harbour Grace and made strenuous efforts to promote a whale hunt in Conception Bay. In its early years, whaling was exceptionally dangerous, and injuries and death were common. The whaling factory in Harbour Grace closed circa 1913, but memories of the industry lived on well past that date—the Harbour Grace Regatta was established using whaleboats for the races, a tradition that persisted up to 1971.

July 17
Harbour Skull — St. John's, 1899

John Taylor, a diver, whilst groping the bottom of the harbour for one of the *Lucerne*'s anchors, made a gruesome find. He came across the skull of a human being, and the remains of a coat a few inches away. Taylor could not locate the anchor but came to the surface with the skull, leaving the coat where it was found. "In all probability, the body must have been lying on the bottom for some time," it was reported, "as the flesh had completely disappeared from the bones."

July 18
Rescued by Danes — Bay Roberts, 1908

The Danish schooner *Hans Emile* arrived at Bay Roberts with more on board than just the salt they were delivering to C. & A. Dawe. Five days earlier, George Grandy and Charles Marshall, two crewmen of the banking schooner *Ruby*, strayed away from their fishing vessel. The men were without food and water for three days and nights and were 80 miles off the coast when picked up by the *Hans Emile*. They were kindly treated by the captain and crew and were taken care of in Bay Roberts until transportation could be arranged to take them back to their home of Grand Bank.

July 19
Whaling Operations — Trinity, 1904

The whaler *Fin* with a Norwegian crew and master, Nils Neilssen, began hunting from Trinity. Coincidentally, they killed a fin whale on the *Fin*'s first voyage and later captured a sperm whale. The community of Trinity became involved in whaling that year when the Atlantic Whaling and Manufacturing Co. Ltd. built a substantial whaling factory at Maggotty Cove, near Fort Point. In its first season, it processed 68 whales (59 fin, five hump, three blue, and one sperm) and produced 115,416 gallons of oil and nearly 300 tons of guano (fertilizer). The factory closed in 1914.

July 20
Flirt with Disaster — Wild Cove, 1878

The schooner *Flirt*, bound for Labrador, was totally lost as she attempted to make the harbour at Twillingate in the darkness. The *Flirt* was owned by John Butler of Harbour Grace and was on a trading voyage laden down with shop goods, provisions, all of which were uninsured. The crew escaped with their lives but had no time to save anything on board, not even their extra clothes.

July 21
Snowstorm in July — Labrador, 1886

A blizzard accompanied by intense cold set in and lasted for two days. Much anxiety was felt for those living in the interior.

July 22
Apparatus for Drying Fish and Other Articles — Washington, DC, 1890

Edward Robinson of St. John's patented his invention of a new and useful "Apparatus for Drying Fish and other Articles or Substances." In addition to drying fish, it could be

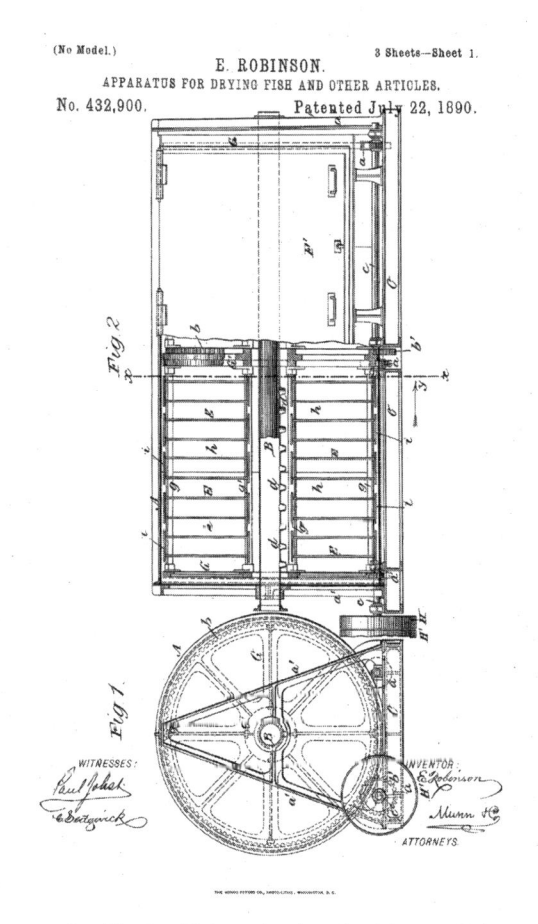

Apparatus for Drying Fish and other Articles or Substances 1890

utilized for drying tea, wool, or fruit. A blast of heated air was used in connection with revolving wire frames or baskets to dry the materials placed within. Robinson was the manager of the Newfoundland Fish Drying Company, which had established a factory at the Jersey Rooms, Burin. Perhaps ahead of its time, the company went into liquidation in 1893, and its "Hot Air Fish Drying Apparatus" went up for sale.

July 23
Deleterious Matter — Windsor Lake, 1896

A report was made of "deleterious matter" floating near the head of Windsor Lake, from which St. John's draws much of its drinking water. The matter in question took the shape of a dead sheep, and people were not happy about it, as "such substances are not calculated to improve the water in hot weather."

July 24
Peculiar Theft — St. John's, 1912

A flag thief was in the wind. A great deal of bunting was used for decorative purposes for the formal opening of the new Seamen's Institute on Water Street. When the bunting was gathered up to be returned to the owners, several flags were missing, including a large Union Jack and a flag belonging to the *Calypso*. Police were on the lookout for a particularly patriotic bandit.

July 25
Shame! Shame! — St. John's, 1892

Peter Leary was severely injured by one Mr. Murphy. Murphy was well-known about town and was described in the language of the day as a "cripple." Leary was intoxicated, and the two got into a disagreement outside McKay's saloon. Murphy struck Leary a violent blow upon the head with his crutch, fracturing his skull and knocking him unconscious. Murphy was about to strike again, but "the witnesses cried shame at him, and then he wanted to fight anyone in the crowd, and threatened several with his weapon." Leary was carried to a drugstore and provided with care. Murphy was arrested by the police and carried off to Fort Townshend.

July 26
A Fine Chance — Somewhere in Maine, 1892

Seeing an opportunity, a farmer in the state of Maine wrote a letter to the mayor of St. John's in the aftermath of the Great Fire of 1892. He had heard of the fire, and he would be glad to give a "suitable female" a good home. Kindly, he offered to employ her at good wages until they knew each other well enough, then he would marry her. She had to be between 25 and 35 years old, weigh from 150 to 175 pounds, and be "plump and light complected" with good character. Pictures could be exchanged, and the writer wished it to be clearly understood that he was "not joking, but in deadly earnest."

July 27
Song of Ice and Fire — St. John's to Boston, 1897

Exactly one month before she was abandoned, the British tramp steamer SS *Furter* struck an iceberg and was forced to put into St. John's for repairs. In spite of the warnings of local mechanics, Captain J. D. Jenkins had only temporary repairs made before setting out again. When a strong northerly gale sprang up on July 25, it was no surprise that the ship sprang a leak. The ship slowly took on water until two thirty on the morning of the 27th, at which point the crew abandoned ship. Their final act was to build a fire on the deck of the steamer to attract the attention of passing vessels, and soon the *Furter* was aflame. Four boats were lowered into the sea. Forty-eight hours later, they were rescued by the British steamer *Sagamore*, out of Liverpool, and were taken to Boston.

July 28
A Shower of Flies — Square Islands and Venison Islands, 1897

A shower of flies, somewhat larger than the common fly, descended upon shipping lanes two miles off the coast of Labrador, a sight never reported before. The insects were somewhat yellow in colour, with two horns protruding from their heads. Sails, decks, water, and everything surrounding were covered with insects as far as the eye could see. Boats and schooners passed through at least seven miles of them, and they were still falling as the boats passed through. A doctor and mail officer collected samples as a curiosity. The event took place after one of the heaviest displays of lightning on record, and it was theorized this was linked to the strange downpour.

July 29
Murderer of Mary Nugent Hanged — St. John's, 1899

Ship's purser and tavern owner Francis Canning was executed for the shooting of barmaid Mary Nugent of Kelligrews. He had shot Nugent from behind, and she lived long enough to identify him at the General Hospital before she died. Her murderer was hanged during the worst thunder and lightning storm in St. John's in 50 years and was buried 30 feet from the gallows within the walls of Her Majesty's Penitentiary.

July 30
Shower of Honey — St. John's, 1862

Much more appetizing than a shower of flies, a shower of honey fell like hailstones from the sky, dotting the leaves of trees. Several prominent gentlemen were out at the time and "had their beavers spoiled." Not all were upset at the strange windfall. One gentleman collected the honey from trees near Carpasian Road and ate it, while a lady living nearby obtained two large tumblers full, which she kept for many days.

July 31
A Visit from Edmond Halley — St. Mary's Bay, 1700

En route from Bermuda to Cape Cod, the *Paramore* was blown off course by a fierce gale and ended up seeking shelter in St. Mary's Bay. The *Paramore* was on a scientific expedition with noted English astronomer, geophysicist, mathematician, and meteorologist Edmond Halley, of the comet fame (though he would not determine the comet's periodicity till 1705). They were guided through a thick fog by French fishermen, and on August 2, they sailed around Cape Race and eventually came into the harbour at "Toad's Cove"—today's Tors Cove. When they arrived, several English fishing vessels fled, fearing them to be pirates, with one Humphry Bryant firing shots through the *Paramore*'s rigging. The ship came to no harm, and the crew spent a few days in Tors Cove, collecting birch wood and "Excellent good water" before sailing back to England.

AUGUST

August 1
Lammas Day — Flower's Cove, 1938

This is the feast of St. Peter-in-Chains in the Roman Catholic Church, Lammas Day in the Church of England. For Canon George Earle, sailing along the coast of the Great Northern Peninsula in the *Argonaut*, it was a day of misery spent in bed, medicated with aspirin and hot wine, in the home of his aunt Dora Richards of Flower's Cove. He wrote:

> I was so sick that I didn't care about St. Peter in fetters or whether Lammas meant loaf-mass or lamb-mass in the early English Church or even about the significance of episcopal consecration. The reality on that day was that I was in torture and couldn't eat and wanted only to get better.

August 2
An Alarm of Fire — St. John's, 1900

At five minutes after 11 on Thursday, an "alarm of fire" was sent in from the firebox at the foot of Patrick Street. By the time men of the Central and West End fire stations arrived, Snow's Cooperage had been completely gutted. The following day, it was revealed that the fire had been started accidentally by schoolboys Frank White, aged eight, James Collins, seven, and E. Collins, five. The threesome were called to the bar at the police court to answer for setting the fire. Inspector

General McCowan acted as prosecutor, pointing out that the owner of the cooperage had no insurance to cover the loss. The judge ruled that the five-year-old was too young to stand trial but that the parents of the other two boys had to pay a bond of $100 each. Today, that would be equal to around $3,000 in modern currency, which may be why your mother told you to never play with matches.

August 3
Blown Over the Parapet — St. John's, 1838

Before the rest of St. John's was up for breakfast, two Royal Artillerymen were already hard at work. John Rowledge, aged 25, and his companion Joseph Hammond, 27, were preparing a gun at the Crescent Battery, one of two batteries on the top of Signal Hill. The gun was to be used that morning in firing a salute over the waking city for the French brigantine *Cert*, which had arrived after sunset the previous evening. As they rammed home the cartridge, it exploded, blowing the two men over the parapet. Companions in life, they were buried together in one grave at the Anglican Cathedral of St. John the Baptist three days later.

August 4
Ran Itself to Death — Torbay, 1900

Doctor Mitchell drove to Torbay with his young chestnut horse, one of the fastest pacers in town and worth about $200. The doctor dismounted near the convent and moved to take off the horse's bridle. At this, the animal bolted into Mr. Liddy's yard nearby and upset a buggy. The vehicle was righted, but the chestnut careened off again, galloping away at a frantic pace toward St. John's. The horse raced on until it smashed into a carriage and fell down dead with exhaustion.

On Sunday, Mr. John Kelly, cab man, also lost a horse. As Kelly was driving along Torbay Road, his animal suddenly fell to the ground and expired. Kelly's explanation for the horse's demise? The day before, it had overexerted itself in hauling home the dead weight of Doctor Mitchell's departed trotter.

August 5
A Solar Eclipse — Burgeo, 1776

The first recorded eclipse of the sun in Newfoundland was observed on this day by explorer and cartographer Captain James Cook. Cook had been appointed by the Lords Commissioners of the Admiralty to survey the sea coasts of "Newfound-land and Labradore." Cook took with him aboard the HMS *Grenville* a set of instruments, among them a brass telescopic quadrant made by astronomer John Bird of London. As the solar eclipse started, Cook took a series of measurements, confirmed by three observers with telescopes who all agreed as to the moments of the event's beginning and end. Later, these were compared to measurements of the same eclipse taken at Oxford by the Rev. Mr. Hornsby, thus establishing the longitude of the place of observance. Today, the island off Burgeo where it all happened is known as Eclipse Island (longitude 57° 36' 54.6" West, in case you were wondering).

August 6
Gigantic Raft — Bonne Bay, 1919

The 15,000-horsepower oceangoing tug *Humber* steamed out of Bonne Bay and headed out across the North Atlantic. It was towing a remarkable structure invented by Ivan A. Bayley of North Sydney: an enormous raft of pit timber 250 feet long, 25 feet deep, and 44 feet wide. It contained 2,000,000 board feet of timber, and once it crossed the Atlantic in 20 days' time, it was estimated that the sale of wood would fetch approximately $250,000.

It had taken the St. Lawrence Lumber and Pulp Company two years to build the massive raft, which featured a tapering stern and smoothly planked bow to render towing easy, the timber bound together by steel rods welded at its many joints. The prodigious undertaking had been conceived by Bayley during the war for the purpose of rendering cargo torpedo-proof and indestructible. It was reported that Bayley's contraption was "impossible to disintegrate or break apart and become loose."

Within four days, the raft had come loose from the tug and gone adrift. When last sighted by a Dutch captain, the indestructible raft was fast breaking up. Thus ended a brave new era in transatlantic freight.

August 7
Light on His Feet — St. John's, 1919

The good citizens of St. John's living in the vicinity of Bannerman Park were scandalized this Monday evening by a sight never before seen in that park. An old, grey-haired man of 75 got on one of the platforms and danced a jig and a two-step. The old man maintained his terpsichorean exertions for several minutes without pause. The many who had assembled were loud in their applause, clapping and cheering on the hearty old man with great enthusiasm.

He returned Tuesday night and did it again.

August 8
Bootlegger Hits the Road — George's Pond, 1900

A man by the name of Haywood, originally of Prince Edward Island, boarded a train and hightailed it to Port aux Basques. From there he sailed onward to Sydney, Nova Scotia. Before that fateful Wednesday, Haywood had been employed as camp cook at the Howard Sawmills in George's Pond. A number of the woodsmen working at the camp had been found intoxicated, and the camp manager followed a boozy trail of clues back to the cook. An enterprising Haywood had been brewing overproof beer and selling it to the parched employees of the lumber camp. The manager had reported the bootlegging to the local magistrate, who was about to hold an investigation. Haywood (and his assistant) caught wind of the impending arrest and fled town, leaving the thirsty woodsmen without a source of brew.

August 9
A Rolling Stone Pleases No Moss — St. John's, 1892

As part of the cleanup following the Great Fire of 1892, a party of men were engaged in demolishing the walls of the waterside stores previously occupied by Harvey and Company. Gun cotton was used, with explosive results. Some of the stones from the walls were blown into the air and reached as far away as Bond Street. A piece of stone weighing six pounds fell within a few feet of a passerby, while another stone thrown from the explosion broke a window in the house of one Captain Moss.

August 10
Wall Falls Down — Botwood, 1897

Edward Wall, Government Inspector of Railway Bridge Construction, was described as a stout, heavy, and entirely sober man. At 20 minutes to six, he climbed up to the top part of the Exploits bridge, a height to which he had never ventured before, close to where Joseph Vokey was working driving rivets. Albert Swartz, another riveter, was working with his "holder up," Thomas C. Murphy of Harbour Main. William Stone was heating up rivets topside of the bridge.

Wall was living alongside the bridge and came every day to inspect the gang's work. On this day, he walked out onto the scaffolding, where the planks were laid out but not fastened down. Vokey saw Wall approach the edge of the planks. Vokey then turned his back and went back to his rivet work; the next thing he heard was the crash of Wall falling to the ground.

The noise startled the other men, who ran off the scaffolding and slid down the posts 65 feet to where Wall lay on the rocks, still breathing and covered in scratches, with his arms broken. A hand cart was sent down the line to telegraph for a doctor, while the riveters fetched a mattress and carried Wall back to the top of the riverbank. Wall asked the men several times how he had fallen, then asked Thomas Murphy to turn him over.

"Turn me over on my left side," he said, "until I die. Goodbye, boys."

Murphy asked him if he had any trouble on his mind, and Wall replied, "No."

Wall lived for an hour more. The doctor, meanwhile, had only made it as far as Norris Arm and was sent word that he was no longer needed. Arrangements were made to send the body on to Whitbourne Sation, from where Undertaker White received the remains for conveyance to town by the incoming train. Wall left behind a wife and eight children, all of tender years.

August 11
Outing at Smithville — St. John's, 1920

The little ones of the Congregational Sunday School assembled at the schoolroom and from there were taken out by motors and other conveyances to the beautiful grounds of Smithville for a picnic. Various games were indulged in, with the teachers joining in the sport, and the catering by the Miss Furlong was more than could be desired.

Smithville Tennis Club, circa 1910

Toward the end of the picnic, one of the children, the son of a local contractor named Thomas, had climbed into a waiting wagon to go home. Suddenly, a football kicked in a field nearby struck the attached horse. The startled animal dashed through the grounds and out the road, dragging Thomas the Younger along. The driver failed to stop the runaway and shouted to the frightened child to lie down, which he did. Just outside of the Smithville gate, the wagon crashed into an electric light pole and was practically demolished.

The children, it was said, enjoyed their outing to the fullest extent, except perhaps for little Thomas, who went home with a bump on his head.

August 12
Youthful Sneak Thief — St. John's, 1914

A nine-year-old waif by the name of Woodland snuck inside the counter of a shop in the West End, opened the cash drawer, and made off with $1.50 in loose change. He was quickly arrested for larceny by a Constable Tobin. It was reported that the authorities scarcely knew what to do with the lad, as it was not the first time that he had been caught for larceny, yet he was too young to be sent to prison. The boy was sparsely clad and had been constantly wandering the streets, hungry. It was suggested that he be sent to an institution and looked after.

August 13
Strange Signs and Tokens — Kelligrews, 1891

Mr. John Haines of Middle Bight, along with several others (including the station master and two ladies from town), was standing on the platform overlooking the Kelligrews railway station.

The group had been standing there for about 20 minutes when one of them directed their attention to a light shining in an old, untenanted house on the south side of the railway track. To their great surprise, they saw a large green light shining through the sashless downstairs window. It illuminated the house so brilliantly that even at such a distance they were able to easily count the clapboards. The light drifted upstairs and shone for a minute. Next, it came out, crossed the track, and disappeared about 70 yards away.

Five green lights shone out like this, at intervals of about three minutes. Then a bright red light appeared, and a noise was heard from inside the house. The red light remained in the house for a minute, then spread out rapidly over the nearby ground.

Five of the braver witnesses walked from the station to about 20 feet from the house. They waited patiently for an hour and, seeing nothing, began to retrace their steps. Suddenly they saw three more lights, one after the other, after which they saw and heard nothing more.

It was said the property had once belonged to Old Man Gillingham and that several unmarked graves were located near the house. After Gillingham's death, the property changed hands a number of times before weird sounds and strange lights were reported. The owner at that time sold the property for the sum of $800 and headed out west, both to earn a better livelihood and to say farewell to the ghosts.

"This is not an idle tale," said Mr. Haines, "for seven of us witnessed it."

August 14
Attempt on the Life of Vicar-General — Shearstown, 1941

The Right Reverend Monsignor Dinn of the parish of North River had gone to Shearstown, Bay Roberts, to call in on one of his parishioners, Robert Bradbury. What transpired is not fully known, but two shots were fired from Bradbury's revolver during the visit. The shots, fortunately, missed their mark, but in the following tussle for control of the weapon, the monsignor was badly bruised about the head and chest before he was able to flee the house.

Magistrate Hawco of Bay Roberts remanded the accused to the Harbour Grace jail.

Bradbury was a veteran of the Great War and was said to be suffering from shell shock. An examination regarding his sanity was made, and three days after the shooting, the veteran was admitted to the Hospital for Mental and Nervous Diseases, diagnosed with paranoia. He died there two years later from complications due to Hodgkin's disease.

August 15
Cupid at the Picnic — Octagon Pond, 1900

The Benevolent Irish Society outing at Octagon Castle was deemed an absolute success. The entire party numbered 191 persons, and almost everyone sat down together for tea at five thirty. This was followed by a variety of games. At about eight o'clock, dancing commenced, which continued till the time of closing. The event was more like an organized ball than an ordinary picnic, in part due to the fine display of summer attire by the ladies in attendance.

Such was the attractiveness of both the occasion and the ladies present that no fewer than three gentlemen were moved to make proposals of marriage. The first was a prominent member of the government, who lost his heart to a handsome young Boston lady. The second was an official of the Municipal Council, who succumbed to the charms of a Prescott Street belle. The third was a bookkeeper in a city office who laid his heart at the feet of a West End brunette.

It must have been some picnic.

Octagon Castle, date uncertain

August 16
Corpse Candle — St. Lawrence, 1924

A St. Lawrence fisherman had been making ready in his house to proceed to the fishing grounds. Suddenly, he was startled to hear the tramp of feet on the stairs. As the fisherman followed the unusual noise, he saw the gleam of a candle move down the stairs, approach and pass through the kitchen door, and drift off toward a nearby churchyard. Two days after this strange sighting, one of the man's sons died unexpectedly. At the time the "corpse candle" had been seen, his son had been in perfect health.

August 17
A Whale of a Submarine — Bay Bulls, 1918

As the First World War wore on and as the effectiveness of Allied troop convoys grew, the German high command decided to take the submarine war directly to the coast of North America. On this date in 1918, a large British tanker was on fire off Cape Hatteras, and a French cruiser participating in activities with American vessels was torpedoed and sank. Both events were front-page news in St. John's, and wild rumours about submarine sightings and missing vessels circulated for a tense 48 hours. In the midst of this panic, the schooner *Klondyke* reported a very suspicious object lying low in the water just off Bay Bulls. Immediately, a force was sent to reconnoitre.

Investigation proved that the lurking German submarine was, in fact, a dead whale, missing its tail.

August 18
Complaint About the Cars — Placentia, 1899

Disgruntled passengers complained of the unclean condition of the railway cars on the Placentia line, insisting that they should be thoroughly scrubbed and properly lighted.

August 19
Daring Act of Turnip Vandalism — St. John's, 1897

Under the cover of darkness, sometime between the hours of 11 and 12 o'clock, audacious vandals entered the garden of Mr. Edward Russell, who owned a farm on Newtown Road. When Russell went into his garden the next morning, he was surprised to see his beloved turnip beds in a terrible state.

Looking over the fence, he saw upwards of $20 worth of destroyed vegetables scattered about the roadside. Russell had his suspicions about "certain parties," while the police stated they had the matter of the violence against the vegetables firmly in hand and hoped the culprit would soon be caught.

August 20
Terror to All Smugglers — Trinity Bay, 1881

Mr. Thomas W. Gaden of the Harbour Grace Customs Department was ordered to Trinity Bay for the purpose of investigating reports of United States bankers and Western Shore traders smuggling "right and left." It was rumoured that the smuggling was being carried on "with a heedlessness of consequences truly characteristic of our American cousins." Mr. Gaden was deemed one of the few government officials whose conduct had always merited the confidence of the public, and opinion was that a better selection could not have been made for the job. Gaden was charged to determine the extent to which smuggling was being carried on, to devise a means to put a stop to the matter, and to teach the desperadoes that they could not violate revenue laws with impunity.

Thus unleashed, Gaden went on the warpath, the former accountant achieving notoriety as "a terror to all smugglers"—searching premises for smuggled goods and seizing illicit tobacco, casks of liquor, hundredweights of cheese, sacks of flour, Schnider rifles, and barrels of sugar buried in cargoes of salt. Hot in pursuit of smugglers of all kinds, he ventured from Trinity Bay to St. John's, Harbour Grace, Witless Bay, Bay Bulls, and beyond.

So feared became Gaden by smugglers that he was sent death threats. In 1895, he received a letter, inscribed on a paper of large dimensions, threatening to seal his doom. The letter was illustrated in a ghastly and blood-curdling manner: a dagger for the terrible deed; a gibbet and a portly man swinging from it by the neck; then a grinning skull and crossbones; and a black coffin bearing a white cross, to contain the remains of the deceased, Thomas W. Gaden, Tide Surveyor of Her Majesty's Customs, "Peace be to his ashes—when he is gone."

A violent end was not to be his fate. After 27 years of unremitting hard work, he was retired and put on the pension list with the beggarly sum of $300 per annum. On Saturday, March 23, 1907, he complained of a cold and retired to bed at seven o'clock. His wife noticed that he grew rapidly worse and decided to fetch a doctor. Mrs. Gaden and her daughter went to Doctor Anderson's surgery and, on returning shortly afterwards to their Prescott Street home, found him dead. Thomas W. Gaden, terror to all smugglers, died in his bed of cardiac disease, aged 60.

August 21
Attacked by Devil Fish — Bay of Islands, 1912

At an early hour, Josiah Sheppard left for the fishing grounds in his dory, towed by his brother Henry in his motorboat. Finding fish scarce in their first location, they decided to move to the grounds off French Island.

Josiah got in the motorboat and proceeded to French Island, taking the dory in tow. Arriving at the grounds, Josiah again got into his dory, and his brother slacked him astern about 200 yards.

Josiah was preparing to put his lines out when a monster of the deep rose to the surface, rearing its fearsome head over the side of the dory. The terrified fisherman described it as a "Devil Fish," with a dreadful mouth measuring about four feet, large eyes, a white bottom, and black back.

The Devil Fish looked first at the half-quintal of fish

lying in the bottom of the dory. Then it looked at Josiah. Thinking the cod looked like a better breakfast than the human, the creature took hold of the dory, throwing Josiah into the sea and disappearing with its snack.

Josiah screamed, and Henry hurried to his assistance. The dory floated to the surface, bottom-up, and bearing a bite mark over two feet wide. Sheppard climbed aboard the upturned dory and from that precarious perch was rescued by his brother.

August 22
More Vegetable Violence — St. John's, 1892

Several of the farmers about Monkstown and Circular Road registered complaints of the depredations committed on their crops by "prowlers" who had been systematically raiding the Georgestown neighbourhood night after night. Fences were broken down, and large quantities of vegetables were taken from the fields. One local newspaper reported, "It would be well for the Inspector to send a constable along this route during the nights, as such would prevent much lawlessness."

August 23
St. John's in St. John's — St. John's, 1899

The *St. John's*—the first car for the new street railway—arrived by train. It attracted a good deal of attention, and "its appointments, which are modern and elaborate, were very much admired and favourably commented upon." At that point, the Water Street line had progressed as far as Adelaide Street, and three gangs of men were dispatched from the West End portion of the tracks to start laying track on Queen's and Military Roads.

August 24
First Chinese Laundry — St. John's, 1895

Two new immigrants opened the first Chinese laundry in Newfoundland. The first to arrive was a 24-year-old man whose long braided queue of hair attracted great public interest. His name was given variously as Tong Toi, Fong Toy, Fong Foi, and Fong Choy. With his partner, Wang Chang (or possibly Su-Ho-Hin), he opened what may have been the Sung-Lee & Co. laundry at the corner of New Gower Street and Holdsworth Street. Chinese-Newfoundland oral tradition holds that Fong Choy was an adventurous and entrepreneurial young man. He had left Guangdong Province for England, then from there to Montreal and Halifax, opening laundries along the way. After some time in Newfoundland, he ventured to Bermuda, where he made his fortune and eventually died at the age of 77. The laundry premises he established in St. John's remained a Chinese-owned business for years afterwards.

August 25
The Great Goobies Cattle Drive — Burin Peninsula, 1964

Harold Lees, a rancher from Saskatchewan, picked up a shipment of 1,000 head of Hereford cattle in Goobies and proceeded to drive them down the Burin Peninsula toward Marystown. Premier Joseph Smallwood, not wanting to miss a photo opportunity, rigged up in western cowboy garb and headed the cattle drive astride a chestnut mare. He rode for about 10 miles with a film crew in tow. Once the cattle arrived, less than a quarter of the planned pasture land had been developed, so hay had to be imported from Canada. The cattle proceeded to eat fatal sheep laurel and marsh grasses, sink into bogs, or get poached by locals. The company liquidated not long after.

August 26
First Across the Brooklyn Bridge — New York, 1876

Brooklyn Bridge during construction, showing the workers' temporary walkways going up to the pier tops and cables being spun

Henry Supple, Jr. of St. John's became the first person to cross New York's East River, on a wire. Supple was a construction foreman on the famous Brooklyn Bridge. Thousands of spectators on both sides of the river watched in awe as Henry, strapped into a bosun's chair, inched his way across a 1,600-foot steel wire that linked Brooklyn to Manhattan. The bridge itself would not be finished for another three years. Henry Supple, Jr. went on to work on other engineering projects and died in New York at an advanced age.

August 27
Billy the Newsboy — St. John's, 1807

Newfoundland's first newsboy, Billy Barnes, appeared on the streets of St. John's. Billy delivered the *Royal Gazette*, which began publication on the same day. The paper had been instituted by John Ryan, who moved to Newfoundland from New Brunswick, where he had been King's Printer.

August 28
New Era of Pleasure — St. John's, 1886

"Coming Through the Rye" with variations on the clarinet was performed by Professor Bennett's Band at the New Era Pleasure Grounds. The Grounds was located in a field just off Freshwater Road, probably near what today is known as the Ayre Athletic Grounds. Professor David Bennett was a military drummer who became music director of St. Bonaventure's College, having been appointed to that position by Bishop John Thomas Mullock in 1863. He was much in demand throughout the Victorian period, performing for the visits of both Prince Hendrik of the Netherlands and the Prince of Wales, at the laying of the cornerstone for the Hospital for the Insane, and at the consecration of the Catholic Cathedral of St. John the Baptist.

August 29
Tale of Two Hermits — Torbay and Battle Harbour

In 1899, it was rumoured that gold had been discovered in the bed of the river running up from Torbay Road, near the town of Torbay. A hermit living in the vicinity had been washing the precious metal out of the sand for some time.

Also on this day, in 1932, the "Hermit Taxidermist of Labrador," Edward Doane, collected the last Canadian specimen of the Eskimo curlew at Battle Harbour. The last confirmed sighting of the species happened on September 4, 1963, when a hunter caught sight of one in Barbados and promptly shot it. The carcass of the bird was presented to American ornithologist James Bond (whose name was appropriated by writer Ian Fleming for a certain fictional British spy).

August 30
A Sad and Serious Case of Insanity — Labrador Coast, 1894

A Newfoundland man fishing on the Labrador became, according to the news of the day, "violently, and we fear, hopelessly mad." The local medical officer was anxious to send him back home but could not find someone to accompany him. As the Coastal Steamship Company refused to allow "the carrying of insane patients unless properly attended," the man had to remain on the coast. Not wanting to see him left behind, but also not wanting to cut their fishing season short, his schooner-mates compromised by confining him to a straitjacket and taking the patient fishing along with them. A Sergeant Lacy was dispatched from Tilt Cove to track him down and see that he got home safely.

August 31
Young Lady Ambulance Driver — France and Belgium, 1916

It was announced that Miss Armine Gosling, daughter of St. John's Mayor W. G. Gosling and noted suffragette Armine Nutting Gosling, had offered her services to the war effort as an ambulance driver. She spent every afternoon at a garage to familiarize herself with the workings of the automobile until she could take a machine apart and repair broken parts as "quickly as any man." Miss Gosling served in Belgium and France with the British Army's Voluntary Aid Detachment, broke her arm in an accident with her ambulance, narrowly escaped her hospital being bombed by the Germans, married a soldier (Captain Denis Keegan), was a championship golfer, moved to Bermuda, wrote a three-act comedy, and went to her heavenly reward at the respectable age of 86.

SEPTEMBER

September 1
Impaled on a Hay Fork — Torbay, 1911

Mrs. Bradbury was in her meadow loading hay on a cart. The horse became restless and would not stand still, so the woman took the hay fork and gave the beast a smack with the handle. The horse, understandably, did not appreciate this, and lurched forward, causing Mrs. Bradbury to fall heavily to the ground. As she fell, two prongs of the fork pierced her, entering her left side and coming out through her back. The woman was "of robust constitution" (feel free to substitute the word "badass") and yanked the hay fork out of her side, resisting the urge to faint from the pain and loss of blood. Her son ran to the house of local constable McGuire, who called for a doctor. She was sent to the hospital and was reported as being in serious condition.

The first of September seems to be an unlucky day to be around farming implements. In 1899, Mrs. Duff was injured in her meadow on Freshwater Road. A family argument over land between uncle and nephew got heated. When Mrs. Duff moved to intervene, she was sliced on her wrist with a scythe. Doctor Tait bound up the wound, and the gentlemen found themselves bound for court.

(*You can follow the further adventures of Doctor Tait on September 28 and November 22.*)

September 2
Can't Say I Blame the Horse — St. John's, 1903

A man employed as a horse driver by a Mr. Score took the animal down to the seashore to give it a wash. The horse did not want to go into the water, so the man beat it and forced it in. When the horse came out, it caught the man by the arm and threw him out into the water. The man, not having learned his lesson the first time, drove the horse into the ocean again, and when the horse came back up on shore, it seized the man by the breast and shook him in the air like a rat. The horse finally threw the man to the ground and was about to trample him when J. Dobbin ran to the man's rescue. Brandishing an axe before the animal's face, Dobbin distracted its attention from the driver long enough to give the horse-beater a chance to escape.

September 3
Work Horse Parade — St. John's, 1919

A much more positive story of interactions between horses and drivers was presented at the Work Horse Parade organized by the Society for Protection of Animals. The object of the parade was to encourage drivers and owners to treat their animals with humaneness and consideration. One of the main supporters of the event was Mrs. Gosling, wife of the mayor, and the governor put the grounds of Government House at the disposal of the Society for the purpose of the parade.

There were 11 classes in the parade and competition, and horses and carts could be decorated or not, as competitors pleased—the only stipulation was that they "must be clean and smart in any case." Nearly 150 horses were involved, drawn up, side by side, to form a square, with the horses' heads facing in. The list of owners and horses shows us what must have been typical horse names for the era: Teddy Bear, Betty, My Lady, Pansy, Dandy, Emilea Lee (an imported Kentucky mare), Bella, Floss, Rosa Belle, Darkey, and several horses named Billy. The Martin-Royal Stores Hardware Co. entered their Jerry, then 32 years old and who had been in their employ for 26 of those years. The prizes, 35 in number, included combinations of cash, rosettes, or medals. First-place horses were given an engraved brass medal, which was attached to the horses' harnesses and worn every day for the following year.

Michael Power, chief agent for the Society for the Protection of Animals, and his son Gerald Power on a horse-drawn vehicle on Scott Street

September 4
Monster in the Lake — Glenwood, 1903

An aquatic monster as big as a punt was seen in one of the lakes of the interior near Glenwood. The beast "caused consternation" among the local guides and wood rangers, who described it as a freshwater serpent.

September 5
A Stone Without a Tomb — St. John's, 1890

Municipal Council had decided to remove the range of old houses at the head of Theatre Hill in order to widen the street. During the course of demolition, the property owner, a cooper named Coady, was pulling down an old ceiling when he dislodged an oblong stone, which proved to be a tombstone, 30 inches high, two inches thick, and eight inches wide. The inscription was obscured by cobwebs and dust, but following some cleaning, it was found to read: "P. BALDWIN. Died, January 16th, 1850, Aged 13 years. Take ye heed and pray for ye know not when the time is. — St. Mark, 13th chap., 33rd vrs." No one in the immediate neighbourhood recalled a family named Baldwin or knew how the stone got there. It was surmised that the stone had been placed there by someone who died before disclosing its presence.

September 6
Quartz from the Moon — St. John's, 1872

As if showers of blood, grubs, and honey, or tombstones falling from ceilings were not strange enough, a rain of quartz fell during a thunderstorm in the vicinity of the Riverhead Convent and along the Marine Promenade. The strange shower consisted of a large number of small pieces of quartz, the largest weighing nearly half an ounce. No one had any idea where the quartz fragments came from, though one journalist had a fantastical theory: "Can it be that gold-miners are at work on some quartz reef in the moon, and that too heavy a charge of nitro-glycerine has hurled the rubbish beyond the attraction of our satellite, till caught by the earth's gravitation it dropped down near Riverhead Convent, Newfoundland?" A bold theory, but only the Man in the Moon knows for certain.

September 7
Saucy Ham Thief — Topsail, 1903

Two boiled hams were stolen from the camp of the Catholic Cadet Corps (whom you met moving a house on May 1), in spite of a sentry standing watch. The brazen plunderer ate the meat to the bones. These he left, licked clean, just outside the camp. The guard was increased the next night, and shortly after midnight an intruder's footsteps were heard approaching.

"Who goes there?" the sentry shouted.

"What in the hell odds is it to you?" replied the stranger as he ran out of sight, never to be brought to justice.

September 8
A Bunch of Bad Apples — St. John's, 1890

Four youths were brought before the court for cribbing crabapples from an orchard in the western suburbs of the town. The two ringleaders were fined $2 apiece, while the other two received a good lecture and were then discharged. Also appearing in court that day were two "female scolds," one of them as complainant against the other. Evidence proved each one as bad as the next, so they were fined $5 each to teach them better manners.

September 9
Incorrigible — St. John's, 1925

A domestic servant by the name of Fitzpatrick found herself before Judge Morris. The day before, she had demolished the door of her employer's residence on Hamilton Street with an axe in order "to gain prompt admission." Doctor Anderson testified that she was an "incorrigible mental degenerate" who required strict discipline. She was sent to the penitentiary for eight days. At some point previously, the woman had annoyed her former employer so much by refusing to get out of bed that he had tied her up with rope and carried her to the police station. Perhaps the girl had reason to smash down his door.

September 10
Happy Hunting — Southern Shore, 1900

Reports circulated that lynx had destroyed a number of partridges on the Southern Shore hunting grounds. Many sportsmen who intended to hunt in that area decided to try their luck elsewhere. While lynx are a native species, they were extremely rare on the island prior to the introduction of the snowshoe hare. Hares were introduced from Nova Scotia as a food supplement and distributed throughout the island between 1864 and 1876 by local magistrates as part of a scheme devised by the Newfoundland Agricultural Society.

Lynx du Canada.

Canadian lynx, illustration circa 1885–1891

September 11
A Fracas — St. John's, 1897

Michael Rourke was heading home, and as he walked along Adelaide Street at about 9:30 p.m., he was accosted by John St. John. The two got into what was described as both a fracas and an affray, two words that need to be used more often. The altercation ended with St. John stabbing Rourke in the back as he tried to run away. Two girls called for a doctor to bandage him up. The doctor, appropriately for the occasion, was named Doctor Stabb.

September 12
Tucker's Town Torments — St. John's, 1898

A chap named Tucker, hailing from Bird Island Cove and sporting a tremendous cane, made himself very noticeable on Water Street. First, he attempted to run off with a pipe he had stolen from a Lebanese peddler selling her wares at Steer's Cove. The woman was having none of it, and as he crossed the street, she captured him and made him give up his loot. Constable Fitzgerald was nearby and quickly brought him to, though he did not arrest him. About 6:00 p.m., he made the mistake of insulting a labourer and was repaid with a tap from the man's number 12 boot to his ribs. Somewhere in his travels, boys stole his cane, and by the time he reached his boarding house, Mr. Tucker was far from feeling well.

September 13
UFOs over Labrador — Goose Bay, 1951

Between 9:00 and 10:15 p.m., two radar operators tracked three unidentified objects over the Goose Bay Air Force Base. No aircraft were known to be in the area except a Douglas C-54 Skymaster en route to landing. Two of the objects seemed to be on a collision course, and when one of the radar operators requested a course change over the radio, one evaded to the right of the other craft. All three objects vanished, without any visual confirmation, despite efforts by the radar crew, tower crew, and the incoming C-54. A very similar encounter, including the radio call and near-miss, had been reported from the exact same location in October 1948.

September 14
Skeleton of a Murderer Unearthed — St. John's, 1896

Workmen opening up the ground near Rawlins Cross made a grisly find. They were digging a trench on Military Road to carry water pipes into a house being made for the Honourable Edward Patrick Morris. About four feet below the surface of the street, they excavated the skeleton of a human body lying at right angles with the cut of the drain. After the men carefully took up the bones and placed them in a box, they were taken to the central constabulary station to be reburied by the authorities.

According to Chief Justice Sir Frederick Carter, the remains were those of Robin Barry, who was guilty of the murder of several children and accused of the murder of a woman named Thomas, his boarding mistress. Barry cheated the gallows by committing suicide, and in consequence, his body was buried in the exact centre of the crossroads with a wooden stake driven through his body in accordance with the custom of bygone days. A mark, long missing, had been put there to denote the spot.

"The boys of those days," said Sir Frederick, "used often to say they saw his ghost but were so accustomed to it, that they didn't mind it."

September 15
Monkey Speedway — St. John's, 1917

Inspector General Hutchings, accompanied by Superintendent Grimes and Detective Sergeant Byrne, made an inspection of the visiting "Wonderland Shows," which included a sideshow, Hawaiian village, and a Ferris wheel, all installed at the Prince's Rink and grounds.

The Inspector General was given a private tour through

the various "girl shows" by the management. To these titillations, the gentleman apparently had no objection, but he was quick to shut down the "Wheel of Fortune" and "Palmistry Camp," as they were not in keeping with regulations regarding games of chance.

Fortunately, "The Monkey Speedway, Where Little Monkeys Race in Automobiles," was given the green light. This consisted of an automobile track, around which four little monkeys drove tiny motor cars. The simian speeders handled their vehicles in an expert manner, and the most successful was deemed to be one named Kelly, who drove car No. 2.

"He is a reckless driver and delights in speeding," one eyewitness wrote, "but although apparently careless, he has avoided accidents."

September 16
Somnambulism — St. John's, 1879

A man named Walsh, while in a somnambulic state, walked over the end of the Job Brothers & Company wharf. The sleepwalker would have been drowned but for the timely aid provided by Walkins, the watchman.

September 17
Feline Firebug — St. John's, 1898

The Spencer Street home of Mr. James Furlong came close to being destroyed by fire, was it not for the aid rendered by Mr. G. Bambrick, who valiantly quenched the blaze with mats and water. The walls and floors of the kitchen were charred, and the curtains burned from the windows. Mrs. Furlong had left some meat on the table, near a lit lamp. A cat had entered the kitchen through an open window, drawn in by the scent of the meat. The cat knocked over the lamp, and the apartment was ablaze within minutes.

September 18
Lo and Behold! — Great Harbour Deep, 1902

Naturalist and geologist James Patrick Howley, along with his crew and his dog Beppo, spent the night on board the schooner *Silver Spray*. They were woken by the nearby sound of an anchor being let go and its chain running out. A hundred yards off, they spotted a vessel of some kind, its sails down, with no lights or signs of life on her deck. In his reminiscences, Howley wrote:

> Our crew, all of whom were extremely superstitious, could not but imagine that the stranger was some phantom ship. I wanted to lower our punt and go over to investigate, but not one of them would come. We soon retired again to our bunks and were not further disturbed during the night. But at early dawn next morning when some of the hands went on deck, Lo and behold! the craft was not there and not a vestige of her was to be seen anywhere around. This, of course, confirmed the crew in their belief that she must have been some unearthly visitor, perhaps the ghost of some lost ship and crew which had come to grief hereabout in years gone by.

September 19
No Big Deal — Witless Bay, 1915

Stanley Mullowney, aged 22, entered the General Hospital to undergo an operation to extract a bullet from his left side.

Earlier that day, Mullowney had been driving a wagon, with a loaded .22 Winchester rifle beside him and its muzzle pointing upward. As he rounded a corner, he hit a big stone. This gave the wagon a heavy jolt, throwing the muzzle of the rifle toward him. It discharged, the bullet entering his body. Unfazed, Mullowney drove himself to the train station, caught the train to St. John's, and walked to the waiting ambulance. The bullet, which had entered a fleshy part of his body, was removed, and he went home a few days later.

September 20
Birthday of Jack Bursey — St. Lunaire, 1903

Jack Bursey, polar explorer, US Coast Guard officer, and dog team driver, was born on this day. When he heard that Commander Richard E. Byrd was planning an expedition to the Antarctic and needed dog drivers and skiers, Bursey was one of 50,000 men to apply. He did not get a position but went to the expedition office and asked one of Byrd's men to see if he could help. Two days later, Bursey had what he would later describe as "probably the shortest interview on record."

> Byrd: "So you come from Newfoundland."
> Bursey: "Yes, sir."
> Byrd: "And you are a dog driver?"
> Bursey: "Yes, sir."
> Byrd: "Have you got adventure in you?"
> Bursey: "Yes, sir. I'm full of it."
> Byrd: "I suppose you can skin a seal."
> Bursey: "Yes, I can do that, too."

He was hired. Jack Bursey went on to accompany Byrd on two different Antarctic expeditions and made one of the longest Antarctic dog-team trips ever recorded. The name of

Bursey's lead sled dog on his first polar trip? St. Lunaire, named after his hometown.

Commander Richard E. Byrd's first Antarctic expedition ship, SS *City of New York*, next to the Great Ice Barrier, Antarctica. September 1929.

September 21
Birthday of Captain William Wilson Kettle — Grand Bay, 1861

Happy birthday to the late Captain Kettle, who died in California at the age of 102. Kettle married twice and was the father of 13 children. He was listed in the Guinness Book of Records as having the most living descendants in a monogamous country (542). Captain Kettle had his own schooner for 20 years and went to the sealing grounds for 48 springs. He took up commercial diving and made his last dive in 1946 at the age of 84. Kettle was buried at Grand Bay in a coffin he had bought 20 years previously.

September 22
The Lantern Parade — Donovans, 1896

About 40 members of the Cycling Club departed St. John's from New Gower Street at about 7:30 p.m. They rode in single file, with 10 yards between each cyclist. The Club had affixed many coloured Japanese lanterns and lamps to the handles of their machines. Crowds thronged the streets to witness the spectacle and "cheered the brilliantly lighted party as they sped along." Dinner was served at Donovans at 10:00 p.m., with a delicious partridge prepared for each. Dinner was followed by toasts, songs, recitations, dances, and piano selections. The party ended at 2:30 a.m. with the National Anthem and Auld Lang Syne, then the club members cycled back home.

September 23
Pea-Blowing Nuisance — St. John's, 1909

It was reported that boys armed with peashooters were making a nuisance of themselves around the city. One little arsehole blew some of these missiles, at short range, at a woman on Hamilton Street. The woman was sitting on her doorstep with her children at the time. The peas struck her painfully between the eyes, practically blinding her and leaving her with one eye much swollen and inflamed.

September 24
Tsunami Drawback — Bonavista, 1848

Between 3:00 and 4:00 p.m., the water in the harbour receded suddenly, to "a frightful extent." Boats tied out on the collar were grounded at their moorings. When the water returned, it did so quickly, rising above the floor level of the local fishing stages. The water rushed up Walkham's Brook and flooded the pond, and continued rising and falling every ten minutes for the rest of the afternoon. Elderly residents said a similar event had taken place in the harbour in 1755, following the destruction of Lisbon by an earthquake. In addition to Bonavista, the effects of the 1848 tsunami were reported in St. John's, Catalina, and Elliston, as well as southern Labrador.

September 25
Pie-Eating Contest — St. John's, 1917

Visiting "Fat Lady" sideshow performer Victoria Young hosted a whort pie–eating competition in three heats, at 8:00 p.m., 9.30, and 10. Eight young hopefuls entered the contest, including the doughty Billy Murphy. The contest drew an interested crowd, most of them there to see Young herself, a 33-year-old American performer born of Belgian parents who tipped the scales at over 500 pounds.

A whort, incidentally, is an older name for what we today would commonly call a blueberry. If you are feeling peckish, you can try this 1900 recipe for Whortleberry Pie:

> Wash and pick over the berries; place them an inch thick on the under crust, covering them thickly with sugar; add a small piece of butter, cover with the upper crust and bake half an hour. Blackberry and

raspberry pies are made the same way. They require no spice; but whortleberries are greatly improved by having a few currants or the juice of a lemon mixed with them. Sift powdered sugar over all fruit pies before serving.

September 26
The London House Mystery — St. John's, 1896

Mrs. Amelia Cairns, the proprietress of the London House millinery establishment, died on this date in her 55th year. For many years, Cairns ran the largest millinery businesses in the city, selling hats, mantles, and seasonal novelties. She arrived from Glasgow circa 1861 and was well-known. Her funeral cortège was followed by a large number of friends and citizens to her final resting place at the General Protestant Cemetery. Miss Muir, her assistant, bought out her business and continued it from the same house with a grand spring opening in April 1897.

The story of Mrs. Cairns, however, did not stop there. She had died without a will, and her estate became the property of the Crown. In 1903, however, a Thomas R. Cairns residing in Scotland claimed to be the next of kin of Amelia's long-lost son, William J. Cairns.

William had vanished somewhat mysteriously in 1892, after writing a letter to his mother saying that she would never see him again and that she should not write to him, as he would never respond. The two had been on affectionate terms, so the letter was very puzzling. When she died, it was presumed that William was dead as well. The court case dragged on and on, the court placing ads in international newspapers and even going so far as to hire the Pinkerton Detective Agency to track down the missing William. The Pinkertons could find no evidence that he was alive or dead, the representatives of Thomas Cairns could not prove that William had died after Amelia (thus inheriting her property), nor could the so-called next of kin prove they were related to William in any way. The estate, worth somewhere between $10,000 or $11,000, remained tied up, the case still unresolved into the 1930s.

If you can prove you are the descendant of Amelia Cairns, milliner, there may be some money in it for you!

September 27
King of Skittles — St. John's, 1898

Mr. John Flynn, of Ordnance Yard, East End, was proclaimed the King of Skittles. Three hundred is the greatest possible number that can be made by one player at a game, which Mr. Flynn did. He was presented with a gold medal by Mr. Lindberg (whom we met on January 20 as a financial backer of skittle alleys). Several players had won skittle bonspiels in the city, but none equalled Mr. Flynn's perfect score.

September 28
Found in a Swoon — Mount Pearl, 1905

While driving his horse along the road to Mount Pearl, Mr. Lester's animal suddenly shied, came to a standstill, and would not move. Lester got out of his carriage and, following the sound of groans, found a young woman with torn clothes lying on the ground "in a swoon." Lester placed her in his vehicle and drove her to the nearest physician, Doctor Tait, at the Lunatic Asylum. The woman, Catherine Walsh, was given restoratives and eventually came to. After a night of care and refreshments at the asylum, she was sent home the next morning.

September 29
Not Your Average Tourist — Bound for Hebron, 1905

Inuit man, woman, and baby at the Pan-American Exposition, Buffalo, NY, circa 1901

A dapper, intelligent-looking gentleman, dressed in the latest New York fashions and speaking with an "enviable American accent," disembarked the SS *Silvia* and presented a local reporter with his card and a fragrant Havana cigar. This was Mr. Jonathan Chickenneck, who, with his companion Mr. Helenak Eventseek, was heading to Hebron to spend a winter vacation. Seven years previously, Chickenneck, only speaking 20 words of English, along with nine other Inuit, had gone to Buffalo, New York, where they were paid $2.50 a day to operate the "Esquimaux exhibits." This was possibly the "Esquimaux Village" at the Pan-American Exposition held in Buffalo in 1901, famous for being the location of the assassination of United States President William McKinley.

Chickenneck had run a number of operations in Buffalo and was returning to Labrador, flush with dough, to escape the heat and do some walrus hunting.

September 30
Kite Season — St. John's, 1897

Kite season was judged to be under way, as evidenced by the number of them in the skies, flown from the heights of the town by local boys. Kites were readily available at local stores. Byrne's Bookstore in 1906 had a selection of linen kites (from 2¢ to 30¢ each) and paper kites (a bargain at 7¢ a dozen). Homemade kites were just as popular—young Arthur Hodge of Fogo had one that measured six feet, which was said to have had two miles of twine on it.

OCTOBER

October 1
Best Late Excuse Ever — St. John's, 1880

An unusual court case played out between Nathaniel Ebbs, plaintiff, and James Hickey, defendant. Ebbs, a fishing servant, sued Hickey for holding back $44 in wages. Hickey had held back the money because Ebbs had missed 13 days of work, without leave. Ebbs contended that he had left his home two hours before dawn for the purpose of going to work and that all he remembered was seeing a funeral procession. At this point, Ebbs claimed, he lost his senses and was carried away by the fairies. A witness testified that he had discovered Ebbs three days afterwards, lying speechless on the ground. Hickey did not deny that his employee had been carried off by the fairies, but he argued that the lost time should be made up nonetheless. It was suggested by one of the lawyers that it appeared to be a clear case of "spiritualism," to which Ebbs asserted he was a strict total abstainer, "except at Christmas." Judge Conroy ruled in favour of the plaintiff, "for amount sued for with the exception of some cash admitted to have been received"—a total of $19.10.

October 2
Tin Men — St. John's, 1903

The employees of all the tinsmith stores assembled at the Mechanic's Hall and voted to form the St. John's Tinsmith's Union, with a Mr. Pike as president. The workers had gone on strike a while before and refused to go back to work unless they were all paid a minimum wage of $1.50 a day. The Union would go on to advocate for the work of local tinsmiths, petition the government to increase duties on imported manufactured tinware, and set standardized price lists for local tin work.

Unidentified tinsmith, possibly in St. John's, though date and location are unknown

October 3
Grand Farewell Concerts — St. John's, 1895

Newfoundland's first opera singer, Georgina Stirling, also known as Miss Twillingate Stirling and Marie Toulinguet, performed her farewell concert. This was given prior to the prima donna's departure to England, where she was booked to sing first in Birmingham, followed by engagements in the midland counties, and then on to Johannesburg, South Africa. Her singing that night was reported to have been better than it ever had been previously. The most popular number that evening was "Ye Mariners of England," which "could not but stir the heart-blood of every Briton, to hear her send forth in her rich powerful voice, this poem of England's might." Stirling appeared in a dress made by House of Worth, the Paris dressmakers and inventors of haute couture, which was rumoured to have cost $1,000 (over $30,000 today).

October 4
Vanishing Train Jumper — Donovans, 1910

Passengers on the outgoing train were startled to see a man jump off the train shortly before reaching that station. Some thought the man had fallen after his jump and suggested he might have been killed. The Reid Newfoundland Company gave Sergeant Sparrow the loan of an automobile, and upon arriving, he made a thorough search for a mile along the track, but the jumper had vanished completely. The mystery was partially solved later when Mr. P. Dunn turned up at his home with some slight bruises and scratches. He had bought a ticket on the outgoing train at 6:00 p.m. to go to Donovans but "changed his mind" when the train drew near the station. Why he decided to jump, rather than disembark at the station, remained uncertain.

October 5
Lawless Locals — St. John's and Musgravetown, 1906

Two accounts of rowdyism made the news. In St. John's, moving-picture spectators at St. Patrick's Hall were disappointed with the quality of their show, and a number of young men got into a racket with the manager. The police were called and quieted the crowd. The manager managed to escape, but not before the malcontents had trashed his projector.

Meanwhile, in Musgravetown, where there were no police, residents complained about the conduct of local boys destroying property and maiming cattle.

October 6
Traverspine Gorilla — Northwest River, 1906

One of the first accounts of interactions with the shaggy, gibbering, manlike monster that would eventually become known in Labrador as the Traverspine Gorilla was printed on this date. The community of Northwest River was abuzz over mysterious footprints left in the neighbourhood, resembling the track left by a barefooted man with the mark of a great claw on each foot. The prints were deeply sunk in the ground as if made by an enormously heavy creature. Fears were stoked when a trapper, who lived 20 miles out, brought his family into the settlement with the story that his grown daughter had seen an enormous figure who had beckoned her to come away with him.

October 7
Spying on the Sex Lives of Caribou —
Sandy River, 1912

The fabulously named Welsh-American naturalist and wildlife photographer Arthur Radclyffe Dugmore (1870–1955) made camp at Sandy River to study the reproductive habits of Newfoundland caribou. "Scarcely a day passed without several being seen," he wrote. "On some days from five hundred to a thousand would pass within sight of me. The season was an abnormal one, the mating and the migration taking place together, a most unusual occurrence."

October 8
The Goat Nuisance — St. John's, 1887

Residents of LeMarchant Road were daily tormented by the ravages of some five or six goats. These beasts freely roamed, unyoked, up and down the street, forever on the watch for gates left open by peddlers or vagrants. Goat complaints were the special purview of Sergeant Peter L'Estrange, goat catcher, Impounder, and Pound-Keeper for the St. John's Municipal Council Sanitary Department. Said to have been of Norman extraction, L'Estrange was formerly of the Royal Irish Rifles, in which regiment he had attained high military honours in the Crimea. His role was to keep the streets free of unwanted creatures such as goats, though one anonymous letter writer was not impressed with his work:

> I have seen L'Estrange, the goatherd, only once on the street the summer, but he can be seen often idling about doorways where goats are not likely to enter or be found.

October 9
Magnificent Mill Menu — Grand Falls, 1909

Paper was first manufactured at the Grand Falls pulp and paper mill, and the assembled guests were royally received and sumptuously dined. Fifty waiters were in attendance and served up the following delectables:

Soup
Julienne.

Fish
Boiled Fresh Salmon. Lobster Mayonnaise.

Entree
Vol-au-vent of Chicken.

Joints
Roast Turkey, Oxford Sausage, Roast Beef, Horseradish, Ham, Champagne Sauce, Glazed Tongue.

Vegetables
Boiled Potatoes. Green Peas.

Relieve
Partridge.

Sweet Course
Ice Pudding.

Savoury Course
Anchovies on Toast.

Dessert
Fruit, Chocolates, Nuts, and Raisins, Cake,
Tea, Coffee, and Aerated Waters.

During the feast, the Church Lads' Brigade Band also served up select music at intervals, and Highland pipers marched around the tables playing stirring Scotch airs. Ice pudding, by the way, is not a typographic error for "rice pudding." Ice pudding is a type of moulded frozen custard, or moulded ice containing preserved or fresh fruit, popular in the Victorian and Edwardian eras.

October 10
Logging Camp Night School —
Ahwachanjeesh Road, 1942

Mr. Arthur Budgell of Springdale started a night class for 36 woodsmen at Bowater's Camp No. 22. At the start of the class, most of the men were not capable of signing their names. For two months, the men gathered nightly for an hour and a half and, at the end, were able to write letters home and make up the amount of wood they had cut. The literacy project, supported by the Department of Education, was so successful it was repeated at other logging camps. Camp No. 22 was situated on Ahwachanjeesh Road, presumably near Ahwachanjeesh Pond northwest of St. Alban's. Ahwachanjeesh is an anglicization of the Mi'kmaq word *Awaqanji'j*, meaning "Little Paddle."

October 11
Something Went Boom — Corner Brook, 1941

Saturday afternoon was cloudy and dull with occasional rain showers. There were no squalls of wind or electrical disturbances, but nonetheless, at 5:25 p.m., a strange phenomenon shook the community. An object was seen falling from the sky, and immediately after, a great noise was heard as it struck the ground near the home of William Snow on Lower Country Road. The impact shattered two windows, lifted a clothesline pole entirely out of the ground, and scattered a pile of lumber in all directions, some of it landing 900 feet away. There was no damage to the house beyond the breaking of the windows and no sign of any impact. The matter was never fully explained.

October 12
What Was It? — Portugal Cove, 1917

Mr. Del. Hibbs, the son of Mr. William Hibbs, local constable and planter, was driving his carriage home when a perplexing incident occurred. It was very dark, and as he progressed homeward, a man of stout build wearing a soft felt hat suddenly appeared just abreast of the rig. As the mare passed the man, it suddenly shied in fright and went over the embankment. Mr. Hibbs immediately thought he had crushed the solitary stranger underneath the carriage. The horse jumped up and bolted. After running some distance, the mare was stopped by the driver, who returned to the spot expecting to find a human being badly hurt or killed. No one could be found. Both man and beast arrived home in a bad state: young Hibbs, who was only 19, was "prostrated from fright and excitement" for hours; the mare, trembling with fright and excitement, would not partake of food. Family and friends believed that something of an occult nature had occurred, and no one could provide an alternative explanation for the strange encounter.

October 13
Luck Ran Out — Flamborough Head, 1896

A codfish, caught off Flamborough Head, was found to have swallowed 59 fish hooks, all of them baited.

October 14
Bad News — Falmouth, UK, 1696

Merchants at the Port of Falmouth were surprised by the contents of a letter brought by ship. It bore the news that a squadron of French men-of-war had surprised 14 of their merchant ships in a bay in Newfoundland and had taken and destroyed all of them as well as some smaller vessels. The letter also stated that the French had landed upwards of 2,000 men and done considerable damage, "but we hope this bad news will not be confirmed." Sadly, the letter likely referred to French attacks by sea under the command of the Governor of Plaisance, Jacques-François de Monbeton de Brouillan, and the start of the Avalon Peninsula Campaign of Pierre Le Moyne d'Iberville. That winter, their raids would devastate the English settlements of Newfoundland.

October 15
Constable Crane Gets His Man — Bay of Islands, 1896

Lawrence Connolly, in remand for larceny, escaped from officials at St. George's Bay. He stole $15, fitted himself out in a new suit of clothes, and vanished. No trace of him could be found. Two days later, Constable Crane heard, casually, that a person resembling the escaped prisoner had been seen at Riverhead, Bay of Islands. Crane immediately disguised himself and went on the hunt. The constable only knew Connolly by description, and Bay of Islands presented many spots for the fugitive to hide. However, after 12 hours of search and inquiry, Crane found the prisoner, asleep, at Woods Island, a distance of 15 miles from where Crane had started his search. Connolly was transported by the *Grand Lake* to St. John's, where he was sent to the penitentiary for six months.

October 16
The Plucking — St. John's, 1895

In the office of the *Evening Telegram*, there was exhibited a very large turnip that had been picked on that day. It was grown on Exon Farm, Long Pond Road, owned by Mr. James T. Southcott, and had been planted on May 20 by Mr. Edward Hanrahan. The turnip was of the purple-top Aberdeen species, weighed 15 pounds, measured 36 inches in circumference, and was "a surprise to look at."

October 17
Foote's Big Potato — Grand Bank, 1903

Not to be outdone, Mr. Thomas Foote, of Grand Bank, made his way to town on the SS *Glencoe*. With him, he brought a special handbag containing the largest potato ever raised in Newfoundland. It weighed two and a half pounds and was 18 inches in circumference. He showed it to several of his friends in town, and all praised him for raising the largest potato in the country. Mr. Foote had harvested 15 barrels of potatoes from planting one barrel of seed.

Four years later, Mr. Reuben Gordon, of Bear's Cove, Harbour Grace, grew a spud, which, though large, was not enough to beat Mr. Foote's. Gordon's tuber measured seven inches in length and nine inches around the largest end and weighed a mere two pounds.

October 18
Killed by the Train — Gaff Topsails, 1900

One of the railway cars of the train bound for St. John's ran off the track, throwing Brakeman Yates under the wheels as it did so. He was killed instantly. An upright and industrious young man, Yates was reported as being well-liked by all with whom he came in contact.

October 19
The *Africa* — St. John's, 1863

The steamer *Merlin* arrived from Halifax, and among its passengers were six divers. They arrived in port to take a look at the packet steamer *Africa*, which was leaking badly. A few days before, the *Africa* had struck Cape Race and had taken serious damage. The divers were paid £5 a day for their work, and by October 26 they had the ship nearly ready to set out to sea once more.

Two years prior, the *Africa* had carried François d'Orléans, Prince de Joinville, to the US Naval Academy at Newport, where he had enrolled his son. Prince de Joinville was a former admiral of the French Navy who had fought with the United States government during the Civil War. He was a writer, talented artist, and friend of Victor Hugo. In 1840, Prince de Joinville had been the one entrusted with bringing the remains of Napoleon from Saint Helena to France.

October 20
Made Right Here — Dorset, 1762

An interesting series of baptisms took place in the parish of Milton Abbas, Dorset. Parents Thomas and Ann Norris were pleased to have baptized six of their children on the same day: Thomas, born 1748; John, born 1753; William, born 1754; Elizabeth, born 1757; George, born 1761; and Joseph, born 1762. All six of the children had been born in Newfoundland.

October 21
The Grandiloquent Zera — St. John's, 1879

Professor Zera, the "Wizard and Ventriloquial King," arrived by the SS *Cortes* and performed in the Athenaeum. If nothing else, Zera was a master of self-promotion, and ads in the local papers implored the public, "don't fail to see the most wonderful conjurer in the world." His performances were, by his own admission, first-class in every respect. He also warned of other so-called magicians in a public address to the people of St. John's, confiding without apparent irony that "quite a number of people are perambulating the land calling themselves magicians, with additional high-sounding titles, and a large display of coloured pictures, who actually possess less real talent than a veritable backwoodsman." These people Zera dismissed as "mere empirics, charlatans and imposters, playing upon the credulity of a few, and utterly unworthy the attention of the public." He signed his letter, "ZERA, Leading Magician and Ventriloquist of the World." Modest chap, that professor.

October 22
Eel in the Plumbing — St. John's, 1906

While putting the water into Mr. Ruxton's house, Springdale Street, the workmen found an eel in the pipe so large that it almost stopped the flow of water completely. Think about that next time you go to sit upon the ivory throne.

October 23
Who Did What? — St. John's, 1902

Male great horned owl, 1734

John McHugh did not have a good day. While visiting the store of Mr. T. Allan, a large horned owl escaped from its cage. The owl, probably frustrated at having been put in a cage in the first place, attacked poor McHugh and cut him badly about the face with its beak. The owl was captured, and McHugh probably thought twice about shopping at Allan's store in the future.

October 24
Birthday of Private Ryan — Blackhead, Conception Bay, 1892

Herbert Louis Ryan was the son of fisherman Robert Ryan and his wife, Naomi. Robert and Naomi had three sons: Herbert, Orlando William, and Norman. When the First World War broke out, Herbert and Orlando signed up out of Halifax as members of the Canadian Expeditionary Force. Norman, the youngest, remained home. Herbert was assigned to the 58th Battalion, Canadian Infantry, 2nd Central Ontario Regiment. Orlando, a good shot, was made a sniper. Frequently exposed to danger, he was the source of a great deal of worry for his mother in Newfoundland. Eventually, Naomi got the message that every mother in her situation must have dreaded. However, it was not the sniper on the front lines who had been shot. Instead, Herbert had been killed in action, on Wednesday, August 28, 1918, at the age of 26. Orlando was still on the front lines. Tragedy followed tragedy, and Norman, the son who had stayed home out of harm's way, perished. He died at age 19 of peritonitis of the bowels, which we know today as complications from a burst appendix. Orlando, the son Naomi had been most concerned about, outlived his brothers and returned home safely from the Great War.

October 25
Bouncer — Bound for Portsmouth, 1901

Bouncer, a Newfoundland dog, headed off to England aboard the *Ophir* in the company of his new owners, their Royal Highnesses the Duke and Duchess of Cornwall and York (later King George V and Queen Mary). The royal couple had made a brief stop in St. John's as part of the final leg of their imperial tour. They had been greeted by the Governor Sir Cavendish Boyle, monster bonfires blazing on the hilltops, and a steady downpour of heavy rain. They were in St. John's for only 48 hours before setting off, but before they departed, a delegation of Newfoundland children had presented them with Bouncer as a gift for the Royal Highnesses' children, along with a small dogcart. According to one story, as Her Royal Highness went to pet the dog, she exclaimed: "Oh, isn't he a beauty!" "Begobs, ma'am," the dog's trainer was said to have replied, "you won't find the likes of him nowhere!"

Bouncer, presented to Prince of Wales in 1901

October 26
Escaped from the Asylum — St. John's, 1903

Kate Trimingham Mullins, who had been missing from the asylum, was tracked down by Sergeant Colliers. She had been spotted by fireman Ed McGinn as he was returning from tea. He followed her quietly, and once he reached the East End Fire Station, he called for the sergeant. When the sergeant found her, she was near the old railway station in the Fort William area. She had evidently been out in the rain all day, as her clothes were saturated. She was taken to the fire station, treated kindly, and driven back to the asylum in a cab, though she claimed she had done no wrong and was not insane. She died there of apoplexy (a cerebral hemorrhage or stroke) four years later at the age of 62 and was buried in Belvedere Cemetery beside the husband who had predeceased her.

October 27
A Tea Time Surprise — Whitbourne, 1895

The patrons of the Globe Hotel were taking tea when they were interrupted by an unexpected visitor. An inquisitive horse put his head completely through a windowpane, sending splinters of glass among the eatables. The horse seemed inclined to devour something from the table inside but, seeing nothing to its liking, withdrew its head. The genteel ladies who had gathered for tea were badly frightened but retook their seats once the equine interloper had removed itself. The dainties besprinkled with glass were removed and replaced by other dishes, and tea time resumed peacefully.

October 28
Doctor Grunia Ferman — St. John's, 1995

At its Fall Convocation, Memorial University of Newfoundland conferred an Honorary Doctorate of Laws upon Grunia Movschovitch Ferman. Born in Novogrudok, Poland, in 1916, Grunia Movschovitch was trained as a physical education teacher. She was pressed into service as a fitness trainer by the Russian Army during its occupation of Poland, and then in 1941, she witnessed the execution of relatives and friends by the Nazis. She escaped into the Naliboki Forest, where she joined the Jewish resistance as a nurse. It was there she met her future husband, Lewis Ferman. In 1947, the Fermans moved to St. John's and established a store on Water Street called Lewis Ferman and Company. They remained in St. John's for 40 years, during which time Mrs. Ferman spent countless hours as a volunteer at hospitals and helped start the city's Holocaust remembrance service.

(L-R) Neighbours Joan Simms, Grunia Ferman, and Doris Snelgrove. St. John's airport, 1995, after Ferman received her honorary doctorate from Memorial University at the Fall Convocation.

October 29
Phantom of George Street — St. John's, 1896

Mrs. R. Brien and Aggie Mearns, of Springdale Street, were walking down the street at about midnight. As they reached the intersection with George Street, Aggie gave a great scream and fainted dead away. She was carried to a nearby house and, when she regained consciousness, told a frightening tale. She had seen the form of a woman from the neighbourhood who had been buried one week before, who raised a ghostly hand up toward her in a threatening manner. Badly frightened, Aggie said she would not venture out after dark again, for fear of beholding the ghost.

October 30
Bad Doggos — St. John's, 1911

John Butler, a servant of William Hall, had to have a wound on his hand cauterized after a run-in with a pack of wild and vicious dogs on Portugal Cove Road. Former residents of the area had moved away several years previously and, upon leaving, had abandoned a number of dogs that had propagated and gone feral. Butler's hand was badly lacerated, as one of the dogs had driven its teeth deep into his flesh. The attack resulted in a public call to have the pack exterminated. Dog attacks along Portugal Cove Road dated back to at least 1889, when a young farmer named Mahon had to use a pitchfork to defend against an attack by two wild dogs along the road.

October 31
Halloween Dinner and Dance — Grand Falls, 1917

The women of the Rebekah Branch of the Oddfellows put on an elaborate dinner and dance for over 100 dancers. The hall was decorated with the pink and green colours of the Rebekah Lodge, but the women had taken the decorations far beyond that:

> The imaginations of the Sisters have been busy as well as their fingers, for all the supernatural occurrences associated with Hallowe'en were represented. The centre of the stage contained the usual witches' cauldron, the stick fire being made very realistic by coloured electric bulbs concealed within it. Flanking the pot were the ghosts with the most approved pumpkin heads. As midnight struck, the lights in the Hall were put out, and only the stage was visible, where a witch was seen stirring the contents of the pot. Then there entered a procession of twelve witches who paraded the hall in ghostly silence, and then proceeded to dispense "Cauld Cannon" to the whole of the assembled company.

Cauld Cannon or colcannon can refer to both Halloween night celebrations, or the casserole-type mixture of potatoes and cabbage typically served at this time of year. If you want to whip some up for your Halloween celebrations, the ladies of the 1956 George Street United Church Women's Association have you covered:

> Today Colcannon is served in Newfoundland at Hallowe'en parties or suppers and little prizes or favours are hidden in the mixture. It can be made from any vegetables though white ones are preferred. Wash and cook the vegetables. Put through a potato ricer. Mix well in a saucepan with 1 dessertspoon of butter for each cup of mixture. Press into a well-buttered dish and bake for twenty minutes. Serve with parsley sauce or meats.

NOVEMBER

November 1
Resplendent — St. John's, 1886

The streets of St. John's were illuminated by electricity for the first time, an event that generated very little media attention. A Newfoundlander living abroad going by the acronym "J. T. O'C." heard about the newfangled lights and wrote the following to the editor of the *Colonist*:

> St. John's must look quite splendid, or perhaps, resplendent, now at nights, since you got the electric lamps in working order. I hope the lights don't flicker much, if they do they will be a nuisance. As here was illuminated by electricity some time ago, but owing to some impurities in the carbons, the lamps would sometimes give but very little light, and also owing to the flickering, some people objected to them, but I am not certain whether they were removed or not. I hope you won't have the same complaint in St. John's. The complaint probably will be that the glare is too strong, and so be injurious to the sight. An objection to electric lighting in some places is that it gives out no heat. However, the people of St. John's can scarcely complain, considering how badly the town had been before lit up by gas.

November 2
Kelly in the Well — Southside, St. John's, 1956

Death lurked for three hours as firemen worked feverishly to free Roy Kelly from the bowels of the earth. Kelly was cleaning out a well some 18 feet below the floor of the basement of his home when the walls suddenly caved in. Kelly was instantly buried beneath over a ton of earth. A child ran for help, and within minutes assistance was on the scene, only to discover that only the top of Kelly's hat was visible above the rocks and clay. They cleared a small space around his head and found he was still alive. When firemen arrived on the scene, they discovered that the shaft was so small that it was impossible to get down to free the trapped man, though they were able to dig out his hands.

    For the next three hours, Kelly dug away at the clay with his bare hands, sending it to the surface in a bucket. After a ton of clay had been lifted out, it was discovered that one of his legs was jammed under a boulder. The firemen lowered a rope, and Kelly tried repeatedly to pull himself up but had to give up and dig some more. At one point, he stopped for a few seconds, and it appeared to his family waiting above that he might collapse. If he fainted, reckoned the rescuers, they might have to break his leg and force it from underneath the boulder. Kelly, however, only needed a rest, and brandy was lowered down to fortify him. Finally, he gave the signal to pull the rope, and within a few seconds, he was on the surface. Kelly showed some signs of fatigue but was calm and otherwise in fair condition.

November 3
Goodness, Gracious, Great Balls of Gas — Stephenville, 1997

A ball of red fire was observed over the ocean across from the airport runway. It hovered there for about two or three minutes and then left without a sound. As it was leaving, it split into two different balls of gas and dropped into the sea.

November 4
Laughter of the Dead — St. John's, 1891

A large and respectable audience gathered at St. Patrick's Hall to hear a phonograph, as exhibited by Mr. Urquhart. Urquhart was there as a representative of the Edison Manufacturing Company, to exhibit the powers of the "wonderful invention of the Wizard of Menlo park." The event had been organized by the Benevolent Irish Society Literary and Amusement Committee. Urquhart came to the stage to speak of the uses to which the phonograph could be put. He apologized in advance for the quality of the sound, as the brass horn for the phonograph had been left behind, and he had arranged local tinsmiths to fashion one out of zinc for the evening. He then proceeded to play a number of recordings, including a hornpipe, marches, a "barnyard solo" with the cackling of hens, a crowing cock, and the gobble of turkeys, as well as an audio recording of Mr. Patrick Brady before his election as an Alderman of New York.

For many, it was the first time they had ever heard recorded audio. One recording, that of a "laughing song," was sung by a gentleman whom, Urquhart told the amazed crowd, had passed out of this world, "but yet his voice lives by means of the phonograph, and can be reproduced any number of times." The recording had "a somewhat gruesome effect on the audience to hear a laugh from the grave." On the whole, however, the audience was surprised and pleased and counted their first meeting with a phonograph a pleasant experience.

November 5
Falling Rocks — Harbour Grace, 1895

A large portion of Harbour Grace Island, about 20 feet in diameter, split off and crashed into the sea. The thousands of tons of rock and earth falling into the ocean made a terrific noise heard all over Conception Bay.

November 6
An Interview with an Alchemist — Mortlake, England, 1577

Adventurer and explorer Sir Humphrey Gilbert (half-brother of Sir Walter Raleigh) met with Mortlake's most famous resident: Doctor John Dee, mathematician, astronomer, astrologer, alchemist, and adviser to Queen Elizabeth I. Dee was greatly interested in the nautical enterprises of the day, as well as being an early advocate of colonization, and was consulted by many voyagers to the west. The exact nature of their talk is unknown, but Dee's diaries suggest that later conversations with Gilbert involved proposed voyages to the Gulf of St. Lawrence. Gilbert would take formal possession of Newfoundland for the English crown on August 5, 1583. Though Dee was a practitioner of the "scryer" (crystal ball) and communed with angelic voices, not even he foresaw that Gilbert would be lost at sea on his return voyage from Newfoundland.

Portrait of John Dee engraved by R. Cooper, circa 1800

November 7
Rare Birds — England, 1503

According to the Privy Purse Expenses, King Henry VII, the first monarch of the House of Tudor, rewarded an unnamed man for bringing him a choice gift. The expense account notes: "To one that brought hawkes from the Newfoundedland, £1." While one pound might not sound like a lot of cash, today it would be the equivalent of over $1,200 Canadian.

November 8
War on Shebeens — St. John's, 1894

Judge Prowse, it was reported, was hard at work doing what he could to stamp out shebeens, taverns or houses where liquor was sold illegally, as well as the illegal brewing of "hop beer," which could contain anywhere from two per cent to six per cent alcohol.

"Judge Prowse is doing good service to St. John's and the entire island in his efforts to eradicate shebeening from our midst," one temperance-minded columnist penned. "The law is a terror to evil doers, and in spite of Anarchist and Socialistic doctrine, is the great physician for human wrongs. Judge Prowse should be upheld in his endeavours to destroy the evil and to save our young men from ruin."

November 9
The Amazing Miss Atlantis — St. John's, 1915

Rossley's East End Theatre, St. John's leading vaudeville, dramatic, and picture theatre, hosted a competition in which the strongest man in the city could not lift the Amazing Miss Atlantis or even push her off one foot. The dainty Miss Atlantis was a visiting sideshow performer who weighed 120 pounds, and in spite of not holding onto anything or being fastened down in any way, the three handsome prizes she offered to local competitors who could lift her off her feet went unclaimed.

In addition to her strength competition, Miss Atlantis appeared on a rolling globe, blindfolded, whilst juggling. The act that caused the great sensation, however, was her "artistic posing" and delightful dances in bewildering costumes representing various statues: the morning dawn; the blind flower girl; Justice; the Greek slave; the Statue of Liberty; the Goddess of War; the Goddess of Peace; Britannia, the Mistress of the Sea; and, in a nod to the local punters, "a Maid of Terra Nova." Miss Atlantis held the audience spellbound for several nights, altering her themes each evening, and making up to five costume changes a show, "even to shoes and stockings."

November 10
First Casket Burial — St. John's, 1878

John F. Meehan of Harvey & Co. was buried in the first casket ever used in the city.

Meehan had been in a delicate state of health all summer and had spent most of the season in Topsail to recuperate. Feeling a bit better in the fall of the year, he had journeyed to Buffalo, NY, where he died suddenly with his wife at his bedside.

"The remains of the lamented deceased will be brought here for interment," his death notice read, "where those who knew and loved him in life will have an opportunity of paying the last mark of respect that can be tendered on this side of the grave."

At the time, most burials in Newfoundland and Labrador used wooden coffins, traditionally with six sides, which were made as needed. Meehan's death in Buffalo ushered in a new age in burials for Newfoundland, as he was shipped home inside a sealed casket. Doctor Almond Fisk received a US patent in the late 1840s for a cast-iron casket that he claimed was airtight and indestructible. Then, during the Civil War era, thousands of coffins were needed to transport dead soldiers, marking the start of the mass-produced (and four-sided) casket era.

The funeral of Mr. Meehan took place from his late residence on Queen's Road at 2:30 p.m. He was 54 years old. His wife, Mary Ann, died in 1901 and was buried alongside him at Belvedere Cemetery.

November 11
A Whaling Yarn — Somewhere in the Arctic Seas, 1894

Captain McKay, of the whaler *Terra Nova*, shared the following story after returning to port. Around the middle of September, they had come up against an unusually large whale, which was killed by the boats of the *Terra Nova*. Once the whale was brought alongside and the work of cutting it up had begun, an obstruction was discovered, lodged in the blubber. When the object was removed, it was found to be an old harpoon bearing the name of the whaler *Jean*. Old Arctic navigators remembered the *Jean* had been lost in the ice some 37 years previously. The steel of the harpoon was as bright as the day it was made, four decades before. The finding of the relic was the subject of much speculation and talk among the whaling crews.

November 12
The Launch of the *Saint Ida* — Gambo, 1890

The *Saint Ida*, a new schooner, glided gracefully and with ease into the water from Murphy's dockyard. She was constructed of hardwood, seasoned birch, juniper timbers, and copper-fastened by shipwright Mr. Dan Blackmore. The *Saint Ida* had a 65-foot keel and a beam of 23 feet. Eleven thousand treenails were used to fasten her planks, besides copper bolts.

> Much credit is due Mr. Blackmore for turning out so staunch and graceful a craft. He is a young man and a native, with no opportunities for acquiring the art of shipbuilding. His work, however, evidences the hand of the skilled workman, and is equal to anything the famed Nova Scotia builders can turn out.

November 13
Unlucky — St. John's, 1899

Friday the 13th was not the luckiest of days for two St. John's men, a Mr. Strang and a Mr. Thomas.

I'll introduce you to Mr. Strang first, a veteran sportsman. The day before, Strang returned from Holyrood with 16 partridges and a snipe. The birds were placed into a bag and safely stored. When he went to retrieve the bag, he found it had been stolen, possibly as a joke. The partridges were returned on Friday the 13th, and then promptly purloined by somebody else that very morning.

Our second victim was Mr. Thomas, or possibly his client. Whilst going up Water Street with 10 barrels of flour on his cart, one barrel was jolted out of place and rolled onto the street. The head of the barrel fell out, and a quarter of the flour went into the mud. Not perturbed in the least, Thomas scraped the flour up out of the mud and put it back in the barrel!

November 14
The Chieftain of the Pudding Race — St. John's, 1890

Those of Scottish heritage were invited to satisfy their cravings at the Atlantic Hotel. Mr. John Whitty, the manager, announced that he was prepared to treat customers to a dish of haggis on the shortest notice. It was not the first time haggis was served at the Atlantic, as the pudding had been made up for the January meeting of the Saint Andrew's Society. One hopes the hungry Scots ate their fill, as, by the following January, Mr. Whitty had moved to Vancouver to become the manager of the Waverley Hotel.

November 15
Letter from the *Saxilby* — Irish Coast, 1933

The SS *Saxilby*, on her way from Wabana to England with a cargo of 6,000 tons of iron ore, was lost with her crew of 27 in a storm 500 miles west of Ireland. Miraculously, a farewell message written by Joe O'Kane, a seaman on the steamer, washed up in a sealed tin two years later, within two miles of his home at Port Talbot, Wales. Fishermen digging for bait found the tin and discovered the tragic message:

> "Steamship Saxilby sinking somewhere off Irish coast: love to sisters, brothers and Dinah — Joe O'Kane."

When police presented them with the tin, O'Kane's bereaved parents recognized the handwriting as that of their son.

November 16
A Mouse Twice Swallowed — Freshwater Bay, 1887

The six-year-old daughter of Mr. Hennessey, of Freshwater Bay, swallowed a mouse. She did not do it intentionally, of course—the girl was sleeping with her mouth slightly open on her bed when the mouse ran down her throat. Her screams quickly brought the family to the room, and after some time the girl threw up the mouse, still alive. A watching cat pounced on the opportunity, and the mouse was downed a second time, this time for good.

November 17
The Tipstaff's Uncle — St. John's, 1870

Patrick Kelly, of Cochrane Street, was buried on this date. His was said to be the last funeral in St. John's at which a clergyman and doctor preceded the cortège on the way to the churchyard. Kelly was the uncle of John Burke, the tipstaff for the Supreme Court. The tipstaff was the 19th-century equivalent of a bailiff, appointed to attend upon judges and take custody of all prisoners.

November 18
The *Riseover* Sets Sail — Seldom-Come-By, 1911

The schooner *Riseover*, under Skipper William Pomeroy, left Seldom-Come-By for St. John's with a cargo of lumber. She sailed into a gale and, at around 2:00 a.m. the next morning, ran aground the "Muddy Shag" and started to fast go to pieces. Knowing the ship was doomed, the skipper gave the order to make a raft out of the lumber on board so they could sail to safety. What transpired next was immortalized in the ballad *The Loss of the Riseover*.

> To save their lives a raft was made
> And that was quickly manned
> By these poor shipwrecked fishermen
> In hopes to make the land
> And as the raft got near the shore
> It quickly broke in two
> And carried off two fishermen
> Of the "Riseover's" crew.
>
> The fishermen who reached the shore
> Their hearts were filled with joy

But changed to sadness quickly
When they heard their comrades' cry.
And as they watched them drive to sea
While they stood on the shore
They saw them wave a fond adieu
Till they were seen no more.

The crew on the larger portion of the raft were eventually rescued by the *Fogota* under the command of Captain Barbour. The other two young men, John Pomeroy, 24 years old, a married man, and Archibald Spracklin, 20, unmarried, were never seen again.

November 19
Phantom Ship Reappears — Near Lewisporte, 1952

At about midnight, George Gale, the port pilot, and Peter Abbott were returning from Twillingate in the former's motorboat. They saw a ship steaming toward them from the direction of Lewisporte with all its lights on, even the lights of the saloon. As she was coming directly toward them, they changed their course, but the ship did the same. Finally, she came so close that they feared a collision was imminent. Gale leaped to the wheel to reverse the craft. Abbott looked up, to see if they could get clear in time, and was amazed to see no trace of the menacing ship. The two men scanned the water carefully but could see nothing. Later, it was determined that no other ship had been in that vicinity for 18 hours.

The vanishing-ship story caused a lot of discussions and some worry. Years previously, there were rumours that a phantom ship had been seen off Sceviour's Island, about seven miles from Lewisporte. Many had forgotten about the tale or had never heard of it until Gale and Abbott's encounter with their phantom ship. The mystery remains unsolved.

November 20
St. Mary's Church — Southside, St. John's, 1859

The first service in the old stone St. Mary's Anglican Church was held. It was built to compensate for overcrowding at the Cathedral and because parishioners on the Southside were inconveniently remote from their church and clergy. After nearly a century of worship, on the morning of Sunday, June 21, 1959, the congregation paraded from the old church to a site on Craigmillar Avenue and broke ground for a new building.

November 21
Six Feet Under — St. John's, 1849

A curious discovery was made opposite the dwelling house of R. Prowse, Esquire, on Duckworth Street. Workers excavating in order to lay pipes for the water company uncovered human bones at a depth of about six feet below the surface.

November 22
Death by Exposure — Goulds, 1900

An autopsy was held on the body of Henry Cooper, who was found dead in Joyce's field, Petty Harbor Road. It was the opinion of Doctor Tait that the man died of exposure. The night before, at 7:00 p.m., Cooper and two other men, William Hefferan and William Chafe, had driven out of town to Petty Harbour. They took along a couple of bottles of spirits and visited various public houses along the road. Their last stop was the house of Emanuel Chafe, where they remained for a considerable time before heading on for Petty Harbour. The night was very dark. The horse, instead of keeping to the road, turned in to Joyce's field, and the heavy carriage promptly sank into a bog. The horse was unharnessed with the hope of getting the carriage out of the muck, but the animal wandered away toward the road, leaving the three men in the field. Cooper went in search of the animal.

The other two men remained in the hooded carriage all night and were thus sheltered from inclement weather. Upon waking up the next morning, they made their way to the road and walked home, believing that Cooper had found the horse and left for home. Cooper had, in fact, found the horse, and had tied it to a tree. It was assumed he then wandered about for some time, lost in the dark. When found, his pants were torn and one of his boots was missing, suggesting he must have travelled a good deal through bog and wood. In searching for the road, he beat himself out and fell down, exhausted. He died there in the cold darkness, only a short distance from a nearby barn. His funeral was held the following day.

November 23
Death of Richard Hakluyt — London, 1616

Richard Hakluyt, writer and promoter of the English colonization of North America, died on this date and was buried three days later in Westminster Abbey. He wrote, edited, and translated numerous works, including the writing of Jacques Cartier and Ferdinando de Soto, which served as source material for William Shakespeare and other authors. His chief work, *The Principal Navigations*, includes a remarkable story about a very early (and moderately disastrous) expedition to Newfoundland. In 1536, leather merchant and sea captain Master Richard Hore proposed a tourist expedition to the New World, and a number of wealthy gentlemen took him up on the promise of adventure. After a number of exploits, the gentlemen arrived in Newfoundland and ran out of provisions. I will let Hakluyt describe what happened next:

> But such was the famine that increased amongst them from day to day, that they were forced to seeke to relieve themselves of raw herbes and rootes that they sought on the maine: but the famine increasing, and the reliefe of herbes being to little purpose to satisfie their insatiable hunger, in the fieldes and deserts here and there, the fellowe killed his mate while he stooped to take up a roote for his reliefe, and cutting out pieces of his bodie whom he had murthered, broyled the same on the coles and greedily devoured them.

When the charcoal-broiling of human flesh came to light, the captain was horrified and made a "notable Oration" on the sins of cannibalism. Fine words, however, buttered no parsnips, and as the famine increased, even the captain agreed that their best course of action was to draw lots on who would be killed and consumed next. Luckily, a French vessel sailed into the harbour. Being good Englishmen, they pirated the ship, commandeering both it and its victuals, and sailed back to England.

November 24
The Savage Pigs of King's Bridge — St. John's, 1890

A great number of pigs wreaked havoc on garden properties along King's Bridge Road. Impounder L'Estrange (whom we met on October 8) was exhorted to round up these villains and hold them till their owners paid a fine. The following spring, the pigs were still at it and had moved into Mount Carmel Cemetery, where they busily set about destroying the sacred grounds. "Mr. LeStrange should go on the war-path," shouted the *Colonist*. Years passed, and still, the pigs kept up their reign of terror, wandering at large. In 1897, two ladies passing down the road met an accident by tripping into a hole made by "those pigs." The ladies were in a bad state after their fall, but emboldened by their success, the pigs expanded their territory. By 1908, feral pigs were tearing up yards, gardens, private grounds, and public roads, not just at King's Bridge, but also Quidi Vidi Road and Winter Avenue. "Residents think it is time that the Council enforce the law," noted the *Evening Telegram*, but little happened.

In response, the pigs, now just being jerks about it, started rooting up the sidewalks along King's Bridge Road.

November 25
Streets' Birthday — St. John's, 1855

Queen's Road as seen from Chapel Street, 1970s

On this date, four streets were officially named: Victoria Street (formerly Meeting House Lane); Cathedral Street (named for its proximity to the Anglican Cathedral of St. John the Baptist); Chapel Street (located between Queen's Road and Bond Street); and Darling Street. Of these, only the first three remain. Darling Street was a name used for that portion of Bond Street which runs from King's Road to Cochrane Street. Today, it is just Bond Street. The current Darling Street, located between Downing Street and Rostellan Street, was named such by the City Council on May 1, 1952. Both Darling Streets were named for Governor Sir Charles Henry Darling, KCB, Governor and Commander-in-Chief of Newfoundland.

November 26
Rare Find — Near Isle aux Morts, 1981

Wayne Mushrow discovered a very rare Portuguese mariner's astrolabe (a navigational instrument) on a shipwreck near Isle aux Morts. The year "1628" and "Y. Dyas" were stamped on the astrolabe, indicating that it was likely made by astrolabe maker Joas Dyas. The ship on which it was found sank sometime after 1638. Though its identity is not known, it is thought to have been a French vessel, based on artifacts found during archaeological excavations.

November 27
Stepped Into History — St. John's, 1887

Two guests were in the gentlemen's parlour of the Atlantic Hotel, and the porter, William Shea, was finishing up work in an adjoining room. Mr. Foran, the owner, went through to see that all guests had retired for the evening. The guests went to bed, and Foran instructed Shea to do the same. Foran then left for his own apartments, turning off the gaslights in the hallway as he did so. Three hours afterwards, at 3:30

a.m., he heard the slight noise made by the elevator as it ascended. A few minutes afterwards, he heard "an exclamation with tones of terror in it cry out, 'Oh!' from the hollow space in which the elevator worked." Mr. Foran reached for a box of matches, as everything was in darkness, then he and Mrs. Foran rushed to the basement of the elevator. There, they found the almost lifeless body of Shea. Doctor Harvey and Father Scott arrived quickly and administered to the man, who died from his injuries seven hours later. It was thought that Shea had called for the elevator carriage and that it had risen, past Shea, to the very top floor. Shea, one floor below, had stepped into the open shaft and to his death. He was described as an industrious young fellow, a kind parent to three children, and a good son.

November 28
Killing Dogs — St. John's, 1891

Two dogs were found poisoned in the vicinity of the White Hills. While sad, even shocking, by today's standards, it was not uncommon in the late 19th or early 20th century to hear or read reports of dogs being poisoned or shot. There was at that time a large problem with feral, or partly feral, dogs, and owners of other animals saw killing dogs a legitimate way of protecting their property. Even dog owners themselves seemed somewhat resigned to the matter. In 1917, for example, a Twillingate writer noted, "We had a lot of trouble last summer with our dogs, for they killed quite a few sheep, hens, etc. around here last summer and no doubt some of our dogs got shot. If they are doing mischief we don't expect anything more for them to get shot." Shootings aside, there were concerns raised about accidental poisonings, either from dead and decaying dogs contaminating water sources or by people unfamiliar with the safe handling of materials like arsenic.

November 29
Gone with the Wind — St. John's, 1890

A terrible storm blew down fences, uprooted trees, and capsized a schooner in the harbour. Most heartbreaking for local saltwater bathing enthusiasts, the bathing house at Chain Rock was swept away. The bathing house was the property of the City Point Bathing Association, and up to the day of the storm, it had been located in a convenient location only one minute's walk from the railway wharf. It was furnished with lifebuoys, ropes, floats, and all accoutrements any young gentleman saltwater bather might require.

November 30
Captain Rupert Wilfred Bartlett — France, 1917

Captain Rupert Wilfred Bartlett of Brigus, brother of Captain Bob Bartlett, was killed by a German sniper on the Masnières-Marcoing Road. "Pat" or "Paddy" to those who knew him survived the evacuation of Suvla Bay, the Battle of Arras, and the capture of Gueudecourt, having been gassed and shot in his right arm in the process. On the day he died, he was said to have gone over the battlefield leading his men, and shouting, "Go for them, Caribous." He was shot in the forehead and died instantly. Bartlett was awarded the Military Cross and Bar, as well as the Italian Order of the Crown of Italy (Cavalier). There is some mystery surrounding his final resting place. Reverend Thomas Nangle recorded his interment in Marcoing Copse Cemetery, but his remains were possibly removed and reburied somewhere else. A small cemetery memorial was erected by his family in his hometown of Brigus.

DECEMBER

December 1
Grenfell Commemorative Stamp — St. Anthony, 1941

The Newfoundland government issued a postage stamp in commemoration of the life and work of Sir Wilfred Grenfell at the start of the 50th year of his work. The stamp was 5¢ in denomination and blue in colour, its design representing Sir Wilfred on the bridge of a Mission vessel surrounded by icebergs. First-day covers for philatelists were available through the St. Anthony post office, featuring the official International Grenfell Association postmark and the seal of the Mission.

December 2
Strongman Show — St. John's, 1909

Professional strongman Al Marx gave his first exhibition in the British Hall, along with his two contortionist daughters and a set of performing dogs. Marx performed various feats of strength. He suspended a large dumbbell of 500 pounds weight across his shoulders, all while supporting a man on the bar of the dumbbell, two men suspended from either hand, and a young lad sitting on his shoulders. Their combined weight seemed not to affect him in the least, and he spun them around for several minutes. He bent heavy iron bars with ease, broke horseshoes in half, and wound a heavy draft chain around his breast and snapped it in two. He then broke a piece of marble and a paving stone with a blow from his fist and passed the pieces around the audience to show that his feat was genuine. For his finale, Marx performed two more exploits. First, he put a 100-pound stone on his head and had a man hit it with a sledgehammer three times before he broke it. He next lay on the stage and had four men put a stone of 600 pounds on his chest. A local blacksmith broke it with four blows of a sledgehammer. Every feat brought thunderous applause.

Aloysius Marx, a dockworker, started his professional career with a boxing match against famed prizefighter John L. Sullivan, the "Boston Strong Boy." Marx lasted exactly 55 seconds against Sullivan but parlayed his loss into a career as a boxer under the name "The Texas Cowboy" and later as a professional athlete, acrobat, and circus strongman. As a strongman, Marx also performed under the name "Nero: The Herculean King." He travelled with his family as the "Marx Brothers Flying Circus" and also teamed up with Luxembourg native John Grün (believed to be the strongest man in the world at the time) as "The Bros. Marx." In 1931, Al Marx died alone at an infirmary in Galveston, Texas.

December 3
Mules and Monkeys — Sangro River, Italy, 1945

The 166th (Newfoundland) Field Regiment had been in Italy since October 1943, and on this day the regiment crossed the Sangro near Ortona. The river crossing took place without incident, except that a mule fell into a hole beside the road and was completely submerged in mud and water. As the Regiment advanced, they found an unlikely friend in an enemy gun position. It was a monkey, which the Newfoundlanders appropriately named "Sangro." Sangro became the 166th (Newfoundland) Field Regiment mascot and was fed a diet of peanuts, roasted potatoes, bully beef, milk, and vermouth. Lance-bombardier Tasker Cook of Woodland Farm, St. John's East, claimed "she's as cool as any gunner in the battery. I hope I can bring her home with me." Gunner Jack Hayworth and Gunner Avalon Frampton, both of St. John's, bunked with Cook and Sangro. "She's a very clean monkey," said Frampton, "and she has never had a flea since we got her."

December 4
Five Happy Couples — Garnish, 1901

A unique event took place in St. Giles' Church. Rev. J. Hewett presided over the marriage of five couples, one wedding at a time, one after the other. In total, there were 44 "bridesboys and girls." The women were dressed in various colours, including mauve, pink, and grey. After leaving the church the five couples retired to their five different houses, where their celebrations continued.

December 5
Royal Designation — Cambrai, France, 1917

The Newfoundland Regiment's involvement in the Battle of Cambrai, which had begun November 20, ended when they were relieved by the 2/11 Royal Irish Rifles. The Regiment distinguished themselves in the battle. There were over 200 casualties. Captain Rupert Wilfred Bartlett (November 30) and L/Cpl. John Shiwak, an Inuk from Labrador and the leading sniper in the Regiment, were two of those killed. The title of "Royal" was bestowed on the Regiment in recognition, in part, for their efforts in this battle. It became known henceforth as the Royal Newfoundland Regiment, the only regiment on which this honour was bestowed during the First World War.

December 6
Marconi's Assistant Arrives — St. John's, 1901

George Kemp, ex–petty officer and assistant to Italian inventor Guglielmo Marconi, arrived by ship in St. John's. His diary for the day indicates:

> We saw at daybreak this morning that there had been a hard frost during the night. We sighted the Block House at St. John's. To the North there were icebergs while, to the South of the Harbour, the spouting of whales was seen. We landed at Shea's Wharf and put up at Cochrane House where Premier Bond had apartments. In the afternoon we went to Block House and to the Club in the evening.

The next day, Kemp would start the process of moving Marconi's equipment, instruments, and kites to Signal Hill, in preparation for receiving their historic transatlantic radio transmission on December 12.

December 7
The Waterford Kitchen — St. John's, 1914

Matron Fanny Field of the Waterford Hospital, "full of zeal and activity," complained to the Board of Works that the facility's kitchen, originally designed to serve 80 people, could no longer cope with the 332 people at the asylum. The total sum of the kitchen equipment with which she was to prepare meals for 288 patients and 44 staff consisted of three boilers, one sink, and a broken-down range that had been discarded from Government House.

December 8
You Will Put Out Someone's Eye — St. John's, 1907

If you value your eyesight, maybe stay away from Hamilton Avenue on Sundays:

> The police should visit Hamilton Ave., especially on Sundays, as boys cause a great deal of annoyance to the residents there. A young fellow threw a snow-ball through a window . . . and nearly knocked out the eye of a lady who was sitting in a chair in the room.

If your mother ever warned you about throwing snowballs, this is why.

December 9
Ice-Creepers — Washington, DC, 1873

Some kind of medal should be awarded posthumously to Mr. Reginald Heber Earle, Esquire, of Water Street, St. John's, inventor, jeweller, and ice-skating aficionado. On this day, Earle registered a patent for an Improved Ice-Creeper, "neat and simple in construction, and convenient in use, and which will enable the wearer to conveniently and safely walk over the smoothest ice." The device screwed on to the wearer's boot and was no doubt inspired by the streets and sidewalks of wintertime St. John's. Earle also invented a screw-on ice skate, two marine distress signals for naval and merchant shipping, improvements for a local skating rink, and a swinging frame and gravity cradle for the improved raising and lowering of boats.

December 10
Merry Christmas from Mr. Delgado — St. John's, 1891

While other downtown merchants were probably thinking about decorating for the joyful Christmas season (see December 20), fruit merchant and entrepreneur Andrew Delgado went off in a totally different, cryptozoological direction. While visiting the French Shore during his summer vacation, Mr. Delgado had picked up from a beach the bones of what he believed to be a sea serpent. He decided the year-end season would be as good a time as any to display them and hung them up on exhibition in his Water Street premises. Nothing quite says Christmas like a sea monster's vertebrae.

December 11
Birthday of Clarence Arthur Hubley — St. John's, 1877

If you've ever had problems with a clogged pipe in St. John's (I'm looking at you, October 22) and needed someone to come sort it out for you, raise a glass to celebrate the birthday of consulting engineer Clarence Arthur Hubley, born this day in St. Margaret's Bay, Halifax County, Nova Scotia. After various jobs as a blacksmith and running freight and passengers on the Yukon River during the Klondike Gold Rush, he settled in St. John's, married Miss Ella Annie Forey, and established what is now the oldest plumbing business in Newfoundland and Labrador. Hubley's Plumbing & Heating has "done plumbing right since 1917" and has been family-owned and operated for four generations.

December 12
They Are Not Departed or Gone — St. John's, 1842

The Sisters of Mercy moved from their temporary home at the bishop's residence to their new convent on Military Road, the first Mercy Convent in North America. The present granite building was opened in 1857, under the guidance of Right Rev. Bishop Doctor John Thomas Mullock, and was designated as a Registered Heritage Structure in 1990.

December 13
Christmas Tree and Fancy Fair — St. John's, 1880

A Christmas bazaar, in connection with the Methodist Church Aid Society, opened in the Temperance Hall and continued for some days. The ladies of the congregation organized a fancy table, where items were sold, as well as a refreshment table. The Christmas Tree and Fancy Fair was apparently a popular fundraising idea for Methodist congregations—the ladies of the Clarke's Beach Methodist Church organized a similar event to raise funds for the enlargement of their church.

December 14
Opening of the Bishop's Palace — St. John's, 1925

The new Bishop's Palace was opened three years after the previous building had been destroyed by fire. The exterior walls were constructed of bluestone quarried on Signal Hill and backed with concrete and trimmed with freestone imported from the Wallace quarries in Nova Scotia. Some of the bluestone from the old Palace was recycled and incorporated in the new building. The building was designed in an Italian Renaissance style but built to last in the Newfoundland climate:

> The general impression made upon the casual observer is that the entire building is built to last, that it is so constructed as to be more than proof against the fierce cold blasts to which it shall surely be subjected during the many winters of its existence.

December 15
Super Speeder — Upper Humber, 1946

A speeder is a motorized vehicle used on railroads to move quickly to and from work sites. Slow compared to a train or car, it is faster than a human-powered vehicle such as a handcar. The Upper Humber speeder worked 1,454 hours between May 9 and December 15. It covered 16,289 miles, made 674 trips, and carried 5,167 men and 855 tons of supplies to the Upper Humber lumber camps.

December 16
Strange Fish Sighted — Somewhere in the Atlantic, 1924

When the United American liner *Reliance* reached port, Captain F. L. Ivenson told of a strange sea monster that he was sure would interest ichthyologists around the world. The sea was particularly calm when he spotted the beast, Iverson said, and he had an excellent opportunity to inspect the strange monster closely through his binoculars. He described the creature thusly:

It was from 6 to 7 feet long, and had a corrugated back looking very much like that of a turtle. It was oblong in shape and fully two feet wide. It had a dorsal fin like a shark and a tapered tail like a lobster. Its colour was pale green. It continued to float peacefully on the water, basking in the warm sunshine until we were within very few feet of it. Only when it saw that it was in danger of being run down did it take a dive under the surface which for speed would have done credit to smallmouth bass.

December 17
Dead-On — St. John's, 1862

Old Mrs. Power died on this date, aged 99 years. Or she possibly died the day before, aged 100 years. We aren't sure. Exact details about Mrs. Power are a little hazy, but we do know that she was famous in St. John's as "The Bullseye Woman," which is much more important. Bull's eyes were a popular pulled-molasses candy. Old Mrs. Power most likely sold her bull's eyes from a huckster shop, a small shop usually located in the front room of a private house, which sold small wares, one-cent candies, chewing gum, bull's eyes, shoelaces, pencils, tobacco, and the like. During the First World War, bull's eyes were included in care packages sent to soldiers at the front, and they continued to be sold in St. John's frontparlour shops well into the mid-20th century. In 1985, the Newfoundland Historic Trust held a bake sale featuring oldtime favourites, and nothing went as quickly as the bull's eyes. If you want to try your hand at making your own, you have then Trust member Martha Entwisle to thank for the following recipe:

Bull's Eyes

1 cup Brown Sugar
1 cup molasses
2 tbsp. lemon juice*
2 tbsp. butter

*substitute 1/2 tsp. Peppermint essence for lemon juice

Combine all the ingredients and boil without stirring until the soft boil stage is reached. Pour onto a greased platter and cool sufficiently until it is easily handled. Grease hands and pull and manipulate until it is a golden brown colour. Pull into a narrow strip and cut into one inch pieces with scissors and arrange onto a greased platter to harden.

December 18
Back to Lapland — St. John's, 1908

A family of Laplanders consisting of Aslak Larsen Somby with his wife, Brita Olsdatter Nango, and their son Per Aslaksen Somby, left by the RMS *Siberian*, en route to Liverpool and from there to Lapland. They had arrived earlier that year as part of a scheme devised by Wilfred Grenfell to introduce reindeer to Newfoundland. The Somby family spent about a week in St. John's and attracted much attention due to their "peculiar dress and high peaked caps." Like the Laplander herders themselves, the reindeer would soon leave as well. Many were poached by hunters, and those that remained were shipped to Labrador and thence to Anticosti Island, where they eventually all died off. In the words of author Arthur Johnson, "It was a dark and very disappointing chapter for Sir Wilfred and the Grenfell Mission."

Reindeer herder Aslak Larsen Somby, circa 1884

December 19
Saved by a Human Chain — Gulf of St. Lawrence, 1908

Two days out from the Bay of Islands, the Newfoundland schooner *T. M. Nicholson* found itself engulfed by roaring seas kicked up by the blizzard that had swept across the Gulf. Four seamen had gone out on the bowsprit to furl the jib: Charles Gregory, Daniel Gregory, Daniel McDonald, and Ben Clifford. Clifford was at the end of the bowsprit when the schooner plunged headfirst down into the inky water. He came up, half-drowned and insensible, hanging head downward with his legs wrapped around the bowsprit.

Charles Gregory, the nearest, bent down and grasped the drowning man, trying to hold him up. Charles Gregory was seized by Daniel McDonald. In turn, McDonald was grabbed by Daniel Gregory, who clung tight to a guy rope with his other hand. The schooner rose and fell in the wild waves, swaying back and forth. At one end of the chain, Daniel Gregory gripped the rope with eyes closed and clothing torn from his body. At the other end, Charles Gregory held fast to Clifford, though he himself was quickly nearing exhaustion.

Captain Gillie had seen the accident and thought the four men had perished. But other sailors rushed forward and after much labour got all four of them aboard, though the vessel was continually washed over by waves while they toiled. No one was lost, and the *T. M. Nicholson* would arrive safely in the port of Boston two days later with its 1,700 barrels of herring intact.

December 20
Christmas Windows — St. John's, 1890

If you think Christmas is becoming more and more commercial, it is part of a trend that started long ago with the Victorian-era shopkeepers of yesteryear. Merchants up and down Water Street decorated their storefronts gaily, all with an eye to tempt holiday purchasers:

> The city stores are all nicely bedecked with goods appropriate to the holiday season, and the slight snow which fell during last night gives the streets a Christmas appearance. The grocers have their nice wares disposed in tempting array enshrined in bowers of evergreen, and the hardware men are not behind them in the display of lamps, skates, cutlery and other arti-

cles suggestive of the coming festive season. The dry goods men have also pretty windows to attract crowds of purchasers along the street. In the East end Prof. Danielle and Mrs. Walsh of the Royal and City restaurants, respectively, vie with each other in the exhibition of choice fruits, vegetables, &c, &c.; there are figures in each window representative of Christmas. Messrs. Garland, Chisholm, Fenelon, Dicks, Milligan and Byrne's bookstores have their toys and Christmas presents for the little ones, scattered in profusion in their windows, and the rosy-cheeked small boy would fain remain the entire day gazing on the stocks from the pavement.

December 21
Burial of John Hearn — St. John's, 1903

The funeral of the late John Hearn, of Hearn and Co., took place from his mother's residence on LeMarchant Road. Hearn had been ill for some time and had travelled to France shortly before in the hope that a milder climate would benefit his failing health. It did not, and he passed away in the city of Tours. His grieving mother, who had accompanied her son to France, returned with his body via Liverpool on the RMS *Corean*, in order that it might be laid beside relatives in Belvedere Cemetery.

Hearn was the lieutenant-bandmaster of the Catholic Cadet Corps, and his hearse and casket were preceded by a detachment of the CCC and the full band of the brigade. Following the graveside service, the Cadets returned to their armoury by way of King's Road and Duckworth Street, playing lively airs along the line of route.

December 22
You Get What You Ask For — St. John's, 1863

Notices were put up around town prohibiting the use of firearms and forbidding "the practice of mumming" over Christmas. Christmas Day that year was reported as having "no news of importance, but indications of a dull festive season."

December 23
Happy Tibb's Eve — Channel–Port aux Basques, 1971

Many Newfoundlanders and Labradorians don't need much of an excuse to have a party. One of the most inventive local reasons might be Tibb's/Tipps/Tib's/Tipsy Eve. One report in the Memorial University Folklore and Language Archive includes this origin story for the day:

> Christmas really starts in my home on Tipps Eve which is the day before Christmas Eve. I have heard that it is called Tipps Eve because when men used to put up their own homebrew etc. they wouldn't drink it before Christmas but I guess most men would sneak a drink or two on this day because they felt that Christmas was close, and they probably got a bit tipsy, thus Tipps Eve.

Take that tale with a grain of salt, however. The phrase "on Tibb's Eve" originally meant "a day that would never come." According to folklorist Doctor Philip Hiscock, the idea of Tibb's Eve as a particular day on the calendar is specific to Newfoundland and Labrador. Sometime around the 1940s, people along the south coast began to associate the evening before Christmas Eve with the phrase "Tibb's Eve" and deemed it the earliest date it was socially acceptable to have a Christmas drink.

December 24
Cantankerous Violinists — King's Cove, 1871

At about nine o'clock on Christmas Eve, a party of 12 or 15 violinists headed by drum, cymbals, and triangle serenaded Monsignor Veitch, the local clergyman. The drum was made from a sawed-off flour barrel with goatskin heads, the cymbals were two pot covers, and the triangle was an old fire-tongs and a piece of an iron rod. From the Monsignor's house, they marched through the community, stopping at the residence of each member of the band for a wee swallow. It was midnight before they reached

Lawton's Bridge, their disbanding point, but by then the combination of moonlight and moonshine had elevated their natural cantankerousness. A terrible row ensued, and when daylight broke Christmas morning, the detritus of their fray was littered about the battlefield. The staves of the drum were scattered over the bridge, and the cymbals and triangle lay at the bottom of the little stream that trickled beneath it.

December 25
Birthday of Richard Brothers — Port Kirwan, 1757

Richard Brothers, naval officer, faith healer, eccentric, and conspiracy theorist, was born in Port Kirwan on Christmas Day. Brothers was born to an English soldier garrisoned in Newfoundland, and as a child he was sent to England for education. He became a midshipman in the Royal Navy at age 13 and rose to the rank of lieutenant. He retired in 1784, married, left his wife, and travelled the Mediterranean before returning to England. At this point, things got interesting. He claimed to hear the voice of an attending angel and declared himself to be the apostle of a new religion and Prince of the Hebrews. He fashioned a rod from a wild rosebush, with which he claimed he would perform miracles and lead the "hidden Israel" to the land of Canaan. No one paid much attention until he prophesied the death of the King and the collapse of the monarchy. At this, he was arrested for treason, a sentence he escaped by being found criminally insane. He was committed as a lunatic to an asylum, where he spent his time designing flags and uniforms for the New Jerusalem. Brothers was released in 1806 when it was decided he was not a menace to society. He died, a lonely figure, on January 25, 1824, possibly the first Canadian to establish a new religious sect.

Richard Brothers as the Prophet of the Hebrews, circa 1795

December 26
Staff Night at the Newfoundland Hotel —
St. John's, 1932

A "right royal celebration" was held at the Newfoundland Hotel for its staff members. The Christmas tree was hung with presents that were distributed to those in attendance, but the most intriguing part of the evening was the reversal of roles that took place. Staff night was the night where the regular staff took over the responsibility for the kitchen, dining room, and waiting services, whilst those staff members did the ordering and feasting (and hopefully the tipping).

December 27
Device for Cutting Ships' Cables —
Washington, DC, 1892

Charles Petrie, blacksmith, and John Squires, both of St. John's, obtained a US patent for a device especially adapted for use in cutting ships' cables. The inventors had noticed that there were times when it was desirable, and even imperative, that a vessel should be quickly released from its anchor. This could be in the event of a sudden storm, when there was no time to haul up the anchor, or when an anchor had become fouled and it was required to cut it away. Squires and Petrie's device comprised of a knife, cord, and lever system that could travel down the cable to a point near the anchor and sever it at that point.

Charles Petrie was born in Bridgeport, Nova Scotia, in 1858. He started a general blacksmithing business on Holloway Street in 1890. Petrie was employed as an engineer at the Reid Newfoundland Company's shops until about 1900, at which point he was appointed as a government railroad inspector. He was known as a very intelligent man and the "inventor of several marine appliances of considerable utility and ingenuity."

December 28
Thrilling Rescue — Between Cadiz and Baltimore, 1905

The Basin, Baltimore, Maryland, sometime between 1900 and 1910

Captain Yetman and his crew, of the schooner *Harold* out of Harbour Grace, had a marvellous escape from death. They had left St. John's bound for Cadiz in early December. On the 11th, the *Harold* was hit by a waterspout, causing every seam in the vessel to open. Waterlogged, and adrift in heavy seas, the half-starved and half-frozen men lashed themselves to the masts and prayed for rescue. They drifted for 17 days before being spotted by the steamship *Koin*. A volunteer crew manned a steel lifeboat, fought their way through a mile of tremendous seas, and cut the ropes that bound the men to the masts. They then rowed the lifeboat back to the safety of the *Koin*, which conveyed the men to Baltimore.

December 29
Photographic Clue — St. John's, 1920

The dauntless Constable Byrne (you will remember him from January 28 and April 1) arrested four young men for complicity in a brace of Christmas Eve burglaries. Mr. W. H. Jackman, whose store was one of those robbed, had found a photograph of a child on the floor of his shop. It was handed over to Byrne, who deduced it had fallen from the pocket of one of the burglars and immediately began tracing it. Byrne discovered that the child in the picture was named Reid, whose mother, Nellie Reid, had been found dead on the Southside the previous spring. Eventually, the ownership of the photo was traced to a man named Neil. With this knowledge, Byrne and his associates searched the lodging house of Neil and the home of a man named McManus. Both dwellings were in the Dardanelles, "the Bowery of St. John's." The stolen property was discovered in a cellar adjacent to the McManus home, covered with earth and protected by a covering of canvas. The burglars were arrested, and Byrne was once again praised for his resourcefulness.

December 30
The Garrison Hill Fire — St. John's, 1883

At about 10:00 p.m., Constable Mifflin was proceeding up Garrison Hill when he heard a man calling for assistance, saying that he was "smothering and burning to death." The constable hurried across the street and observed a man, William Kelly, with his hands up through a coal chute, holding on by the edge. Stooping down, Mifflin discovered the cellar to be in flames. He took the man by the arms and tried to pull him out, but the chute was too small. The officer then knocked at the door, found it closed, and forced it open. In a corner, he found a hatchway leading to the cellar, from which smoke and flames poured.

The constable took a nearby ladder, put it down the hatchway, and descended, but the smoke was too much for him. He ran up the ladder, pulled off his overcoat, threw it out into the street, and made a second attempt to reach the chute below. This time he narrowly escaped suffocation but managed to escape from the cellar and get out into the open air. There, Mifflin rushed to some nearby scaffolding, grabbed a five-foot-long timber, and used it to bust a hole into the basement wall. He jumped through the hole, pulled the man out of the chute, and handed him up through the hole to waiting bystanders. They then pulled out the gallant constable himself.

It seems Mr. Kelly had been attempting to put out a fire in his coal bin when his retreat through the hatchway got cut off. In sheer desperation, he had tried to escape through the coal chute and had gotten stuck.

December 31
A Disgrace to the City — St. John's, 1897

A number of lads celebrated a little too hard on New Year's Eve and were found drunk on Water Street. They were deemed "a disgrace both to themselves and those who sold them the liquor, who should be punished if found out." The boys ranged in age from 12 to 16.

And with that, our year of history, mystery, and more comes to an end, with another year set to begin. Happy New Year, and keep an eye on your 12-year-olds.

ACKNOWLEDGEMENTS

Thanks to Kelly Jones for her help, patience, and editing; George Jones for introducing me to the practice of packing dead men in salt; Katie Crane for alerting me to the story of the man buried with a stake through his body; Alanna Wicks, Archives Technician with City of St. John's Archives, for her photo help; Brenda Simms Flood for the chat about (and photo of) Grunia Ferman; Julie Pomeroy for information on Fanny Goff; the staff at Downhome for their continued support of my writing; Jim Miller for information on the Trinity whaling operations; Nicole Penney at MUNFLA for tracking down files; Linda White at Memorial University's Archives and Special Collections for her help with the tinsmith photo; Shane Heard at *Them Days* for finding the photo of the *Harmony*; Wade Greeley at The Rooms for the museological gossip on the supposed Peddle sword; and everyone at Flanker Press for their help and hard work!

BIBLIOGRAPHY

JANUARY

1 – Higgins, Jenny. "The Arms, Seals, and Emblems of Newfoundland and Labrador." Heritage Newfoundland and Labrador. Heritage.nf.ca.

2 – "Mary Travers (1783–1854)." Heritage Newfoundland and Labrador. Heritage.nf.ca. Reprinted from the Women's History Walking Tour Booklet. Women's History Group, 1999; Updated August 2013.

3 – "Saw Tracks of Two Moose." *Western Star*, 1906-01-03.

4 – "Interesting Particulars of the Death of One of the Oldest Inhabitants, Broad Cove." *Colonist*, 2.5 (08 January 1887): 4.

5 – "Arrest of Two Small Boys." *Colonist*, 6.3 (05 January 1891): 4.

6 – "Bazar St. Patrick's Hall." *Colonist*, 5.255 (06 November 1890):4.
"Xmas Tree at Torbay." *Colonist*, 6, no.3 (05 January 1891): 4.

7 – "Historic Relic." *Evening Telegram*, 1920-01-07: 6.
Maunder, John E. "The Newfoundland Museum: Origins and Development." Fall 1991. [Originally published in printed form]. Therooms.ca.
"Penney/Piddle." Newfoundland Family Histories: Families linked to the Noels & Newells. Familiesofnfld.wordpress.com, January 6, 2015.

8 – "The New Curling and Skating Rink: Flooding the 'Outer Circle.'" *Evening Telegram*, 1883-01-08: 4.

9 – "Fire Destroys LSPU Hall." *Western Star,* 1922-01-18: 1.
"Origin of Fire Unknown." *Evening Telegram,* 1922-01-09: 4.
"Row on Water Street." *Evening Telegram,* 1922-01-09: 4.

10 – "Snow Drifts." *Evening Telegram,* 1921-01-11: 6.

11 – "Planes to Locate Seals." *Evening Telegram,* 1921-01-11: 4.

12 – James Ryan Ltd. Diaries, Bonavista, 1912. Maritime History Archive.

13 – "Alleged Brutality of Husband." *Evening Telegram,* 1923-01-12: 4.
"Body Exhumed." *Evening Telegram,* 1923-01-15: 6.
"Enquiry Closed." *Evening Telegram,* 1923-02-03: 6.
"Hearing of Nolan Case." *Evening Advocate,* 1923-01-29: 6.
"Nolan Acquitted." *Evening Telegram,* 1923-02-26: 5.
"Nolan Granted Bail." *Evening Telegram,* 1923-01-25: 6.
"Police Take Coffin Case." *Evening Telegram,* 1923-01-13: 4.
"Prisoner Brought in." *Evening Telegram,* 1923-01-17: 3.
"Subpoenas Issued." *Evening Telegram,* 1923-02-22: 6

14 – "Auction Sales!" *Evening Telegram,* 1920-01-30: 1.
"Runa's Story." *Evening Telegram,* 1920-01-14: 5.

15 – "Local Varieties." *Evening Telegram,* 1884-01-18: 4.

16 – "Local Happenings." *Evening Telegram,* 1901-01-16: 4.

17 – "Baby Stamp Dead." *Evening Telegram,* 1907-01-17: 4.
"Baby Stamp Not Dead." *Evening Telegram,* 1907-01-16: 4.
"Local Happenings." *Evening Telegram,* 1907-01-15: 6.

18 – "Another Stage in the Newfoundland Elopement Case." *Evening Telegram,* 1883-02-16: 4.
"The Newfoundland Elopement." *Evening Telegram,* 1883-02-05: 1.

19 – "A Strange Incident." *Evening Telegram,*1900-01-19: 4.

20 – "Bavarian Beer Depot." *Colonist,* 2.146 (4 July 1887): 4.
"From Little Bay." *Evening Telegram,* 1883-09-24: 4.
"From Little Bay: The event of the season here." *Evening Tele-*

gram, 1885-10-20: 4.
"Local Varieties." *Evening Telegram*, 1883-12-27: 4.
"Notre Dame Jewelery Store." *Twillingate Sun*, 12 January 1889: 2.
"A shop at Little Bay…" , *Colonist*, 2.17 (22 January 1887): 4.
"The skittle-alley…" *Twillingate Sun*, 12 February 1887: 3.

21 – "Notes from Melrose." *Evening Advocate*, 5.26 (1918-02-01): 5.

22 – "Blue Ribbon Coin-Op Laundry Opens in Gander." *Daily News*, 1962-01-26: 10.

23 – "A Recluse for Five Years." *Evening Telegram*, 1925-01-23: 6

24 – "A Fishing Story." *Evening Herald*, 16.186 (1905-08-09): 4.
Journal of the House of Assembly of Newfoundland 1904 (5th Session), page 131.
"Likely Story." *Western Star*, 1906-01-24: 4.
"Professor Muller's Tame Whales." *Harbor Grace Standard*, 1905-08-11: 2.
"The Searchlight." *St. John's Daily Star*, 1918-03-23: 7.
"Whale Milk." whalefacts.org. Web accessed 21 November 2019.

25 – "In Jail for Dancing." *Evening Telegram*, 1900-01-25: 4.

26 – "Years Gone By." *Evening Telegram*, 1908-01-13: 4.

27 – "Arrival of the Clipper Brigantine Miriam." *Evening Telegram*, 1882-01-27: 4.

28 – "Sensational Arrests!" *Evening Telegram*, 1916-01-29: 8.

29 – "MURDERED!! A Cold Blooded Crime. Brained With An Iron Bar." *Twillingate Sun*, 1894-02-17: 2.

30 – Jarvis, Dale. "He Left His Mark. The remarkable life of Frederick G. Chislett, tombstone designer and ice-skating champion." *Downhome*, 30.6 (November 2017): 134-137.
"Six Hour Race." *Evening Telegram*, 1905-01-31: 4.

31 – "Marine Notes." *Evening Telegram*, 1906-01-19: 3.

"Marine Notes." *Evening Telegram*, 1906-01-30: 3.
"Marine Notes." *Evening Telegram*, 1906-01-31: 3.
"Marine Notes." *Evening Telegram*, 1906-02-21: 3.
"Young Lads Missing." *Evening Telegram*, 1906-02-01: 3.

FEBRUARY

1 – "Landslide at Gambo." *Western Star*, 1906-02-07: 4.

2 – F.G.M. "Wood Preparing." *Western Star*, 1951-02-23: 10.
"Motor Vessel Trepassey Hails For One Live Moose, Rescued From Waters of Humber Arm." *Western Star*, 1951-02-23: 1.
Raines, Charles. "Commentary." *Western Star*, 1951-02-23: 10.

3 – "The Daily News." *St. John's Daily News*, 1868-02-06: 2.
"Local Happenings." *Evening Telegram*, 1899-02-03.
"We were visited…" *St. John's Daily News*, 1868-02-08: 2.

4 – "Derelict Reported." *Evening Telegram* (St. John's, N.L.), 1920-05-07: 8.
"Foreign News." *St. John's Daily Star*, 1920-02-07: 9.
"Local Schooners Lost." *Evening Telegram*, 1920-02-05: 6.
"Monchy's Crew in New York." *Evening Telegram*, 1920-02-10: 3.
"Monchy's Crew Reach U. S. Port on Steamer Persian Prince." *St. John's Daily Star*, 1920-02-10:1.
"To-day's Messages." *Evening Telegram*, 1920-02-05: 7.

5 – "Moascar Isolation Camp – Ismailia, Egypt." springfieldcollege.contentdm.oclc.org
"Mrs. M. Bastow." *Evening Telegram*, 1916-03-15: 7.
"Profiles: James Carroll." discoveringanzacs.naa.gov.au

6 – "Shower of Blood." *Evening Telegram*, 1890-02-15: 1.

7 – "Bonspiel for the Poor." *Evening Telegram*, 1883-02-06: 1.
Dohey, Larry. "A skating rink in Bannerman Park?" ArchivalMoments.ca July 30, 2015.

8 – "At the TA Hall." *Evening Telegram*, 1900-01-23: 4.
"At the Theatre." *Evening Telegram*, 1900-01-24: 3.
"Local Happenings." *Evening Telegram*, 1900-01-18: 4.

"Local Happenings." *Evening Telegram*, 1900-02-08: 4.
"Saturday's Smoker." *Evening Telegram*, 1900-01-22: 4.
"Serpentine dance." wikipedia.org

9 – "Athenaeum Entertainment." *Evening Telegram*, 1883-02-08:1.
"Athenaeum Hall." *Evening Telegram*, 1883-02-08: 4.
"Last Evening's Touroscopic Entertainment." *Evening Telegram*, 1883-02-10: 4.

10 – "Airplane Flies to Alexander Bay and Back." *Evening Telegram*, 1922-02-10: 4.
"Splendid Flight." *Evening Telegram*, 1922-02-11: 4.

11 – "Blaze at Tub Factory." *Evening Telegram*, 1923-02-12: 3.
"Glorious Weather." *Newfoundland Weekly*, 6.5 (1929-08-24): 1.
"Wanted." *Evening Telegram* (St. John's, N.L.), 1925-06-05: 1.
"Wanted Immediately." *Evening Telegram* (St. John's, N.L.), 1912-03-08: 9.

12 – Sparks, Brad. No. 1155. Comprehensive Catalog of 1,700 Project Blue Book UFO Unknowns: Database Catalog. Version 1.27 (Dec. 20, 2016).

13 – "The Dwelling." *Twillingate Sun*, 16 Feb 1952: 4.
"Househaul." *Twillingate Sun*, 23 Feb 1952: 4.
"Johnny Poker, Ohhhhh!" *Twillingate Sun*, 11 Feb 1950: 4.

14 – "A Decided Novelty." *Evening Herald*, 10.37 (1899-02-14): 4.
"Local Happenings." *Evening Telegram*, 1899-02-14: 4.
"Weighing Party." *Evening Telegram*, 1899-02-15: 4.

15 – O'Neill, Paul. *A Seaport Legacy: The Story of St. John's, Newfoundland.* Erin, Ontario: Press Porcepic, 1976. Page 571.

16 – "According to…" *Twillingate Sun*, 1888-02-28: 3.
"Curious Phenomenon." *Evening Telegram*, 1888-02-18: 4.
"The Great Meteorite." *Colonial Commerce*, 26 (1916-1917): 36.
"Grubs From The Sky." *Western Star*, 1941-01-22: 6.
"Grubs in by Air." *Twillingate Sun*, 1946-02-23: 4.

17 – "The Imperial." historicplaces.ca

18 – Devine, Maurice A.; O'Mara, Michael J. *Notable events in the history of Newfoundland: six thousand dates of historical and social happenings*. St. John's: Devine & O'Mara, 1900.

19 – Mosdell, HM. "Railway Snow Blockade." *When Was That?* St. John's: Trade Printers and Publishers, 1923. Page 113.

20 – "Our Letter Box." *St. John's Daily Star*, 1918-03-06: 2.

21 – *The Book of Newfoundland*, vol. 4. Smallwood and Thoms, eds. St. John's: Newfoundland Book Publishers, Ltd: 1967. Page 518.

22 – "Original Newfoundlanders, Inc." *Newfoundland Weekly*, 1.12 (1941-02-22): 5.

23 – "United Society's Hearse." *Twillingate Sun*, 1884-02-23: 3.

24 – "Notes from the Past." *Evening Telegram*, 1920-02-24: 4.

25 – "100 Guineas Reward!!" *Patriot and Terra-Nova Herald*, 1846-03-04: 3.

26 – Periodical accounts relating to the missions of the Church of the United Brethren established among the heathen, 8 (1821-1823): 182; 10 (1826): 254; 12 (1831): 447; 14 (1836): 308; 19 (1849): 425; 20 (1851): 330; 28 (1871-1873): 282.

27 – "Chronology of Selected Historical Events." trinityhistoricalsociety.com

28 – "Capt. Mylius and Capt. Moore." *Evening Telegram*, 1886-06-05: 4. "Eight Days in the Ice Jam." *Evening Telegram*, 1882-03-13: 1.

MARCH

1 – "Green Island (Catalina) Lighthouse." www.lighthousefriends.com/light.asp?ID=1250
"Speech of Minister of Marine and Fisheries." *Evening Advocate*, 7.146 (1920-06-30): 3.
"To Mariners: No. 1, 1883." *Terra Nova Advocate*, 5.22 (1883-03-03): 1.
"To Mariners: No. 2, 1885." *Harbor Grace Standard*, 1885-02-28: 3.

2 – "Woman Fined For Beating Taxi Driver." *Western Star*, 1949-03-08: 2.

3 – Jarvis, Dale. "Some outlandish reasons for the sky lighting up." *Telegram*, 9 March 2009.

4 – "Magistrate's Court." *Daily News*, 1955-03-10: 3.

5 – "Raw Potatoes Her Only Food." *Western Star*, 1905-03-08: 4.

6 – "The Green Lantern." *Evening Telegram*, 1920-03-06: 5.
"Opens New Store on Theatre Hill Today." *St. John's Daily Star*, 1920-03-06: 8.
"Yesterday's Fire." *Evening Telegram*, 1922-08-10: 4.

7 – "Strange holes, UFOs, and water-sucking aliens." www.nlunexplained.ca, 25 March 2013.

8 – "Lioness on Ship." *Evening Telegram*, 1921-03-08: 4.

9 – "Carrier Pigeons at the Icefields." *Evening Telegram*, 1894-03-09: 4.
James Ryan Diary, 1896 April 10th. Maritime History Archive.
"Trinity." *Evening Telegram*, 1922-04-29: 5.

10 – "England Births and Christenings, 1538-1975," database, FamilySearch.org.
Howley, MF. "Paper no. 145 : Extracts from the registers of The Church of England, St. John's, Newfoundland." Shortis Papers, 3.1.

11 – "Lost 'mid the fog." *Evening Telegram*, 1898-03-12: 4.

12 – Journal of the House of Assembly of Newfoundland, 1912, p45.
"News from the Outports." *Daily Globe*, 1.79 (1925-03-21): 2.
"Sir Robert Bond." *Evening Telegram*, 1912-02-28: 6.
"Tuberculosis." *Encyclopedia of Newfoundland and Labrador*, volume 5, Poole, Cyril,
Cuff, Robert, eds. St. John's, Harry Cuff Publications Ltd., 1994. Page 430-434.

13 – "Hand Caught In Mixing Machinery And Badly Damaged." *Daily Globe*, 1.66 (1925-03-07): 4.

"Surgeons Decide To Amputate Hand." *Daily Globe*, 1.73 (1925-03-1): 7.

14 – "Japanese Tea Party." *Evening Telegram*, 1907-03-15: 6.

15 – Devine, Maurice A.; O'Mara, Michael J. *Notable events in the history of Newfoundland: six thousand dates of historical and social happenings*. St. John's: Devine & O'Mara, 1900.
Statutes of Newfoundland, 1841.

16 – *The Book of Newfoundland*, vol. 4. Smallwood and Thoms, eds. St. John's: Newfoundland Book Publishers, Ltd: 1967. Page 541.
"New Miss Toronto." *Toronto Star* Archives, Accession Number tspa_0020344f, Toronto Reference Library.
"Virginia Martin." *Daily News* (St. John's, N.L.), 1963-10-07: 3.

17 – "Local and other items." *Colonist*, 1.10 (18 March 1886): 1.

18 – Dohey, Larry. "What happened to Sheelagh's Day?" ArchivalMoments.ca, March 16, 2019.

19 – "Labrador Holds First Dog Derby." *Western Star*, 1935-03-20: 1.

20 – "Young Anarchists." *Evening Telegram*, 1896-03-21:4.

21 – "Sunk in Harbour." *Evening Telegram*, 1912-03-21: 4.

22 – Smith, Reverend Canon. "Paper no. 111: A Bit of the History of Portugal Cove, Conception Bay." Shortis Papers, 3.1.
"The Story of Fanny Goff – The Most Beautiful Woman in Newfoundland." Storyboard Notes, Town of Portugal Cove–St. Philip's, courtesy Julie Pomeroy.

23 – "Found Dead in the Woods." *Evening Telegram*, 1909-03-23: 5.

24 – "Ghosts in Trinity Bay." *Daily Globe*, 2. 66 (1926-03-24): 5.

25 – "A Strange Find." *Evening Telegram*, 1917-04-25: 4.

26 – "Personal Notes." *Evening Telegram*, 1909-03-26: 4.
"Pork and Cabbage Supper." *Evening Telegram*, 1909-03-26: 6.

27 – "Curious phenomenon." *Evening Herald*, 5.73 (1894-03-29): 4.

28 – "Had Long Tramp." *Evening Telegram*, 1912-03-29: 6.

29 – "Police Start Drive on Drinkers of Canned Heat." *Sarasota Journal*, 1962-01-05: 4.
"Spontaneous Combustion." *Evening Telegram*, 1920-03-29: 6.

30 – "Men Go Overboard." *Evening Telegram*, 1910-03-31: 5.

31 – "Local Happenings." *Evening Telegram*, 1897-04-01: 4.

APRIL

1 – "Exciting Chase and Capture." *Evening Telegram*, 1910-04-01: 6.

2 – "They Stole his 'Flippers.'" *Evening Telegram*, 1898-04-02: 4.

3 – "Lamb with Two Heads." *Evening Telegram*, 1911-04-03: 4.

4 – The "Caroline Brown." 1872, July. Hon. Sir H. Hoyles, C. J. Decisions of the Supreme Court of Newfoundland: The Reports, 1864-1874. Page 477-479.
"Our Heroes and Notable Events at the Sealfishery." Shortis Papers, 2. 2: Paper No. 446.

5 – Devine, Maurice A.; O'Mara, Michael J. *Notable events in the history of Newfoundland: six thousand dates of historical and social happenings*. St. John's· Devine & O'Mara, 1900.
"Gored by a Bull." *Evening Telegram*, 1889-04-05: 4.

6 – "Local Happenings." *Evening Telegram*, 1904-12-27: 4.
"Local Happenings." *Evening Telegram*, 1904-12-28: 3.
"Local Happenings." *Evening Telegram*, 1905-04-06: 4.

7 – Chevalier, H. Emile (Henri Emile), 1828-1879. "Terre-Neuve : souvenirs de voyage." Revue moderne, 50 (1869): 597-626. Balsara, Aspi (translator), 2013. Page 3.

8 – "City Council Meeting." *Evening Telegram*, 1911-04-08: 3.
"Objects to Blubber." *Evening Telegram*, 1911-04-08: 3.

9 – "Girl Breaks Window." *Evening Telegram*, 1909-04-10: 4.

10 – "First Arrivals From Seal Fishery." *Harbor Grace Standard*, 1908-04-10: 4.

11 – Coish, Della, ed. "Tragedy at the Ice." *Tales of Fogo Island*. Fogo Island: Fogo Island Literacy Association, 1999.

12 – "Man Was Almost Buried Alive." *Evening Telegram*, 1915-04-12: 4.

13 – "Harbour Grace Historical Notes." *Daily News*, 1956-01-14: 11.

14 – "Slate Quarry Operations." *Evening Telegram*, 1900-04-14: 4.
"Special Section: Random Island." *Decks Awash*, 12.2 (1983): 3-44.

15 – "Local Happenings." *Evening Telegram*, 1902-04-15: 4.
"Organ Presented." *Evening Telegram*, 1902-04-12: 4.

16 – "A Light Needed." *Evening Telegram*, 1906-04-16: 3.

17 – "Accident at Wedding." *Evening Telegram*, 1907-04-18: 4.

18 – "What Is It?" *Western Star*, 1952-04-22: 1.

19 – "Fish Biscuit Co." *Evening Telegram*, 1897-05-11: 4.
"House of Assembly." *Evening Telegram*, 1907-03-15: 6.
"List of Unclaimed Letters." *Evening Telegram*, 1897-09-09: 3.
"Native Products." *Evening Telegram*, 1897-02-23: 4.
"Notes and Comments." *Evening Telegram*, 1897-04-19: 4.
"Peat Fuel." *Delta News*, 1902-08-23: 3.
"Sahlstrom's Fish Biscuit Co., Ltd." *Evening Telegram*, 1897-06-30: 1.
"Sahlstrom's Fish Biscuits." *Evening Telegram*, 1897-05-03: 3.
"Two Treasure Houses." *Evening Telegram*, 1897-09-25: 3.

20 – Jarvis, Dale. "A birch broom made by Nigola 'Nickly' Jeddore, of Conne River." Heritage Update, 073 (September- December 2017): 8-10.

21 – "At the TA Hall." *Evening Telegram*, 1898-04-22: 4.
"Hypnotic Tests To-Night." *Evening Telegram*, 1898-04-18: 4.

"Hypnotism." *Evening Telegram*, 1898-04-23: 3.
"In a pleasant sleep." *Evening Telegram*, 1898-04-21: 4.
"Telephone Test." *Evening Telegram*, 1898-04-19: 4.

22 – "Birth on Train." *Plaindealer*, 11.17 (27 April 1918): 2.
"News Briefs." *St. John's Daily Star*, 1918-03-26: 8.

23 – "Local Happenings." *Evening Telegram*, 1897-04-24: 3.

24 – "Community Delighted." *Evening Telegram*, 1900-04-25: 4.

25 – "Clever Capture." *Western Star*, 1906-05-02: 4.
"'Loaded' Concertinas." *Evening Herald*, 7.105 (1906-05-05): 5.

26 – "Improving Gov't House Grounds." *Newfoundland Weekly*, 6.40 (1930-04-26): 3.

27 – "Local Occurrences." *Evening Telegram*, 1896-04-28: 4.

28 – "Meting Out Justice." *Evening Telegram*, 1898-04-29: 4.

29 – "Cappoquin House." Lordbelmontinnorthernireland.blogspot.com, 2019-04-17.
"Keane baronets." wikipedia.org
"Local Happenings." *Evening Telegram*, 1899-04-29: 4.
Seary, E; Kirwin, William; Lynch, Sheila. *Family Names of the Island of Newfoundland*. Montreal: McGill-Queen's Press, 1998. Page 516.
"Will of John Cronin from Newfoundland will books volume 1 pages 485 & 486 probate year 1846." ngb.chebucto.org, Page Contributed by Judy Benson and Ivy F. Benoit. Page Revised by Ivy F. Benoit (April 26, 2003).

30 – "Carbonear News." *Evening Telegram*, 1899-05-03: 4.

MAY

1 "Ill. Grace Notes." *Evening Telegram*, 1912-05-03: 7.

2 – "Train Runs Into a House." *Evening Telegram*, 1908-05-02: 4.

3 – "Newfoundland War Vets' Flipper Supper." *Newfoundland Weekly*, 6.41 (1930-05-03): 2.

4 – *The Book of Newfoundland*, vol. 5. Smallwood, Thoms, and Power, eds. St. John's: Newfoundland Book Publishers, 1975. Page 514.

5 – "Local Happenings." *Evening Telegram*, 1897-05-06: 4.

6 – "Woodpile Falls On Boy." *Evening Telegram*, 1908-05-06: 4.

7 – "Light Keeper Badly Injured." *St. John's Daily Star*, 1916-05-18: 8.
"Some People You Know." *St. John's Daily Star*, 1916-06-06: 8.

8 – "Local Happenings." *Evening Telegram*, 1903-05-08: 4.

9 – "Meteor." *St. John's Advertiser*, 1.12 (1875-05-14): 2.

10 – "Canning Blueberries." *Newfoundland Weekly*, 6.42 (1930-05-10): 2.

11 – "Saw a Large Whale." *Evening Telegram*, 1897-05-13: 4.

12 – "American Seaplanes Arrive at Trepassey." *Evening Telegram*, 1919-05-12: 4.
"Curtiss NC-4." wikipedia.org

13 – Prowse, D. W. *A history of Newfoundland from the English, colonial, and foreign records.* 3rd Edition. St. John's: Dicks and Company, 1971. Page 488-489.

14 – "Obscene Letters." *Evening Telegram*, 1896-05-15: 4.

15 – "An Act Respecting Health and Public Welfare (Passed May 15, 1931)." Statutes of Newfoundland, 1931. St. John's: Government of Newfoundland, 1931.

16 – "The Legend of St. Brendan the Navigator." dalejarvis.ca, Thursday, 12 October 2017.

17 – "Curious Find." *Harbor Grace Standard*, 1893-05-19: 4.

18 – "Phrenology." *Evening Telegram*, 1882-05-19: 4.

"Professor Fowler and the MPs." *Evening Telegram*, 1882-05-23: 4.

19 – "Miraculous Escape From Death." *Evening Telegram*, 1924-05-26: 10.

20 – "Very Large Turnip." *Evening Telegram*, 1895-10-16: 4.

21 – "Mail Bags Astray." *Evening Telegram* (St. John's, N.L.), 1900-05-21: 4.

22 – Kean, Abram. *Old and Young Ahead.* London: Heath Cranton, 1935. Page 38.

23 – "Cam Phillips in the Trenches." *St. John's Daily Star*, 1915-06-30: 8.

24 – Jarvis, Dale. Personal Files.

25 – "Alleged Bigamist." *Evening Telegram*, 1908-05-30: 6.
"Arrested for Bigamy." *Western Star*, 1908-05-27: 4.

26 – "The Velocipede." *Patriot and Terra-Nova Herald*, 1869-05-31: 1.

27 – "Young Newfoundlander." *Evening Telegram*, 1892-06-29: 4.

28 – "Strange Phenomenon." *Evening Telegram*, 1908-05-29: 8.

29 – "American Naturalist Instantly Killed." *Colonist*, 6.90 (20 April 1891): 1.
"Brown-throated wren." wikipedia.org
"Daring Act." *Evening Telegram*, 1889-07-19: 4.
"Local Varieties." *Evening Telegram* (St. John's, N.L.), 1889-05-29: 4.

30 – "Police Court." *Evening Herald*, 1.116 (1890-05-30): 4.

31 – "The New Coffee Tavern." *Weekly News*, 1.10 (1894-05-31): 2.

JUNE

1 – "Dead Man on Board." *Evening Telegram* (St. John's, N.L.), 1904-06-02: 3.

2 – "Inhabited Iceberg Drifting Off-shore." *Daily News*, 1962-06-02: 3.

3 – "One of the most…" *Evening Herald*, 1.116 (1890-05-30): 4.
"Henry Taylor…" *Evening Herald*, 1.129 (1890-06-14): 4.

4 – "A Waterford Man…" *Evening Herald*, 1.120 (1890-06-04): 4.

5 – "Brief Notes of News." *Evening Herald*, 2.129 (1891-06-05): 4.

6 – "Brief Notes of News." *Evening Herald*, 2.130 (1891-06-06): 4.

7 – Brief account of the missionary ships employed in the service of the Mission on the coast of Labrador, from the year 1770 to 1877. London: Brethren's Society for the Furtherance of the Gospel, 1877. Page 9-10.

8 – "Car Owned by Sir John Crosbie Destroyed." *Newfoundland Weekly*, 4.46 (1928-06-09): 4.

9 – "Human Skull Found." *Enterprise*, 1.67 (1897-06-12): 3.

10 – "Message from the Sea." *Western Star*, 1905-06-14: 4.

11 – Devine, P.K. "Paper no. 199 : The Bonavista Railway, a Contract With Ancient Times." Shortis Papers, vol. 01. Page 2.

12 – "Terribly Tragedy on Newfoundland Railway." *Enterprise*, 1.68 (1897-06-16): 4.

13 – "Chief Scout Passes On." *Western Star*, 1941-01-15: 1.

14 – "Strange Coincidence." *Twillingate Sun*, 1952-06-14: 4.

15 – "Moravian Church Mission Ships." wikipedia.org
Periodical accounts relating to the missions of the Church of the United Brethren established among the heathen, 27 (1868-1871): 203.

16 – "The General Water Company." *Patriot and Terra-Nova Herald*, 1862-05-23: 3.
"Notice." *Record*, 2.35 (1862-06-14): 3.

17 – "Havoc of Lightning at Avondale." *Evening Telegram*, 1911-06-19: 4.
"Struck by Lightning." *Evening Telegram*, 1911-06-19: 6.

18 – Devine, Maurice A.; O'Mara, Michael J. *Notable events in the history of Newfoundland: six thousand dates of historical and social happenings*. St. John's: Devine & O'Mara, 1900. Page 242.
Molloy, David John. *The First Landfall: Historic Lighthouses of Newfoundland and Labrador*. St. John's: Breakwater Books, 1994. Page 76.

19 – Murphy, James. *Murphy's Old St John's*. St. John's: Evening Herald Office Print, 1916. Page 21.

20 – "Bait Question." *Evening Telegram*, 1897-04-19: 4.
"From St. Pierre." *Evening Telegram*, 1890-07-08: 4.
"A large number…" *Colonist*, 5.141 (1890-06-21): 4.

21 – "Summer Solstice Brings Winter Weather." *Evening Telegram*, 1923-06-25: 4.

22 – "Vivat Regina." *Enterprise*, 1.70 (1897-06-26): 4.

23 – *Boston Gazette and County Journal*, 1775-10-09. "Newfoundland Voyages in Foreign Newspapers and Journals." NL GenWeb.

24 – "St. John's Day." *Colonist*, 6.144 (1891-06-25): 4

25 – "Echoes From Everywhere." *Colonist*, 6.144 (25 June 1891): 4.
Karstensen, Rebecca. "Sleep Tight, Don't Let the Bed Bugs Bite – A Myth Debunked."
Wylie House News and Notes, 2018-01-18. Libraries.indiana.edu.

26 – Korneski, Kurt. 2013. "Railways and Rebellion: The 'Battle of Foxtrap' Reconsidered." Newfoundland and Labrador Studies 28 (1).

27 – Crellin, John K. *Home Medicine: The Newfoundland Experience*. Montreal: McGill-Queen's Press, 1994. Page 209.
Lacey, Laurie. "Micmac Medicine." *Decks Awash*, 6.2 (March 1977): 16.
Prowse, D. W. *A history of Newfoundland from the English, colonial, and foreign records*. London: Macmillan, 1895. Page 109.

28 – Coish, Della, ed. "The Good Sheppards." *Tales of Fogo Island*. Fogo Island: Fogo Island Literacy Association, 1999.

29 – Anderson, Henry H. "Log - Boston Harbour to Mugford Tickle." *Them Days*, 20.1 (Fall 1994): 36-44.

30 – "The Forest Fires." *Evening Telegram*, 1892-07-04: 4.

JULY

1 – Sparks, Brad. No. 650. Comprehensive Catalog of 1,700 Project Blue Book UFO Unknowns: Database Catalog. Version 1.27 (Dec. 20, 2016).

2 – "Motor Cycle Trip." *Evening Telegram*, 1923-07-03: Motor Cycle Trip.

3 – "Local Occurrences." *Evening Telegram*, 1895-07-03: 3.
Devine, Maurice A.; O'Mara, Michael J. *Notable events in the history of Newfoundland: six thousand dates of historical and social happenings*. St. John's: Devine & O'Mara, 1900. Page 127.

4 – Baring-Gould, Sabine. *Cornish characters and strange events*. London: John Lane The Bodly Head, 1909. Page 261-267.

5 – "Seaman." Gateway Arch National Park, Missouri, National Parks Service. NPS.gov.
"Seaman (dog)." wikipedia.org

6 – "Citizen Complains." *Evening Telegram*, 1923-07-06: 6.

7 – "Forest Fire Roundup." *Daily News*, 1962-06-11: 3.
"Magistrate's Court." *Daily News*, 1962-07-07: 2.

8 – "New Motor Sprinkler." *Evening Telegram*, 1919-07-09: 4.

9 – Jarvis, Dale. Personal Files.

10 – Rule, U.Z. *Reminiscences of My Life*. St. John's: Dicks & Co, 1927. Page 13-14.

11 – "Editorial Notes." *Evening Telegram*, 1899-09-21: 4.

"A Sea Monster Seen by Three Hundred." *Tasmanian News*, 1899-09-23: 4.

12 – "A craze for speed." *Decks Awash*, 14.5 (September-October 1985): 57-58.

13 – "Eight Year Old Boy Spends Night in Woods." *Evening Telegram*, 1908-07-13: 4.

14 – Journal of the House of Assembly of Newfoundland, 1846. St. John's: House of Assembly, 1846. Page 41.

15 – "Building Church By Selling Fish." *Western Star*, 1949-03-08: 5. "Fish-a-trip Donation Rebuilds Nfld. Church." *Western Star*, 1951-07-20: 1-2.

16 – Jarvis, Dale. "Drown'd by the stroke of a whale, 1782: the grave of Jonathan Webber." ichblog.ca, 2019-05-07.

17 – "It Was a Skull." *Evening Telegram*, 1899-07-18: 4.

18 – "Castaway Bankers at Bay Roberts." *Evening Telegram*, 1908-07-18: 4.

19 – Miller, Jim. Trinity Historical Society, personal communication, 2019-07-11, with notes from Dr. John Mannion.

20 – "Loss of a Schooner." *Harbor Grace Standard*, 1878-08-10: 3.

21 – "Chronicle of Events: July." The Annual Register, Volume 128. A Review of Public Events at Home and Abroad For the Year 1886. London: 1886.

22 – "Local Varieties." *Evening Telegram*, 1889-06-12: 4.
United States Patent No. US432900A.
"Valuable Machinery." *Evening Herald*, 4.181 (1893-08-11): 1.

23 – "Local Occurrences." *Evening Telegram*, 1896-07-23: 4.

24 – "Peculiar Theft." *Evening Telegram*, 1912-07-24: 6.

25 – "Local Notes." *Morning Despatch*, 1.9 (1892-07-26): 4.

26 – "A Fine Chance." *Morning Despatch*, 1.9 (1892-07-26): 2.

27 – "SS Furter Abandoned." *Evening Telegram*, 1897-08-09: 4.

28 – "Shower of Flies." *Evening Telegram*, 1897-08-11: 4.

29 – O'Neill, Paul. "CANNING, FRANCIS," in *Dictionary of Canadian Biography*, vol. 12, University of Toronto/Université Laval, 2003, accessed December 10, 2019, http://www.biographi.ca/en/bio/canning_francis_12E.html.

30 – "The Army Grubs." *Harbor Grace Standard*, 1888-03-03: 3.
"The Musty Past." *Evening Telegram*, 1883-08-09: 4.

31 – Broughton, P. "What Brought Edmond Halley to Newfoundland." *Journal of the Royal Astronomical Society of Canada*, 89:1.652 (February 1995): 18.
"Halley's Comet." wikipedia.org

AUGUST

1 – Earle, Canon George. "The 1938 Journey of the *Argonaut*." *Newfoundland Quarterly*, 85.2 (Fall 1989): 7-10.

2 – "An Alarm of Fire." *Evening Telegram*, 1900-08-02: 4.
"No Insurance." *Evening Telegram*, 1900-08-03: 4
"Meting Out Justice." *Evening Telegram*, 1900-08-04: 4.

3 – Grist, John. "Letter to Bishop Howley." *Evening Telegram*, 1899-02-17: 4.
Howley, M. F. "Paper no. 145 : Extracts from the registers of The Church of England, St. John's, Newfoundland." Shortis Papers, vol. 03, pt. 01.

4 – "Ran Itself to Death." *Evening Telegram*, 1900-08-06: 4.

5 – "Eclipse of the Sun." *Encyclopedia of Newfoundland and Labrador*, volume 1. St. John's: Newfoundland Book Publishers (1967) Ltd., 1981. Page 667.
Cook, James, and Bevis, John. XXIV. An observation of an eclipse of the Sun at the Island of New-found-land, August 5, 1766, by Mr. James Cook, with the longitude of the place of

observation deduced from it. Communicated by J. Bevis. Philosophical Transactions, vol 57 (31 December 1767): 215-216.

6 – "Gigantic Raft." *Evening Telegram*, 1919-08-12: 9.

7 – "Dancing at Seventy-five." *Evening Telegram*, 1919-08-07: 6.

8 – "This Man Skipped." *Western Star*, 1900-08-10: 4.

9 – "Local items." *Morning Despatch*, 1.22 (10 August 1892): 4.

10 – "Depositions Made." *Enterprise*, 1.86 (1897-08-21): 3.
"Local Happenings." *Evening Telegram*, 1900-03-23: 4.
"Edward Wall Killed." *Evening Telegram*, 1897-08-11: 4.
"Exploits Bridge Gone." *Enterprise*, 1.86 (1897-08-21): 3.

11 – "Narrow Escape." *Evening Telegram*, 1920-08-12: 7.
"Outing at Smithville." *Evening Telegram*, 1920-08-12: 7.

12 – "Youthful Sneak Thief." *Evening Telegram*, 1914-08-13: 4.

13 – "The Supernatural." *Evening Telegram*, 1891-08-17: 4.

14 – "Attacks Priest." *Western Star*, 1941-08-20: 7.
"Attempt On Life Of Monsignor Dinn." *Newfoundland Times*, 1.35 (1941-09-06): 1.
"Newfoundland Vital Records, 1840-1949," database with images, FamilySearch.org. Deaths 1943-1944, Certificate Number 102025 -102800 > image 63 of 787; Provincial Archives, St. John's.

15 – "B.I.S. Outing." *Evening Telegram*, 1900-08-16: 4.
"Cupid at the Picnic." *Evening Telegram*, 1900-08-17: 4.

16 – A.G.G. "Superstitions and Traditions of Newfoundland." *Newfoundland Weekly*, 1.5 (1994-08-16). 3.

17 – "Cruiser is Sunk by Sub." *St. John's Daily Star*, 1918-08-19: 1.
"Dead Whale." *St. John's Daily Star*, 1918-08-19: 8.
"Large Tanker Attacked by Sub." *St. John's Daily Star*, 1918-08-19: 1.
"U-Boat Sinks Another Tanker." *St. John's Daily Star*, 1918-08-19: 1.

18 – "Local Happenings." *Evening Telegram*, 1899-08-18: 4.

19 – "Daring Act." *Evening Telegram*, 1897-08-19: 4.

20 – "Died." *Evening Telegram*, 1907-03-25: 8.
"From Harbour Grace." *Evening Telegram*, 1885-09-03: 4.
"House of Assembly." *Harbor Grace Standard*, 1901-09-13: 3.
"Local Occurrences." *Evening Telegram*, 1895-09-12: 4.
"Local Occurrences." *Evening Telegram*, 1895-09-18: 4.
"Mr. Gaden Dead." *Evening Telegram*, 1907-03-25: 7.
Newfoundland Vital Records, 1840-1949.
"One Other Seizure." *Evening Telegram*, 1895-10-04: 4.
"Seizure of Tobacco." *Evening Telegram*, 1895-09-05: 4.
"Smuggling in Trinity Bay." *Evening Telegram*, 1881-08-20: 4.
"Spirits and Sugar." *Evening Telegram*, 1896-10-24: 4.
"The Tide Surveyor's Doom." *Evening Telegram*, 1895-11-21: 4.
"Yet Another Seizure." *Evening Telegram*, 1895-09-11: 4.

21 – "Attacked by Devil Fish." *Western Star*, 1912-08-28: 1.

22 – "Local events." *Morning Despatch*, 1.32 (22 August 1892): 4.

23 – Devine, Maurice A.; O'Mara, Michael J. *Notable events in the history of Newfoundland: six thousand dates of historical and social happenings.* St. John's: Devine & O'Mara, 1900. Page 157.
"Local Happenings." *Evening Telegram*, 1899-08-24: 4.

24 – Chang, Margaret. "Chinese Pioneers in Newfoundland." *Evening Telegram*, 11 February, 1978.
"Fong, Toy." *The Book of Newfoundland*, vol. 5. St. John's: Newfoundland Book Publishers (1967), Ltd., 1975. Page 565.
"Two Chinamen in the City." *Evening Telegram*, 1895-08-19.

25 – "Cattle Ranching on the Burin Peninsula." *Southern Gazette*, 16 December 2014.
Connelly, Martin. "Introducing the Brunette Island Bison." *Newfoundland Quarterly*, 104.4 (Spring 2012): 18-22.
"Head 'Em Out." *Decks Awash*, 21.6 (November-December 1992): 14.

26 – Murphy, Michael F. "The Remarkable Feat of Henry Supple, Jr." *Atlantic Guardian*, 11.4 (June 1954): 28-30.

27 – "Newspapers." *Decks Awash*, 10.01 (February 1981): 4-6.
Thoms, James R. Newfoundland *Who's Who : Centennial edition 1967-1968*. St. John's: E.C. Boone Advertising Ltd., 1968. Page xviii.

28 – "Association Football in St. John's: The Pioneer Years, 1870-1896.." The Free Library. 2019 Newfoundland and Labrador Studies, Faculty of Arts Publications 25 Jan. 2020, Thefreelibrary.com.
Cyril Byrne, "BENNETT, DAVID," in *Dictionary of Canadian Biography*, vol. 13, University of Toronto/Université Laval, 2003, accessed July 10, 2019, http://www.biographi.ca/en/bio/bennett_david_13E.html.
"Local Varieties." *Evening Telegram*, 1886-08-30: 4.

29 – "Doane, Ernest B." *Encyclopedia of Newfoundland and Labrador*, vol. 1. St. John's: Newfoundland Book Publishers (1967) Ltd. 1981. Pages 628-629.
"Gold at Torbay!" *Evening Telegram*, 1899-08-29: 4.
Sutter, Glenn. "The Eskimo Curlew: 50 Years Gone?" www.royalsaskmuseum.ca, 9 September 2013.

30 – "A Sad Case." *Weekly News*, 1.23 (1894-08-30): 8.

31 – "Broke Her Arm." *St. John's Daily Star*, 1917-12-28: 8.
"Miss Armine Gosling." *St. John's Daily Star*, 1916-11-29: 8.
"Somewhere in Belgium." *Cadet*, Volume 5, Number 2, July 1918 11.
"War News." *Evening Advocate*, 9.212 (1922-09-20): 4.
"Young Lady to Qualify As Ambulance Driver." *St. John's Daily Star*, 1916-08-31: 8.

SEPTEMBER

1 – "Cut with a Scythe." *Evening Telegram*, 1899-09-01: 4.
"Impaled on Hay Fork." *Evening Telegram*, 1911-09-04: 7.

2 – "Had a Narrow Escape." *Evening Telegram*, 1903-09-03: 4.

3 – "Work Horse Parade." *Evening Telegram*, 1919-08-16: 6.
"Work Horse Parade." *Evening Telegram*, 1919-09-03: 5.
"Work Horse Parade." *Evening Telegram*, 1919-09-06: 4.
"Work-Horse Parade Yesterday." *Evening Telegram*, 1919-09-04: 8.

4 – "Local Happenings." *Evening Telegram*, 1903-09-04: 4.

5 – "Mr. Coady's Very Curious Find." *Colonist*, 5.203 (1890-09-06): 4.

6 – "The Weather – Remarkable Shower of Quartz." *Patriot and Catholic Herald*, 30 (1872-09-10): 4.

7 – "Camp Plundered." *Evening Telegram*, 1903-09-07: 4.

8 – "Local Varieties." *Evening Telegram*, 1890-09-08: 4.

9 – "An Incorrigible." *Evening Telegram*, 1925-09-10: 6.
"Smashed the Door With an Axe." *Evening Telegram*, 1925-09-09: 4.

10 – "Canada Lynx." Fisheries and Land Resources. www.flr.gov.nl.ca
Joyce, Tammy Lee. "Impact of Hunting on Snowshoe Hare Populations in Newfoundland." T. N.p., 2002. Web. Retrospective Theses and Dissertations, 1919-2007.
"Local Happenings." *Evening Telegram*, 1900-09-10: 4.
"Snowshoe Hare." Fisheries and Land Resources. www.flr.gov.nl.ca

11 – "Shocking Stabbing Affray." *Evening Telegram*, 1897-09-13: 3.
"Stabbed with a Knife." *Evening Telegram*, 1897-09-13: 4.

12 – "Struck the Wrong Town." *Evening Herald*, 9.213 (1898-09-13): 4.

13 – Sparks, Brad. No. 471. Comprehensive Catalog of 1,700 Project Blue Book UFO Unknowns: Database Catalog. Version 1.27 (Dec. 20, 2016).

14 – "Execution." *Evening Telegram*, 1899-07-29: 4.
"Skeleton Found." *Evening Telegram*, 1896-09-14: 4.
"Strange But True." *Evening Telegram*, 1896-11-25: 4.
"That Skeleton." *Evening Telegram*, 1896-09-15: 4.

15 – "Big Attendance at Wonderland." *St. John's Daily Star*, 1917-09-21: 10.
"Wonderland Shows." *Evening Telegram* (St. John's, N.L.), 1917-09-15: 8.
"Wonderland Shows." *St. John's Daily Star*, 1917-09-19: 8

16 – "Somnambulism." *Evening Telegram*, 1879-09-20: 1.

17 – "It Was The Cat." *Evening Herald*, 9.218 (1898-09-19): 4.

18 – Howley, James Patrick. *Reminiscences of forty-two years of exploration in and about Newfoundland*. Section 05: 1897-1911. St. John's: English Language Research Centre, Memorial University of Newfoundland, 2009.

19 – "Victim of Peculiar Shooting Accident." *St. John's Daily Star*, 1915-09-20: 8.

20 – Hanrahan, Maura. "Polar labour: Jack Bursey." captainbobbartlett.com, 2018-11-21.
"Jack Bursey." wikipedia.org

21 – "Dies at 102." *Daily News*, 1963-01-28: 3.
"Grand Bay East and Grand Bay West." *Decks Awash*, 18.6 (November-December 1989): 12-14.

22 – "The Lantern Parade." *Evening Telegram*, 1896-09-23: 4.
"The Wheelmans Dinner." *Evening Herald*, 7.223 (1896-09-23): 4.

23 – "Pea Blowing Becoming a Nuisance." *Evening Telegram*, 1909-09-23: 6.

24 – "From the Public Ledger." *Weekly Herald and Conception-Bay General Advertiser*, 6.308 (1848-10-04): 2.
Ruffman, Alan. "Newly-recognized tsunami in Atlantic Canada." *Atlantic Geology*, 23.2 (August 1987): 106.

25 – "Big Attendance at Wonderland." *St. John's Daily Star*, 1917-09-21: 10.
"Circus Closes Soon." *St. John's Daily Star*, 1917-09-26: 8.
Nelson, Harriet Schuyler. *365 desserts; A dessert for every day in the year*. Philadelphia: G.W. Jacobs & Co., 1900.

26 – "Died Suddenly." *Harbor Grace Standard*, 1896-10-02: 4.
"Funeral of Mrs. Cairns." *Evening Telegram*, 1896-09-28: 4.
"In Re AMELIA CAIRNS, BROWNING v. WINTER." Court. June 28, 1906. Decisions of the Supreme Court of Newfound-

land : the reports, 1904-1911. Browning, DM, ed. St. John's: J.W. Withers, King's Printer, 1912.
"In Re Cairns Estate." *St. John's Daily Star*, 1918-03-01: 2.
"London House!" *Evening Telegram*, 1890-09-29: 1.
"London House." *Evening Telegram*, 1896-09-18: 1.
"London House 1897 Spring Opening." *Evening Telegram*, 1897-04-13: 1.
NL GenWeb. Avalon South Region ~ St. John's District. St. John's - General Protestant Cemetery Interments, 1893 - 1896. http://sites.rootsweb.com/~cannf/sj_cem_gp1893.htm
"She Buys Now." *Evening Telegram*, 1897-02-09: 4.
"Supreme Court." *St. John's Daily Star*, 1918-02-14: 8.
"Table I. (B)." Newfoundland and Labrador Budget Speech 1932, page 42.

27 – "King of Skittles." *Evening Telegram*, 1898-09-27: 4.

28 – "Found in a Swoon." *Evening Telegram*, 1905-09-29: 4.

29 – "Two Esquimaux Here." *Evening Telegram*, 1905-09-29: 4.

30 – "Current Happenings." *Evening Herald*, 8.230 (1897-10-01): 3.
"Fogo Chronicles." *Evening Telegram*, 1899-05-15: 3.
"For the Kite Season." *Evening Telegram* (St. John's, N.L.), 1906-08-20: 1. Adv. 4 Page 9.

OCTOBER

1 – "Central District Court." *Evening Telegram*, 1880-10-01: 1.
"Central District Court." *Register*, 1.14 (1880-10-01): 1.

2 – "Budget Speech." *Evening Telegram*, 1904-04-04: 3.
"Local Happenings." *Evening Telegram*, 1905-01-14: 3.
"Tinsmiths All Out." *Evening Telegram*, 1903-10-02: 4.

3 – "Another Musical Feast." *Evening Herald*, 7.241 (1895-10-04): 4.
"Events and Echoes." *Evening Herald*, 7.240 (1895-10-03): 4.
"Grand Farewell Concert." *Evening Herald*, 7.240 (1895-10-03): 1.

4 – "Strange Report." *Evening Telegram*, 1910-10-05: 4.
"Turned Up O.K." *Evening Telegram*, 1910-10-05: 4.

5 – "Policeman Needed." *Evening Telegram*, 1906-10-05: 4.
"Row at St. Patrick's Hall." *Evening Telegram*, 1906-10-05: 4.

6 – "An Arctic Mystery." *Evening Telegram*, 1906-10-06: 3.

7 – Dugmore, Arthur Radclyffe. *The romance of the Newfoundland Caribou: an intimate account of the reindeer of North America*. London: William Heinemann, 1913.

8 – "The Goat Nuisance." *Evening Telegram*, 1887-10-10: 4.
"Sir Shea's Election." *Evening Telegram*, 1885-10-08: 4.
"Word in Explanation." *Evening Telegram*, 1884-07-24: 4.
Year book and almanac of Newfoundland, 1896. St. John's: J.W. Withers, Queen's Printer, 1896. Page 172.

9 – "Memorable Day for Nfld." *Evening Telegram*, 1909-10-09: 6.
Murphy, James. *Historical events of Newfoundland*. St. John's: J. Murphy, 1918.

10 – Hewson, John. "The Name Presentic and other Ancient Micmac Toponyms." *Newfoundland Quarterly*, 77.4 (Winter 1981-82): 11-14.
"Logging Camp School." *Western Star*, 1943-03-27: 8.
"Night School in Logging Camp." *Western Star*, 1942-12-18: 3.

11 – "Strange Phenomenon." *Western Star*, 1941-10-15: 1.
"Very Latest Explanations." *Western Star*, 1941-10-22: 1.

12 – "What Was It?" *St. John's Daily Star*, 1917-10-13: 2.

13 – "Editorial Notes." *Evening Telegram*, 1896-10-13: 4.

14 – Post Man and the Historical Account, Issue 226 (October 17, 1696 - October 20, 1696).

15 – "How Constable Crane." *Evening Telegram*, 1896-10-31: 4.
"Two Prisoners." *Evening Telegram*, 1896-10-27: 4.

16 – "Very Large Turnip." *Evening Telegram*, 1895-10-16: 4.

17 – "Harbor Grace Notes." *Evening Telegram*, 1907-10-14: 4.
"Local Happenings." *Evening Telegram*, 1903-10-19: 4.

18 – "Killed by the Train." *Evening Telegram*, 1900-10-19: 3.

19 – "François d'Orléans, Prince of Joinville." wikipedia.org
"From the United States." *St. John's Daily News*, 1861-09-25: 2.
"The Musty Past." *Evening Telegram*, 1883-09-07: 4.

20 – Newfoundland Baptisms 1699 & 1762, Transcribed from the Parish Registers held at the Dorset History Centre by Kim Parker. NL GenWeb. http://sites.rootsweb.com/~cannf/pw_dorsetmanl.htm

21 – "Don't fail..." *Evening Telegram*, 1879-10-20: 1.
"Prof. Zera." *Evening Telegram*, 1879-10-16: 1.
"Zera." *Evening Telegram* (St. John's, N.L.), 1879-10-21: 2.

22 – "Large Eel in Pipe." *Evening Telegram*, 1906-10-25: 4.

23 – "Events and Echoes." *Evening Herald*, 13.248 (1902-10-24): 3.

24 – Jarvis, Dale. "Finding Private Ryan: A forgotten Broad Cove memorial gets a new home." *Downhomer*, 16.1 (June 2003): 60-62.

25 – Maniate, Peter. "Newfs Given to Visiting Royalty." *Newf News*, March/April 2015. hannibalnewfs.com
Wallace, Donald Mackenzie, et al. *The web of empire: a diary of the imperial tour of their Royal Highnesses the Duke & Duchess of Cornwall & York in 1901*. London: Macmillan, 1902. Page 431-434.

26 – "Kate Mullins Found." *Evening Herald*, 14.248 (1903-10-27): 4.
"Newfoundland Vital Records, 1840-1949," Film Number: 002168728, FamilySearch.org.

27 – "Newsy Notes From Whitbourne." *Evening Telegram*, 1895-11-01: 4.

28 – Convocation, 1995, Fall. St. John's: Memorial University of Newfoundland, 1995.
"Hidden sign reveals history of influential Jewish couple in St. John's." CBC News – Posted: Oct 02, 2018. CBC.ca.

29 – "Another Ghost Story." *Evening Herald*, 7.256 (1896-10-31): 4.

30 – "Fight with Wild Dogs." *Evening Telegram*, 1889-07-09: 1.
"Wild Dogs About." *Evening Telegram*, 1911-10-31: 6.

31 – Balleny, JH. "Odd Fellowship of Grand Falls." *St. John's Daily Star*, 1917-11-09: 4.
Cook Book featuring favourite Newfoundland recipes. Revised Edition. St. John's: George Street United Church Women's Association, 1956-1957.

NOVEMBER

1 – "Letter from a Newfoundlander Abroad." *Colonist*, 1.230 (1886-12-09): 4.

2 – "Buried Alive in Well and Survives." *Daily News*, 1956-11-03: 1.

3 – Jarvis, Dale. Personal Files.

4 – "Bazar Notes." *Newfoundland Colonist*, 6.252 (1891-11-04): 4.
"Local and Other Items." *Newfoundland Colonist*, 6.252 (1891-11-04): 4.
"The Phonograph Entertainment At St. Patrick's Hall." *Newfoundland Colonist*, 6.253 (1891-11-05): 4.
"The Phonograph Exhibition At St. Patrick's Hall." *Evening Herald*, 2.254 (1891-11-05): 4.

5 – "Harbour Grace Historical Notes." *Daily News*, 1956-01-14: 11.

6 – Gosling, William Gilbert. *The Life of Sir Humphrey Gilbert, England's first empire builder*. London: Constable, 1911. Page 131-132.
"John Dee." wikipedia.org

7 – Prowse, D. W. *A history of Newfoundland from the English, colonial, and foreign records*. London: Macmillan, 1895. Page 4.

8 "Shebeens." *Weekly News*, 1.33 (1894-11-08): 2.

9 – "Amusements." *Evening Telegram*, 1915-10-26: 5.
"Amusements." *Evening Telegram*, 1915-11-04: 4.
"Amusements." *Evening Telegram*, 1915-10-18: 4.
"Amusements." *Evening Telegram*, 1915-10-13: 5.

"Amusements." *Evening Telegram*, 1915-10-22: 4.
"Rossley's East End Theatre." *Evening Telegram*, 1915-11-08: 3.
"Theatres." *St. John's Daily Star*, 1915-11-10: 7.

10 – "Anniversaries of Notable Events." *Evening Telegram*, 1915-11-10: 7.
"Belvedere RC Cemetery - St. John's - St. John's East District - SECTION VI." Newfoundland's Grand Banks, ngb.chebucto.org.
"Local and Other Items." *Terra Nova Advocate And Political Observer*, 3.89 (1878-11-09): 2.
"In Memoriam." *Terra Nova Advocate And Political Observer*, 3.83 (1878-10-19): 2.
"Local and Other Items." *Terra Nova Advocate And Political Observer*, 3.83 (1878-10-19): 2.
Weber, Austin. "The History of Caskets." *Assembly Magazine*, 2009-10-2. Assemblymag.com.

11 – "A Whaling Yarn." *Weekly News*, 1.36 (1894-11-29): 7.

12 – "Launched at Gambo." *Evening Herald*, 1.255 (1890-11-13): 1.
"The Saint Ida Launched at Gambo." *Evening Telegram*, 1890-11-13: 4.

13 – "Local Happenings." *Evening Telegram*, 1899-10-13: 4.
"Who Stole the Birds?" *Evening Telegram*, 1899-10-12: 4.

14 – "Brief Notes of News." *Evening Herald*, 1. 256 (1890-11-14): 4.
"Local and Other Items." *Newfoundland Colonist*, 6.283 (1891-12-11): 4.
"Saint Andrew's Society." *Evening Herald*, 1.15 (1890-01-29): 4.

15 – "Message in Tin Picked Up on Welsh Coast." *Western Star*, 1936-05-20: 1.
"Nfld. Iron Ore Cargo Goes Down in Mid Atlantic." *Western Star*, 1933-11-22: 1.

16 – "Local and Other Items." *Colonist*, 2.262 (1887-11-22): 4.

17 – "Anniversaries of Notable Events." *Evening Telegram*, 1915-11-17: 8.
Directory for the Towns of St. John's, Harbor Grace, and Carbonear, Newfoundland, for 1885-86. St. John's: John Sharpe,

1885. Page 37.
Russell, Judy G. "The duties of the tipstaff." *The Legal Genealogist*, Jan 29, 2014. Legalgenealogist.com.

18 – "Great gloom…" *Harbor Grace Standard*, 1911-11-24: 4.
Peacock, Kenneth. *Songs of the Newfoundland Outports.* Vol.3. Ottawa: National Museum of Canada/Bulletin No. 197, Anthropological Series No. 65, 1965, p.958.
"Terrible Experience of Crew of the Schr Riseover." *Evening Telegram*, 1911-11-24: 6.

19 – "Phantom Ship Reappears Near Lewisporte." *Western Star*, 1952-11-21: 1,15.

20 – Dooley, Danette. "Church of St. Mary the Virgin turns 150 years old." *Telegram*, 2009-06-27. Pressreader.com.
"History." The Anglican Parish of St. Mary the Virgin. Stmarythevirgin.ca.

21 – "The Following…" *Weekly Herald And Conception-Bay General Advertiser*, 8.367 (1849-11-21): 3.

22 – "Cooper's Death." *Evening Telegram*, 1900-11-22: 4.
"Autopsy Held." *Evening Telegram*, 1900-11-22: 4.

23 – Hakluyt, Richard. "The voyage of M. Hore and divers other gentlemen, to Newfoundland, and Cape Briton, in the yere 1536 and in the 28 yere of king Henry the 8." in The Principal Navigations, Voyages, Traffiques, and Discoveries of the English Nation Made by Sea or Overland to the Remote & Farthest Distant Quarters of the Earth at any time within the compasse of these 1500 Yeares. Perseus Digital Library. Perseus.tufts.edu.
"Richard Hakluyt." wikipedia.org

24 – "Brief Notes of News." *Evening Herald*, 1.264 (1890-11-24): 4.
"Here and There." *Evening Telegram*, 1909-10-12: 6.
"People at…" *Colonist*, 6.88 (17 April 1891): 4.
"Residents Complain." *Evening Telegram*, 1908-03-19: 4.
"Those Pigs." *Evening Telegram*, 1897-09-27: 4.

25 – "Anniversaries of Notable Events." *Evening Telegram*, 1915-11-25: 4.

City of St. John's Archives. History: Street Names, Areas, Monuments, Plaques. St. John's: September 25, 2012.

26 – "Province receives heritage treasures." News Release NLIS 3, June 13, 2001. Department of Tourism, Culture and Recreation. Gov.nl.ca.
Town of Isle aux Morts. "Our History." Isleauxmorts.ca.

27 – "Anniversaries of Notable Events." *Evening Telegram*, 1915-11-27: 6.
"Shocking Accident." *Evening Telegram*, 1887-11-28: 4.

28 – "Cruelty to Animals." *Evening Advocate*, 1917-02-28: 6.
"Local and Other Items." *Newfoundland Colonist*, 6.247 (1891-10-29): 4.

29 – "Badly-needed Institution." *Evening Telegram*, 1889-06-12: 4.
"Effects of the Storm." *Evening Telegram*, 1890-12-01: 4.

30 – "Bartlett, Rupert Wilfred." Military Service Files database, The Rooms,
https://www.therooms.ca/sites/default/files/bartlett_rupert_wilfred_0-17_or_166.pdf
https://www.therooms.ca/sites/default/files/bartlett_rupert_wilfrid_166.pdf
"Captain Rupert Bartlett MC and Bar." *Evening Telegram*, 1917-12-12: 6.
"Farewell Reception." *Evening Herald*, 6.29 (1918-09-23): 6.
"Late List of Casualties." *St. John's Daily Star*, 1917-12-12: 2.
Smith, Nicholas. *Fifty-two years at the Labrador fishery*. London: A.H. Stockwell, 1936. Page 197.

DECEMBER

1 – "First Day Covers Grenfell Commemorative Stamp." *Among the Deep Sea Fishers*, 39.4 (January 1942): 104.

2 – "Al Marx: Strongman, Acrobat and Heavyweight Contender." Farabaugh.org.
"Strong Man's Show." *Evening Telegram*, 1909-12-04: 6.
"Wonderful Show by Strong Man." *Evening Telegram*, 1909-12-03: 5.

Wood, John. "Aloysius Marx." 2019-03-10. Oldtimestrongman.com.

3 – Fraser, Allan M. *History of the participation by Newfoundland in World War II*. Edited and with an Introduction by Peter Neary and Melvin Baker, 2010.
"Ten Tales of Newfoundlanders Overseas." *Newfoundland Quarterly*, 44.4 (April 1945): 14-20.

4 – "Five Happy Couples." *Evening Herald*, 12.301 (1901-12-24): 4.

5 – "Battle Honour: Cambrai 1917." Rnfldr.ca.
Tait, Robert. *Newfoundland: a summary of the history and development of Britain's oldest colony from 1497 to 1939*. Harrington Park, New Jersey: Harrington Press, 1939. Page 203-205.

6 – *George Kemp Diary 1901*. Centre for Newfoundland Studies - Digitized Books. Page 195.

7 – O'Brien, Patricia. *Out of Mind, Out of Sight: A History of the Waterford Hospital*. Newfoundland History Series 5. St. Johns: Breakwater Books, 1989. Page 133-134.

8 – "Police Should Go There." *Evening Telegram*, 1907-12-12: 4.

9 – "The Father of the Happy Thought." *Evening Telegram*, 1887-01-27: 4.
United States Patent No. US145340A.
"Miscellaneous Inventions." *Scientific American*, 1882-03-25: 183.
"Mr. Reginald H. Earle..." *Evening Telegram*, 1909-06-15: 7.

10 – "Local and Other Items." *Newfoundland Colonist*, 6.282 (1891-12-10): 4.

11 – "Hubley's Plumbing & Heating: Four Generations in St. John's." Hubleysplumbing.ca.
Who's Who In and From Newfoundland 1937. Hibbs, Richard, ed. St. John's: R. Hibbs, 1937. Page 133.

12 – "Early History." Sisters of Mercy of Newfoundland. Sistersofmercynf.org.

"Our Lady of Mercy Convent and Chapel." Heritage Newfoundland and Labrador. Heritage.nf.ca.

13 – "Christmas Tree." *Evening Telegram*, 1880-11-26: 3.
"Xmas Tree and Fancy Fair." *Evening Telegram*, 1891-10-07: 4.

14 – "The New Palace." *Adelphian*, 18.5 (1925): 42-43.

15 – "Chips." *Western Star*, 1946-01-11: 10.

16 – "Sighted Strange Fish in Atlantic." *Evening Telegram*, 1924-12-16: 3.

17 – Entwisle, Martha. "Newfoundland Historic Trust Bake Sale." *Trident*, 10.2 (1985-09): 4.
"For Our Men in the Fighting Line." *Evening Telegram*, 1916-11-04: 1.
Huckster Shop. JH JH 2/70, 1970/02. Dictionary of Newfoundland English Word Form Database.
"The Musty Past." *Evening Telegram*, 1883-08-16: 4.

18 – Johnson, Arthur. "Hugh Cole's Reindeer Trek Down the Northern Peninsula." *Newfoundland Quarterly*. In three parts: 64.4 (Winter 1965-66); 65.1 (Fall 1966); and 65.2 (Winter 1966-1967).

19 – "Saved By a Human Chain!" *Evening Telegram*, 1908-12-21: 6.

20 – "The Holiday Display." *Colonist*, 5.293 (20 December 1890): 4.

21 – "Laid to Rest." *Harbor Grace Standard*, 1903-12-23: 4.
"Local Happenings." *Evening Telegram*, 1903-12-07: 3.
"Obituary." *Adelphian*, 1.1 (1904): 49.

22 – "The Musty Past." *Evening Telegram*, 1883-09-13: 4.

23 – Herridge, Paul. "The Origins of Tibb's Eve." *Southern Gazette*, 2009-12-22.
Kirwin, William. "Folk Etymology: Remarks on Linguistic Problem-Solving and who does it." Lore and Language, 4.2 (1985-07): 18-24.

24 – Lawton, J.T. "King's Cove - The Royal Port." *Newfoundland Times*, 1.36 (1941-09-20): 7.

25 – "Richard Brothers." wikipedia.org
"Richard Brothers (1757-1824)." OliverCowdery.com – The Premier Web-Site for Early Mormon History.

26 – "Staff Night at the Newfoundland Hotel." *Newfoundland Weekly*, 8.25 (1932-01-09): 2.

27 – "Notice." *Evening Telegram*, 1892-02-20: 2.
"Obituary." *Evening Telegram* (St. John's, N.L.), 1915-02-24: 3.
United States Patent No. US488847A.

28 – "Thrilling Rescue." *Western Star*, 1905-01-18: 4.

29 – "Detective Byrne Arrests Burglars." *Evening Telegram*, 1920-12-30: 6.

30 – "The Garrison Hill Fire." *Evening Telegram*, 1883-01-08: 4.

31 – "Snap Shots About Town." *Evening Telegram*, 1897-01-02: 4.

IMAGE CREDITS

01-01 Coat of Arms of Newfoundland and Labrador. Wikimedia Commons, the free media repository. 20 Jan 2019

01-15 Royal Newfoundland Constabulary on horseback at the Parade Grounds, circa 1910s. City of St. John's Archives Photo #01-13-072, Magone Collection.

01-27 The waterfront at Delgada, in the Azores, between 1909 and 1919. Library of Congress Prints and Photographs Division Washington, D.C.

02-05 James Carroll, 15th Australian Infantry Battalion. Discoveringanzacs.naa.gov.au.

02-00 Garment for serpentine dancing, invented by Marie Louise Fuller of New York, 1894. United States patent #US518347.

02-09 Illustration of the new Touroscope, 1880. The Philadelphia Photographer, 17, 1880: 380.

02-17 Imperial Tobacco Company building, prior to its conversion to residential units. Heritage Foundation of Newfoundland and Labrador slide collection, FPT2144_43.

02-18 Winter on Quidi Vidi Lake. City of St. John's Archives Photo #01-13-010.

03-01 The Champion Automatic Fog horn, patented in Canada in 1876. The "champion" automatic fog horn [microform] : Smith & Booth's patent, supplied by the "Neptune" Fog Horn Company Limited. 1878.

03-09 Engraving of "carrier pigeons" (most likely homing pigeons), with messages attached. *Harper's New Monthly Magazine*, No. 275 (April 1873).

03-19 Sybil Hillier with Don and Edgar, Great Northern Peninsula. Photo courtesy Gary Green.

04-02 A group of men on a St. John's dock processing seals. City of St. John's Archives Photo #01-13-063.

04-05 3-year-old Holstein-Friesian bull, 1887.The breeds of livestock, and the principles of heredity (1887). Commons.wikimedia.org.

04-10 Breaking out through the ice—the sealing fleet leaving St. Johns. Harper's weekly, v. 28, 1884 April 5, p. 221. Library of Congress Prints and Photographs Division Washington, D.C.

04-26 Royal Visit of Queen Elizabeth and King George V to Government House, 1939. City of St. John's Archives Photo #01-72-004. Photographer: Summers, William.

05-12 Navy-Curtiss Flying Boat NC-1 in Trepassey, Newfoundland, Canada on a leg of its transatlantic journey in May 1919. Flickr Commons, 2017. Library of Congress Prints and Photographs Division Washington, D.C.

05-16 St. Brendan's legendary voyage, showing Mass being said on the back of a whale. Image circa 1621. Library of Congress Prints and Photographs Division Washington, D.C.

05-25 Petrie Crossing, passenger train shot, May 1959. CN Images of Canada Collection, ID Number X-45184.

06-13 Lady Baden-Powell. Bain News Service, George Grantham Bain Collection, Library of Congress Prints and Photographs Division Washington, D.C.

06-15 The Moravian mission ship *Harmony* somewhere near Nain on the coast of Labrador. D965. *Them Days* Archives, Kate Hettasch collection.

06-27 Advertisements like this one for Ayer's Sarsaparilla were common in the Newfoundland newspapers of the 1890s. Library of Congress Prints and Photographs Division Washington, D.C.

07-01 Convair B-36 Peacemaker in flight. Commons.wikimedia.org

07-05 Newfoundland dog, lithograph created between 1830 and 1835. Newfoundland dog / from nature and on stone by T. Doughty. Childs & Inman, lithographer. Library of Congress Prints and Photographs Division Washington, D.C.

07-07 A 1,000-gallon Mack sprinkler in action, 1917. Frederick Clarence Stilson, World Digital Library.

07-22 Apparatus for Drying Fish and other Articles or Substances, 1890. United States patent #US432900A.

08-11 Smithville Tennis Club, circa 1910. City of St. John's Archives Photo #01-62-001.

08-15 Octagon Castle, date uncertain. Centre for Newfoundland Studies photo 0703004/Archivalmoments.ca.

08-26 Brooklyn Bridge during construction, showing the workers' temporary walkways going up to the pier tops and cables being spun. Appletons' cyclopaedia of applied mechanics, vol. 1. Benjamin, Park, ed. New York: D. Appleton and Company, 1880.

09-03 Michael Power, Chief Agent for the Society for the Protection of Animals, and his son Gerald Power on a horse-drawn vehicle on Scott Street. City of St. John's Archives Photo #01-80-001.

09-10 Canadian lynx, illustration circa 1885–1891.Trousset, Jules. Nouveau dictionnaire encyclopédique universel illustré. Paris: La Librairie Illustrée, 1885-1891.

09-20 Commander Richard E. Byrd's First Antarctic Expedition ship SS *City of New York* next to the Great Ice Barrier, Antarctica. September 1929. Library of Congress (2016/03/10) / Lot 4499-15. National Museum of the U.S. Navy.

09-22 An unidentified member of the Branscombe family, circa 1897–1899. City of St. John's Archives Photo #01-01-018. Eleanor Byrne collection.

09-29 Inuit man, woman, and baby at the Pan-American Exposition, Buffalo, NY, circa 1901. Johnston, Frances Benjamin, photographer. Esquimaux Village. Photograph. Retrieved from the Library of Congress.

10-02 Unidentified tinsmith, possibly in St. John's, though date and location are unknown. 26.02.010 People, Unidentified. Tinsmith. Coll- 137. Geography Collection, Archives and Special Collections, Memorial University.

10-25 Bouncer, presented to Prince of Wales in 1901. Peter Maniate/ Hannibalnewfs.com.

10-23 Male Great Horned Owl, 1734. Albin & Derham, A Natural History of Birds, London, 1731-1738.

10-28 (L-R) Neighbours Joan Simms, Grunia Ferman, and Doris Snelgrove. St. John's airport,1995, after Ferman received her honorary doctorate from Memorial University at the Fall Convocation. Photo from the collection of Brenda Simms Flood.

11-06 Portrait of John Dee engraved by R. Cooper, c1800. Royal College of Physicians.

11-25 Queen's Road as seen from Chapel Street, 1970s. City of St. John's Archives Photo #01-37-042. St. John's Heritage Foundation collection.

12-18 Reindeer herder Aslak Larsen Somby, c1884. The J. Paul Getty Museum, Los Angeles.

12-25 Richard Brothers as The Prophet of the Hebrews, c1795. Library of Congress Prints and Photographs Division Washington, D.C.

12-28 The Basin, Baltimore, Maryland, sometime between 1900 and 1910. Detroit Publishing Company photograph collection (Library of Congress).

PHOTO BY KELLY L. JONES

Dale Jarvis is the provincial folklorist for Newfoundland and Labrador, helping communities to safeguard traditional culture, the first full-time provincially funded folklorist position in Canada.

He holds a B.Sc. in anthropology/archaeology from Trent University and a M.A. in folklore from Memorial University. Dale is a past president of the Newfoundland Historic Trust and has contributed as a board member and volunteer to many local arts and heritage organizations. He regularly teaches workshops on oral history, cultural documentation, public folklore, and intangible cultural heritage.

By night, Dale is the proprietor of the St. John's Haunted Hike ghost tour and raconteur of local tales. As a storyteller, he performs recitations of ghost stories, stories of the fairies and little people, tales of phantom ships and superstitions, and legends and traditional tales from Newfoundland, Labrador, and beyond. His repertoire includes long-form folk and fairy tales from the island, with a wide-ranging knowledge of local legends, tall tales, and myths. Author of several books on Newfoundland and Labrador ghost stories and folklore, he is a tireless promoter of local culture.